Joachim Braun   Gustav Heinemann

JOACHIM BRAUN

GUSTAV HEINEMANN
The
Committed President

FOREWORD BY SIEGFRIED LENZ

TRANSLATED FROM THE GERMAN
by R. W. LAST

OSWALD WOLFF

LONDON

Published in Germany 1972
by Verlag C. F. Müller, Karlsruhe
under the title »Der unbequeme Präsident«

ISBN O 85496 256 5

MADE AND PRINTED IN GERMANY BY
C. F. MÜLLER, GROSSDRUCKEREI UND VERLAG GMBH, KARLSRUHE

Contents

Foreword

No caps are flung into the air when he appears, there is no rejoicing at a gesture from his hand; he is not cheered to the echo, and his appearance is not likely to spark off an epidemic of blind adulation. Even the way he walks leaves a great deal to be desired: his gait has none of the measured portentousness of the statesman, it lacks massive dignity, nor is it the weary rhythmical tread of the ceremonial occasion — no, the Federal President walks to the rostrum quite normally, if a little stiffly. There is no attempt at disguise or a display of fine feathers; there are no rows of glinting insignia proclaiming an elevation above the plane of ordinary mortals effected at second hand, no isolation shielded by protocol which might give one cause to suspect that the holder of the highest office in the land has a hot-line to the deity. With Gustav Heinemann, normality is the order of the day, and since he became Federal President and the people's President, the nation has been encouraged to recognise that there is really nothing out of the ordinary in the office of President.

Admittedly, his attempts to retrieve the presidency from its dizzy heights and bring it down among ordinary men, to deprive it, so to speak, of its mysterious remoteness, have made Gustav Heinemann something of a challenge for many citizens of our Federal Republic. We are called upon to yield up long-cherished notions and at the same time to accustom ourselves to behave in a manner appropriate to the age we live in. The image that the authority of the state has been pleased to give itself has been too deeply engrained in us: withdrawn, in munificent isolation, caught in the gilded cage of a rigid ceremonial system which laid down precisely the degree of proximity permitted to the presence of the great. And pomp and circumstance were all part of this image, which — whether begged, stolen or borrowed — was not by any means designed exclusively for the benefit of the high and mighty, but to dazzle the common folk like a ray of reflected glory. There are not a few who consider that they are only being fittingly represented by means of a public display on the part of the head of state and who only come to revere him if this display occurs in due accordance with the prescribed rules and regulations.

And now this man comes along insisting on calling many things into doubt, and asking himself specific questions, as he is fond of doing at the beginning of his speeches — even confronting himself, the holder of the highest office in the land, with such questions. Authority which raises doubts in the mind? An elected power, which seeks to share or hand over responsibility? Gustav Heinemann, who has declared himself to be the people's President, calls upon each and every one of us to show the door to any notions of a state authority larger than life and resplendent with pomp and pageantry.

Instead, he sees the relevance of his office as one of tirelessly underlining the acknowledged opportunities of a free democracy, of rendering the power base of the state superfluous by means of freely assumed responsibility. A nice turn of phrase, so it seems; but anyone who examines the unexplored possibilities of our democratic constitution will be amazed to find just how justified Gustav Heinemann is in making such a statement. The more people who are prepared to have confidence in themselves and to assume a degree of responsibility, the more we can dispense with the state. And that the state is not an object of affection, or perhaps that affection is not something one should feel for it, has been aptly expressed by Heinemann himself, who once declared that he loved his wife, but that he did not love the state.

When has a German head of state ever spoken in such terms? It was inevitable that the man who was to be the representative of a "difficult fatherland" would strive, despite the opposition he encounters, to recast the image of his office and bring it into line with the exigencies of our age. Other nations, whom experience had led to be somewhat suspicious of German declarations of sincerity, soon realised the kind of concept of the state which was here being expressed. Gustav Heinemann was discreetly able to increase his stock of confidence in Holland, and he was also welcomed by Danish journalists as a "provo" among heads of state. This open goodwill was expressed to a President who condemned any pretentiousness on the part of the state, and who, it was well known, directed his most urgent attention towards the grey fringes of human society, to the outsiders and the misfits. It is as if Heinemann had reawakened the spirit of Protestantism that had long languished as a misfit itself, and blended it into his own social policies.

This bold and above all uncomfortable spirit of Protestantism makes itself felt almost as soon as the people's President mounts the rostrum. I admire him as a speaker, I sense disquiet and expectation emerging almost of their own volition when he refers to the dates of German history, addresses himself to the theme of brotherhood in a speech or takes an anniversary as an opportunity for drawing attention to some unpleasant facts. What a strange mixture of a voice which speaks of burning issues in tones reminiscent of the schoolteacher; what a contrast between an unpolished, almost leisurely delivery and words which leave no one with an unruffled conscience. He is a disturber of smugness, a man who not only exhorts and protests, who not only moderates and causes doubt and disquiet, but who is also prepared to point the finger at himself: it was Gustav Heinemann who asked himself publicly why he had not offered more resolute resistance during the time of the Third Reich. A head of state who admits that he is not satisfied with himself is a phenomenon which many citizens can identify with, not least the large numbers skilled in suppressing the past and forgetting the unpleasant memories.

For if one asks by way of comparison who can adequately represent us in Germany at this time and what his style should be, then one would readily have to admit that we do not want regal socialising, no heavy-footed military legend in his own lifetime, nor do we want a stylised man of honour who after the usual time so confuses himself with his office that he regards all he does as a personal favour. What we really need, it seems to me, is a sovereign civilian, a sceptical, awkward representative, a man as ready to question himself as he is others and who, so to speak, is prepared to do some honest rattling of the skeletons in the German cupboard. So is Gustav Heinemann the right President for us? I believe that he largely corresponds to our requirements and more: every time he takes up a cause, he reminds us of the tasks which our society confronts. And this applies to political as well as social and moral undertakings.

But Heinemann's persistent warnings do not make me forget Heinemann the believer, the man who once proposed that Germany in defeat should join together to form an almost unbelievable community, namely a community of guilt. He has made it clear to all who believed that they had retained their innocence in a time of extreme lawlessness that the sole credible possibility of confronting an existing guilt is to recognise it and to take it upon oneself. A "community of suffering" prepared to face a "common guilt" — this was a truly Christian answer to the experiences of our recent history.

It is remarkable that, in the context of the way Heinemann performs his office, there is not the least temptation to talk in terms of the limited powers of his office, or the restrictions imposed upon it by the constitution. He consistently advises his fellow citizens to accept and explore the extraordinary opportunities of democracy, and he has put his own advice into practice: he makes the fullest use of the opportunities of the highest office in the land to the point of zealous excess. Whether he is trying to persuade people to understand the feelings of demonstrating students, whether he is explaining the lot of the foreign worker, whether he is washing the patina from historical monuments or stressing the rights of the outsider: the highest office in the land does at least have the effect of lending its holder's words a greater weight, at least some attention is paid to them, and Gustav Heinemann says what it seems to him needs saying. And he has succeeded in making his office lose some of its remoteness while at the same time retaining its dignity and standing. It seems to me that Gustav Heinemann has undertaken no mean task in his untiring efforts to inform, to plead the cause of humanity, and to promote among his fellow-citizens a spirit of self-confidence and responsibility.

Gustav Heinemann's special credibility is not least due to his refusal either to become a prisoner in the gilded cage of his high office or to recognise the force of the supposed obligations of his position. He actually asks whether he has to put up with the presence of photographers, even on official occasions. He even stops his state car in Bonn so that he can pass the time of day with a couple of strolling writers. And he even claims the right to let it be known when a conversation is boring him.

No, Gustav Heinemann certainly is not a "well-trained" President. Remote affability is as far from being his nature as ceremonial smugness. He is often enough pointing the finger against ingrained intractability. Frequently he is disconcerted by excessive applause. The honest amateurishness of certain gestures of his will be just as persuasive and convincing as they were on the last occasion.

It is clear that in his endeavour to be a people's President he depends not least upon us, his fellow citizens. We are challenged to compare and to judge. We are urged to determine for ourselves what is appropriate and what best suits our needs. The concept of the highest office in the land as expounded by Heinemann is one of collaboration. We should not withold it from him.

Why it is so worthwile to do so is demonstrated by Joachim Braun in this study of Heinemann. It is a carefully drawn and sympathetic picture composed of a wide diversity of elements: a biographical account and a study of Heinemann's development as a politician, a study of his character and of his activities in Bonn, a portrait of his family and an analysis of his office — all explored and evalued with great insight, not least the outstanding moments of political decision linked with the name of Gustav Heinemann. The parts fuse together into a portrait of an "awkward President", to whom we can only do full justice becoming "awkward citizens" ourselves.

Siegfried Lenz

A Protestant in the liberal Tradition

Gustav Heinemann has never been an easy man; not for his enemies, nor for his friends, and probably not for himself either.

Ever since he entered political life he has been a controversial figure: when he was Minister for Home Affairs in Adenauer's first cabinet and offered his resignation after only a year in protest against Adenauer's German policy; when he founded and led a splinter party and became acquainted with the lot of the political outsider in seven years of opposition outside parliament; when although a shrewd critic of the Social Democrats, he joined their ranks, but only after they had broken with their anti-clerical tradition and made their peace with the economic system of the Federal Republic; or again, when he was Minister of Justice in the grand coalition and set in train a whole package of reforms which were not entirely popular with the public at large — from liberalising the laws on sexual conduct, giving equal rights to children born out of wedlock, to the reform of the criminal code and penal system.

Gustav Heinemann was also a controversial figure as a candidate for the office of Federal President, not among the Social Democrats who elected him unanimously, but in the ranks of the Free Democrats whose political leadership had to summon up every last ounce of energy and all their powers of persuasion to ensure that their delegates gave Heinemann united support. And he was certainly controversial as far as the CDU and the press that supported them were concerned. In those circles his candidacy was regarded as an affront. The choice between Gustav Heinemann and Gerhard Schröder was not just a simple choice between two men who appeared equally well qualified for the highest office in the land — it was a confrontation between twenty years of CDU rule on the one hand and twenty years of opposition to this rule on the other, between what had become of Germany since 1949 and what might have been, between the fear of experimentation and the longing for a great change.

The outcome of a presidential election had never been so wide open. It was clear that the Christian Democrats would vote solidly for their candidate. The twenty-two delegates of the NPD had also made it known that they would vote for Gerhard Schröder. So the question was how the FDP delegates in the Federal assembly would cast their votes. If they gave Gustav Heinemann their wholehearted support, then he would gain victory at the polls. But if only a few of them voted for Gerhard Schröder that would mean the Social Democrats had failed to fill the highest office in the land for the first time with one of their own ranks.

At a quarter to seven in the evening of 5 March 1969 Gustav Heinemann strode to the rostrum of the West Berlin Ostpreussenhalle and spoke these words:

> I should like to offer my thanks to all those who voted for me for the trust which they have placed in me. I fully respect those who decided to cast their votes elsewhere. It is my hope that it will be possible to work together with them as well in fruitful co-operation in facing the common tasks which lie before us all.

After three nerve-racking polls the majority of delegates had decided in favour of Gustav Heinemann. The result was close enough: 512 votes for Heinemann, and 506 for Gerhard Schröder. No wonder the CDU found it hard to respond to the respectful gesture which Heinemann had made in their direction. There was too wide a gulf between the Christian Democrats and the man who had once been one of their number and was now about to take over the presidency as a Social Democrat. Even the years of collaboration in government at the time of the grand coalition had altered little in this mutual antipathy.

The CDU had not forgotten that, after his break with Adenauer, Heinemann had become one of the bitterest critics of the Christian Democrats in the fifties. They had not lost the memory of that famous speech before the

14

Federal parliament on 23 January 1958 in the course of which Heinemann — who had joined the ranks of the SPD by this time — settled his account with his adversary Konrad Adenauer. Nor had they forgotten that it was Heinemann's entry into the SPD and his collaboration on the Godesberg reform programme which had helped to enable the Social Democrats to draw support from the middle class electorate, to turn a class party shackled with tradition into a modern popular party and to take the first steps which led to the ultimate removal of the CDU from office.

Now that Heinemann had been victorious over Gerhard Schröder a few short months before the general parliamentary elections, it began to look as if a change of government in Bonn was on the cards. For the first time since the Federal Republic came into being a coalition of SPD and FDP outvoted the Christian Democrats in a national political decision. Even the support of the NPD votes was not enough to prevent the defeat of the CDU. All those involved were clear in their minds that on 5 March 1969 in Berlin more had taken place than just a change in the office of Federal President.

Reactions at the Berlin elections made it clear how enormously varied responses to Gustav Heinemann actually were. Those who had campaigned for his election were proud, happy and relieved. The defeated party on the other hand were sorely disappointed, not a little bitter and even angry. Filbinger, the Prime Minister of Baden-Württemberg, spoke after the election of the gulf that divided Gustav Heinemann and the system of values of the CDU. Franz Josef Strauss even summoned up the spectre of the Third Reich. Strauss countered Heinemann's all too artlessly expressed statement that what had taken place was "a little matter of a change of power" in due accordance with the rules governing parliamentary democracy with these words:

> I am not happy to hear the phrase "change of power" uttered in the context of presidential elections . . . In Germany, we are very sensitive to phrases like seizure of power, or change of power.

By altering one word in the phrase, Strauss was drawing a parallel between the democratic decision of the Federal assembly and Hitler's seizure of power. This insidious play on words was greeted with applause from his audience.

But the writers of the left and the liberal journalists who supported Heinemann also found it at times difficult to restrain their language in the opposite direction. Even as critical a man as Hermann Schreiber found himself rhapsodising Heinemann. Schreiber reacted to Heinemann's statement that he did not regard himself as a State President, but would rather be a People's President, in the following glowing terms:

> That is good news indeed. If it were to be the rule in this country that we, the citizens, are the state, then these words of Gustav Heinemann give us an opportunity, the like of which is rarely seen in our democracy. Let us grasp it — let us grasp the state, for it is ours.

Over three years have passed by since then. Three years, in which the political face of the Federal Republic has undergone a radical transformation. The change of power of which Heinemann spoke after his election has taken place. At the time of the presidential election, the CDU still drew the Federal Chancellor from their ranks, but eight months later they found themselves on the opposition benches. In the German Federal parliament there is no grand coalition any more, but a confrontation between two almost equally balanced forces. The opposition outside parliament, which three years ago was at the height of its public success, has shrunk into insignificance. In the universities, teach-ins and mass demonstrations have given place to the quiet but determined activities of Marxist minority groups.

And now Gustav Heinemann has more than half of his term of office behind him. In this period, the voices of admirers and detractors alike have become more moderate. If the public opinion polls are anything to go by, the overwhelming majority of the population of the Federal Republic are satisfied with the way Gustav Heinemann is filling his office. But neither the more subdued tone of the commentators nor the approbation of the opinion polls can disguise the fact that many Germans find it hard to get on with this man, that as Federal President he continues to be a provocative figure

1945: mayor of Essen

in the eyes of many of his fellow citizens, and that he remains, as he always has been, an awkward man to have as their representative.

What is the reason for this? Is it because his manner is plain and matter-of-fact, that he simply is not a vital figure, a man with winning ways and heart-warming amiability? Or is it because, in a country in which political parties are still more or less regarded as life-long bonds of political loyalty, he has changed party four times, but without ever having been in the one party which nearly everyone joined a generation ago, namely the NSDAP? Or is it because, in the period of reconstruction, of which we are so proud, he campaigned against just about everything which was sacred to the majority of Germans at that time — against an unpolitical selfish pursuit of prosperity; against the tendency to sweep under the carpet the experiences of the Third Reich; against the assumption of the title Christian by a specific political party; against confusing the conflict between East and West with a struggle between Communism and Christianity; against a German policy of illusory strength, which constantly harped on reunification, although it was known only too well that reunification would never be attained by such means; against a need for security based rather on weapons than on a balancing of interests in Europe?

Or perhaps the reason was that Gustav Heinemann never tired of denouncing the German tradition of submissiveness to authority nor of exhorting his fellow citizens to assume a greater degree of moral responsibility and to exploit their political franchise; or again, that even as Federal President he has not rested content with a representative role and with delivering non-committal speeches on formal occasions, but has pointed to harmful elements in the German community and, when the need arose, also named those responsible.

Or is it because, as Rolf Zundel once wrote, it is not just the fact that this President is answerable to his office, but that the political community of the Federal Republic is also answerable to its President?

It is rewarding and significant questions such as these which this German politician has brought out into the open.

For all that, Gustav Heinemann did not originally intend to enter politics, that is to say, he had never made up his mind to become a politician. The profession which the grammar-school boy Gustav Heinemann had elected to follow was that of lawyer. He was not particularly clear in his own mind as to what such a profession entailed. There were no members of the legal profession in his family, nor even anyone with an academic background. His forebears were tradespeople and craftsmen. His grandfather on his father's side had eked a living as a butcher in Eschwege in Hesse; and his grandfather on his mother's side had been a thatcher in Barmen. His father, Otto Heinemann, had gone to elementary school and had worked his way up to the position of head clerk in the international Krupp concern. Gustav Heinemann had been the first member of the family to enjoy a university education. He chose to study jurisprudence, not so much because the law interested him as an academic subject, but because following this course was the only way of becoming a practising lawyer. And that was what he wanted to become, in order to be independent, to be his own master. He was not the least inclined to become someone at the lower end of a chain of command, a subordinate, who would work his way slowly and loyally up the ladder in a large hierarchy, nor would he in all probability have been successful in such a role.

The attraction of the law was that it offered him early independence, and also that the lawyer had "something to fight for, something to get his teeth into". Max Weber was one of young Heinemann's teachers in Munich. It was he who taught him that politics was like tenaciously drilling through hard planks of wood, with passion, but at the same time with a keen and accurate eye. "This business of tenaciously drilling," he admitted later, "stuck in my mind somehow."

He had his share of tenacious drilling, but not in politics to begin with. Heinemann's wife once said of her husband's past that in the early days he had not taken the least interest in politics. That is certainly an overstatement. Even as a child in his parents' home he was exposed to political influences. His father Otto Heinemann was councillor in Essen for a radical middle-class party. He revered Bismarck as the man who united the Reich, but loathed the sabre-rattling arrogance of Wilhelm II. Because of the oppressive conditions laid down in the Versailles peace, he regarded it as a disgrace for Germany; but he did sigh with relief when the news of the acceptance of the treaty came through. He saw through the myth of the "stab in the back" of the 1918 defeat, and honoured Friedrich Ebert as preserver of the Reich in difficult times. His political confession of faith ran as follows: "To be German and a nationalist, my fatherland above all; to feel, think and act with a social awareness; equal rights and responsibilities for all."

In the mouth of a Heinemann those words — "to be German and a nationalist, my fatherland above all" — have more the ring of Hoffmann von Fallersleben than German nationalist arrogance, more like the black, red and gold patriotism of the 1848 generation than the black, white and red brand of nationalism. And "equal rights and responsibilities for all" was scarcely a conservative point of view in the days when there were three classes of voters.

The tradition of the 1848 revolution was handed down to Gustav Heine-mann even more strongly by his mother's side of the family than by his father. His great-grandfather on his mother's side, Jakob Walter, fought at the barricades along with his two brothers. During the Baden revolution in 1849 one of the brothers was shot by the Prussians and seriously wounded in Waghäusel; he lies buried in Rastatt. The second fled through France to America. To this day Gustav Heinemann has preserved some of his letters, in which his ancestor wrote to the brother remaining at home that, despite the burden of poverty, he did not wish ever to return to Germany, for in America he had freedom of speech.

His grandfather, Gustav Walter, was just seven years old in 1848. He gained his revolutionary experiences with Garibaldi in Italy. Gustav Heinemann can still clearly recall how his grandfather used to rock him on his knee and teach him the Hecker song, the hymn to the leader of the Baden radicals, the Mannheim lawyer Friedrich Hecker, written by the Frankfurt poet Wilhelm Sauerwein.

Gustav Heinemann traces what he himself calls his "forty-eight cast of mind" back to this black, red and gold tradition among his ancestors. His criticism of the tradition of the authoritarian state and of the close relationship between the church and the governing powers, his support for the constitutional state and for the active involvement of the citizen in the democratic process, his demand for national unity: all these convictions, which are expressed time and again in Heinemann's speeches, were solemnly sworn to before the national assembly in St. Paul's church in Frankfurt. At that time in those brief weeks at the beginning of 1848, when the dream of a democratic revolution in Germany appeared to be on the verge of becoming a reality, a constitutional document was drafted in St. Paul's church, which, fUI IIIU IIIUL IIIIIU III ßwIIIIdIIy'ß IIIwIIIIy, wIIß IIIIIIIIIdI IIy II dIUIdIdIdIIIIIIN of basic rights. Freedom for the individual, for economic life, freedom of religious confession, of learning and of the press, legal guarantees against arbitrary arrest and infringement of liberty by the police or the courts, equality under the law by the abolition of all class privileges: that is the forty-eight tradition, even though this constitution never gained the force of law.

But Heinemann would naturally scarcely have felt at home with the liberal centre of that time, that liberalism of the gentry which in the words of Golo Mann sought the consent of the old authority for the new freedoms. He would certainly have been found among the left-wing members of the national assembly, among those men who aspired towards full-blooded democracy and a socialist order in society, and who, after the collapse of St. Paul's, fought for their convictions at the barricades.

So Heinemann was exposed to more than enough political influences in his parental home, and during his student days he also rubbed shoulders with politics. He was a black, red and gold student, a convinced republican and in Marburg deputy chairman of the German democratic student group (the first chairman was the later CDU politician Ernst Lemmer, one of the few men in the CDU who maintained a genuine friendship with Heinemann even after his break with Adenauer). An errand as a courier caused him to become briefly caught up in the confusions of the Kapp putsch, and he even had to spend a night under lock and key as a result. When he was a student in Munich he attended a party gathering of the National Socialists, who at that time were at the very beginning of their active political life, one evening was more than enough for him to make up his mind once and for all about Adolf Hitler.

But all these excursions into politics remained isolated incidents on the periphery of his student days, which he spent in Münster, Marburg, Göttingen, Munich and Berlin. He completed his study of economics, which he pursued at the same time as that of jurisprudence, as early as the year 1922 in Marburg by gaining the degree of Doctor rer. pol.; in the same year came his first state examination in jurisprudence, followed in 1926 by the second examination; in 1929 he graduated in law in Münster. After his 1926 examination he entered the chambers of a criminal lawyer in Essen as a partner. He was only able to obtain fully qualified status as a lawyer by making an appeal, because the authorities were not willing to release the young lawyer from the civil service without further ado. But he had his way, and the professional ambition of the grammar-school boy had been achieved.

But his legal career lasted a mere two years. In 1928 the Rhine steel works in Essen offered Heinemann, who was only twenty-nine years old at the time, a three-year contract as an industrial lawyer with power of attorney and a respectable income. Heinemann accepted, with the added condition of three month's notice on either side. He remained with Rhine Steel for over twenty years; in 1936 he gained a representative position on the board and in 1945 as head of the central administration obtained a permanent place on the board. In addition to his work for Rhine Steel, Heinemann wrote, when still quite a young man, a variety of legal texts which ran into several editions, including commentaries on medical service and dental service law, and which are still regarded as standard works today. And between 1933 and 1939 he was also engaged in lecturing on economic and mining law, at the University of Cologne. It was in the Ruhr industry that he considered his professional obligations lay. Even in 1949 he was not prepared to give up his position at Rhine Steel in favour of a brief from the Federal assembly, although he had in the meantime taken an active part in politics as chief mayor of Essen and as Minister of Justice in the Land government of North Rhine-Westphalia.

Only when Konrad Adenauer summoned him to be Minister of Home Affairs in the first Federal government did Heinemann take his leave of industrial management. Adenauer must have put a considerable amount of pressure on him, because Heinemann was not interested in the prospect of a career in Bonn. He had carved himself out a career long since. He was one of the most important men in the Ruhr, and is known by just political respect and a good position and would have been more than content to continue working on the reconstruction of the German economy.

To play an active part in the work of reconstruction: that was also the reason why he served his home town between 1946 and 1949 as chief mayor. (In North Rhine-Westphalia chief mayors are not career politicians, but a kind of honorary head of the community. So they continue to follow their normal employment.) The British occupation forces had invited him to take the office of mayor in 1945, because he was well known as an opponent of the National Socialists. At the first local elections he was confirmed in office, after the CDU, of whom he was one of the founder members in Essen, had gained an absolute majority in the council. Like his fellow citizens in Essen, Heinemann had taken his spade in his hand, to help clear aside the rubble. The British military government, against whom he campaigned vigorously for a halt to the dismantling of industrial installations, was obliged to face the fact that they had appointed an awkward individual as mayor. Heinemann told them often enough that even as the occupying power in a defeated country they were not able to do everything they wanted. But Heinemann did not hold on to his post out of political ambition. He was an industrialist and wanted to remain in that profession.

It was in Düsseldorf in 1948 that he showed for the first time just how independent an attitude he had when it came to political office. At that time he had been Minister of Justice for North Rhine-Westphalia for a year. His predecessor, Dr. Sträter, did not gain a mandate at the first free election in the Düsseldorf Land parliament, and in accordance with the will of the British forces of occupation was not permitted to continue in office as a Minister. Heinemann stepped into the breach because the chaotic situation in the legal administration with its confusion in the courts, in the public prosecutor's offices, and in the prisons, did not allow a vacancy for the office of Minister to remain unfilled. But he declared that he would step down in favour of Dr. Sträter as soon as the British accepted one single member of the goverment who did not have a mandate from the delegates. A year later this happened. Heinemann stepped down. Konrad Adenauer, at that time party chairman of the CDU in the Düsseldorf Land parliament, could not believe the news that Heinemann had been true to his word and bet upon it, for surely no one who had wormed his way into ministerial office would voluntarily yield his position. Adenauer lost his bet.

So it was neither the tradition of the black, red and gold in his parental home nor political ambition which finally made Heinemann turn politician. There was another motive force at work within him. Heinemann became a politician out of a sense of Christian responsibility. The young Gustav Heinemann, who was bent on a middle-class career, would not have made much sense of that, and for the quite simple reason that at that time he was not a Christian.

The attitude towards Christianity in Heinemann's parental home was one of tolerant but sceptical detachment typical of the liberal bourgeois at the turn of the century. It is true that young Gustav was confirmed, as was only right and proper, but the father of the household did not go along to the confirmation service in the church.

Otto Heinemann had become estranged from the church in his home of Eschwege even as a child, and in his youthful years was connected with the "Society for ethical Culture," and subsequently in Essen with the German League of Monists under the scientist Ernst Haeckel, whose anti-Christian philosophy enjoyed enormous popularity before the First World War. In his memoirs, Heinemann's father, writing as an old man, admitted that he "had been a seeker all my life and had never really settled the question of religion." He read Schopenhauer and Kant, and occupied himself with Confucius and Buddha. In his eyes, Jesus Christ was a founder of one religious movement among many, his command of neighbourly love "the ethical goal of all the great religions, not just of Christianity." In his view, Christianity "was not appropriate to our age, at least not in its orthodox form, with its belief in miracles, its heaven and hell, Adam and Eve as the first human beings, and then the fall from grace and its consequenses." What he wished to see taking place within the Christian churches was a "fundamental reformation: the replacement of an excess of metaphysics by realities."

---

1. On the Feldherrnhügel.

2. Heinemann's great-grandfather on his mother's side, Jacob Walter, who fought at the barricades with his two brothers in the revolution of 1848—49. During the Baden uprising of 1849 one of the brothers was wounded by the Prussians in Rastatt and died shortly after. The other fled to America where subsequently all trace was lost of him. He wrote this letter to the brother who remained at home in Barmen.

3. Self-expression: good; Singing: poor. Entries from the nine year-old Gustav Heinemann's school report.

4. When he was sixteen, Gustav Heinemann wrote a drama entitled: "Konradin the last of the Hohenstaufens." This is the first page from the original manuscript. Fifty-five years later it was given its première on the occasion of Heinemann's seventy-second birthday in the Villa Hammerschmidt.

Zeugnis

für *Johann Heinemann*

Klasse VA **Abteilung**

I. Halbjahr des Schuljahres 19 08/09.

I. Betragen:
II. Ordnungsliebe:
III. Aufmerksamkeit:
IV. Fleiß:
} Gut.

V. Leistungen:

1. Religion:	4. Raumlehre:
a. Bibl. Geschichte:	5. Geschichte:
b. Katechismus: } Gut.	6. Erdkunde: } Gut.
c. Kirchenlied:	7. Naturbeschreibung:
2. Deutsch:	8. Naturlehre:
a. Lesen: } Gut.	9. Schönschreiben:
b. Sprachlehre:	10. Zeichnen: } Im gz. gut.
c. Mündl. Ausdruck: Sehr gut.	11. Gesang: *Mangelhaft*
d. Rechtschreiben: Gut.	12. Turnen: *Genügend*
e. Aufsatz:	13. Weibl. Handarbeiten:
3. Rechnen:	
a. Kopfrechnen: } Gut.	
b. Schriftl. Rechnen:	

VI. Schulversäumnisse: 9 Halbtage mit Entschuldigung,
     Halbtage ohne Entschuldigung.

VII. Besondere Bemerkungen:

Rüttenscheid, d. 30. Sept. 1908

Der Rektor: Hauptlehrer: Der Lehrer:

Brinker   *Abramson*

Unterschrift der Eltern: *Heinemann*

1. Aufzug.

1. Szene. Im Hofe des Herzogs Ludwig von Bayern.
Königin Elisabeth und Ludwig.

E. Nein, nein, ich werde ihm auf jeden Fall abraten; das Unternehmen ist zu waghalsig.

L. Halt Ihr .... ?

E. Nein. Er weiß überhaupt nicht davon, daß wieder eine Gesandtschaft aus Italien angekommen ist.

L. Wollt Ihr sie ihm gar nicht vorstellen?

E. Am liebsten möchte ich es nicht tun! Schon beim ersten Male wäre er gleich aufgebrochen, ohne sich um Anzug und Gefolgschaft zu kümmern. Nur mit Mühe konnte ich ihn zurückhalten.

L. Ich glaube, er traut es sich noch zu, ganz allein den Kampf gegen Karl v. Anjou und den Papst zu bestehen.

E. Er hat echtes Hohenstaufenblut in seinen Adern. Ich weiß noch recht gut, wie er als kleiner Bub hierher kam. Vierzehn Jahre ist es nun schon her und oft genug seit er mich in dieser Zeit in Angst und Verzweiflung

-1-

It was in such an atmosphere that Gustav Heinemann grew up. After his confirmation he had virtually no further contact with the church. As a young man, he belonged like his father to the League of Monists. Before his marriage to Hilda Ordemann, the daughter of a Bremen merchant, he was obliged to promise his future father-in-law that he would not seek to prevent his bride-to-be from attending church. He did not find it difficult to give such an undertaking, because although he was not a supporter of the church, neither was he a militant atheist, rather a religious seeker like his father.

Heinemann has never spoken at length about how he turned to the Christian faith as a grown man. What is clear is that he did not experience conversion, a sudden illumination of faith. It is not possible to pin down his change of heart to a specific time and place. Looking back, he recalled that he "gradually came round to the acceptance of the fact that the gospel is both truth and reality."

There were three people involved in this change, as a result of which Heinemann became a man of the church "after man years of complete alienation and enslavement to so-called modern ideas of enlightenment and all kinds of rationality; they were has wife, the Essen parish priest Friedrich Gräber and the Swiss Professor of Theology Karl Barth.

Hilda Heinemann came from a Bremen business family. Her father was a corn merchant, her mother a parson's daughter from Berne. Her elder sister, Berta Staewen, rebelled against the conventional Christianity of the parental home and subsequently worked on the social rehabilitation of prisoners in the Berlin-Tegel prison, long before such phrases as social rehabilitation had entered the popular vocabulary; and through Berta, Hilda Heinemann came into early contact with the left-wing Protestant, anti-Wilhelminian ideas of religious Socialism. She undertook the study of theology, German language and literature and history, and passed her examinations in Marburg under Rudolf Bultmann. It was there that she met Gustav Heinemann. One of the books from her student days which she brought with her when she married was the second edition of Karl Barth's commentary to the Epistle to the Romans, a book which at the beginning of the twenties caused a revolution in evangelical theology and which Heinemann preserves to this day as one of the treasures of his library.

In Essen the Heinemanns belonged to the parish of Essen-Altstadt, where the parish priest was Friedrich Graeber. In the first years of marriage, Hilda Heinemann went alone to the church services. When she was a young girl, their eldest daughter Uta, who now teaches Catholic theology in the college of education in Neuss, once asked her parents in puzzled tones: "Is it true that only mothers go to church?" At some time or another Hilda Heinemann must have taken her husband along to church with her, and from that time on he continued to attend of his own free will.

In any event, his meeting with Pastor Friedrich Graeber was decisive for Heinemann. There were two aspects of the man that fascinated him: first, that he was able to preach in such a down-to-earth and concrete fashion that his congregation were able to recognise their own situations in his exposition of the gospel, and secondly, that the... "was able to involve his listeners in his own activities." Up until that time, Heinemann had not found either of these qualities in the church.

What he learned from Pastor Graeber above all was the down-to-earth view of man revealed in the Bible. "My view is that the gospel encourages us to adopt a most realistic approach to judging mankind. We are aware of man's limitations, and that he is not ordained to be completely released from such constraints." This was how he expressed as an older man his conviction, the insight which Friedrich Graeber had revealed to him. But, for the Christian, this matter-of-fact view of man is not the last word: "God respects each and every one of us as a person. He grants us freedom of action. We recognise the fact that we travel along many false pathways and God accompanies us along them with His supreme offer of reconciliation through His son. It is up to us to recognise that and make it a reality."

Heinemann wanted to make is a reality. He turned his back on religions scepticism and became a committed churchgoer. In 1933 he became a presbyter in his parish of Essen-Altstadt, which was soon to split. One group supported the German Christians, the other, with Graeber and Heinemann among them, joined the Confessional church as an independent evangelical Presbyterian parish. Heinemann became a member of the Consistory and legal adviser to the Confessional church. In addition, he worked on the editing of a church information service paper which for years was duplicated in the cellar of his house in the Schinkelstrasse in Essen. Ernst Lemmer, Heinemann's student friend from the Marburg days, was a journalist in Berlin at the time, and was thus able to give wider publicity to many reports from the Confessional church which were passed on to him by Heinemann.

In 1936 Heinemann was offered the post of member of the governing body of the Rhine-Westphalia coal syndicate. For a man of 37 years this would have signified an enormous advancement in his career. He accepted on condition that he be permitted to continue his work for the church. But he rejected the offer when it became clear that his condition would not be accepted.

In 1934 Heinemann had participated in the synod of the German Evangelical church. It was there that he met the spiritus rector of the Confessional church, the Swiss theologian Carl Barth, and this meeting marked the beginning of a friendship which was to last right up until Barth's death. Barth was Heinemann's own personal teacher of theology. (His enormous study of ecclesiastical dogma is not to be found in Heinemann's library in Essen, but — as a kind of theological hand-luggage — in his official residence in the Villa Hammerschmidt in Bonn.) In Barmen Karl Barth was a decisive figure in the formulation of the theological declaration which employed the Bible to attack the heresies of the German Christians which were coloured by National Socialist doctrine. The "Barmen Declaration" has now become part of church history.

This declaration, which consisted of six propositions, came to play an important role for Heinemann. In the second proposition it is staded that Jesus Christ is the master of all life and therefore also of the realm of politics:

"As Jesus Christ is God's guarantee for the forgiveness of all our sins, so He with the same seriousness is also God's powerful claim over our entire lives." And further: "We reject the false teaching that claims that there are areas of our lives in which not Christ but others are our masters."

The significance of this confession of faith in Jesus Christ as the sole master of all life made in the year 1934 can be gauged by comparing it with a speech given in the same year at the University of Leipzig by the historian Helmut Berve:

> This faith in Germany, which is demonstrated to be true belief by virtue of the unconditional, resolute will to sacrifice which it engenders, has been bestowed upon us by the great change which was wrought in the year 1933; and it alone is the key to the future. Not only because it moves mountains, but because it restores meaningfulness to life, and thus makes life worth living once more ... Therefore we should not dismiss men as profaners of the word of God when, in their great enthusiasm, they speak of their faith in the German Reich of the future, which in many respects that find a more honourable faith than that of any specific religious denomination, in the same terms that the Bible employs to speak of the kingdom of Heaven.

The fifth proposition of the Barmen declaration attacked this religious transfiguration of a political movement: "We utterly reject the false teaching that a state can or should reach out beyond its normal sphere of influence to become the sole and all-embracing system for human life, and seek to fill the functions of the church." This Barmen declaration spelled out for Heinemann what it meant to be a Christian and a citizen at one and the same time. It led him during the period of the Third Reich into active participation in the struggle for the church and after the collapse of the Third Reich into active involvement in politics.

The Barmen Declaration is one of the events which left their indelible mark on Heinemann for the future; the other is the Stuttgart Declaration of Guilt. On 18 and 19 October 1945 the second session of the newly-formed council of the Evangelical church of Germany took place in Stuttgart; the membership included the bishops Lilje, Dibelius, Wurm and Meise, Pastor Niemöller and Gustav Heinemann. Members of the Ecumenical Council also joined this session, coming to Germany for the first time since the war. The Declaration was directed to them as representatives of Protestant churches throughout the world (and thereby indirectly to the world at large):

> We are all the more grateful that they have joined us, because we and our nation are not only living in a great community of suffering, but also share a common guilt. It grieves us greatly to have to state that through us untold suffering has been brought upon many nations and many lands. What we have often borne witness to in our parishes we now express openly in the name of the entire church: it is true that for many long years we have fought in the name of Jesus Christ against the spirit which found its terrible expression in the National Socialist tyranny; but we accuse ourselves of not having confessed our faith more courageously, for not having praised more sincerely, for not having believed more joyfully, and for not having loved more deeply.

The declaration closed with a sentence which brought together the confession of guilt on the part of the church and a political hope for peace and reconciliation:

> We hope in God's name that through the common work of the churches the spirit of force and vengefulness, which seeks to rise up again today, will be scattered to the winds, and that the spirit of peace and love, in which alone tormented humanity can be restored to health, will prevail once more.

Both these declarations — from Barmen and Stuttgart — had in common the fact that they were supported by representatives of the three big Protestant groups, that is, the Reformed church, the United Protestants, and the Lutheran church. Both had in common the fact that they reposed on the witness of the Bible as the sole foundation; and both affirmed the responsibility of the Christian in the sphere of politics, even though they were not able to state precisely the nature of this responsibility. The Stuttgart declaration went further in that it did not just speak in terms of members of the church in its admission of the political failure of the church, but spoke for all Germans when it emphasied a "community of suffering" and a "common guilt."

Heinemann affirmed this notion of a common guilt time and time again. Even when he became Federal President, he stated in a speech in 1969 in memory of 20 July 1944 that he was still pursued by the question as to why he personally did not offer more opposition during the time of the Third Reich. It is true that he himself had from the outset had nothing to do with National Socialism, true also that he had to face setbacks in his career and considerable personal risk in his work for the church, but Heinemann did not actually belong to the actual political resistance movement against Hitler. His signature to the Stuttgart declaration, which self-righteous apologists of German history soon twisted into an admission of involvement in the collective political guilt of all Germans, was at the same time a confession of his own past inadequacies.

Thus it is that Barmen and Stuttgart are the two events in Heinemann's life without which he can be understood neither as a Christian nor as a politician. Barmen signified the drawing of a strict line of demarcation between church and state, but at the same time an awareness of responsibility on the part of the Christian in politics. Stuttgart signified a common guilt, a change of heart, a new beginning. Taken together, the two stood for politics founded upon a sense of Christian responsibility. Not Christian politics; that is something Heinemann has never engaged in.

Even in the early post-war years, when he was simultaneously president of the synod of the Evangelical church in Germany and a key figure in the Rhineland CDU, he rejected the notion of Christian politics. In 1948 he said: "I declare that, although I am a leading member of this party, I consider that a Christian party is a fundamentally unsatisfactory solution." He had joined the CDU, of which he was a founder member in his home town of Essen, because he regarded it as an historical opportunity that after four centuries Catholics and Protestants were to undertake joint political responsibility in Germany — and also because he was not drawn to either of the other parties. He was not sympathetic towards the SPD, because it had at that time not yet freed itself from the Marxist inheritance of a materialistic concept of history, and also because Heinemann regarded their views on nationalisation to be ill-founded. Nor did he like the FDP, because the anti-clerical stance of liberalism was ill-attuned to his concept of politics based on Christian responsibility.

No Christian politics: what Heinemann meant by this was that on the secular plane of politics the Christian should conduct his arguments with his reason, not with his faith. "The Bible is not a recipe book, where one can look up a topic in the subject index and find the appropriate course for action in the body of the text." — This was how he himself has expressed it on occasion. Whether pensions should be raised or rates of exchange allowed to float, whether a tax should be imposed at one level or another, or how the quality of the educational system should be improved: decisions of this order cannot be based on passages from the gospels. "Politics on the basis of a sense of Christian responsibility" means something different: and that is the conviction that the church and Christians are not there for their own benefit and that, on the other side of the coin, politics is not subordinate to any immutable laws in the face of which Christian responsibility is obliged to remain silent.

It was this attitude which soon led to a break with the party that called itself Christian. Of course, Heinemann's difference with Adenauer had concrete political grounds. Adenauer put his faith in integration with the West and hoped the Federal Republic would attain sovereignty by the offer of a German contribution to the defence system by the Western Allies. Heinemann feared that the goal of reunification would be put beyond reach if the West Germans rearmed. These were political grounds for disagreement. But the fact that, two years after his resignation from the cabinet, Heinemann finally left the CDU in 1952 and became one of its sternest critics, is not entirely unconnected with the fact that the majority of the CDU regarded their policies — and especially their foreign policy — as based on "Christian politics" and commended them to the electorate as such. Heinemann spoke out strongly against this claim:

> Anyone who pursues political objectives with Christian watchwords is sinning against his own words and, moreover, is discrediting his political decisions. It is far from being a Christian duty to defend the policies of the government without exception; it is quite possible to oppose them with a sense of Christian responsibility.

He did not see the cold war between East and West in terms of a struggle between Christianity and Marxism:

> Marxist substitute religion and the Bolshevist system are one and the same thing in the Soviet Union. But that does not justify trying to make Christianity and NATO into one and the same thing. The Christian idea becomes thoroughly debased whenever it is turned into a political weapon, no matter against whom.

Heinemann expressed his attitude towards Christian politics most forcibly in the course of the famous debate during the night of 23 January 1958, in which he stood at the rostrum of the Federal parliament as a Social Democrat deputy for the first time after years of opposition outside parliament. He quoted an issue of the Evangelische Verantwortung (Evangelical Responsibility), the organ of the Evangelical study group of the CDU, which contained the statement that in Christianity the West had an additional weapon against the anti-Christ, against the "monster in the East", and continued:

> I request my friends in the CDU and the party's evangelical wing to see to it that such attitudes are done away with once and for all. It is not a question of a fight of Christendom against Marxism (Shouts from the CDU/CSU: But?) — but of the recognition that Christ did not die to oppose Karl Marx, he died for us all. (Storm of applause from the SPD and FDP. Disarray in the centre.)

As Heinemann campaigned in the political sphere against appropriating the name of Christ for a given set of policies, so too did he campaign within the Evangelical church against the widespread tendency for uncritical support for the prevailing policies. He recognised the danger of a return to the old confederacy of throne and altar, and exhorted the church to keep a greater distance between itself and the state. "Do people really fail to see that the philosophy which dominates us all consists of three principles: a high standard of living; an army to protect it; and churches which give their blessing to both?" This was too much for his ecclesiastical colleagues in the Evangelical church to endure for long. In 1955 he was voted out as president of the synod.

As Minister of Justice Heinemann had demonstrated most vigorously that the Christian politician should not regard himself as a representative of clerical interests, and above all that he is not there in order to make the ethical principles of the church binding upon the populace by translating them into legislation. In the reforms which he put through, his intention was to preserve and maintain the philosophical and religious neutrality of the Basic Law of the Federal Republic and at the same time to make the liberal and socially conscious spirit of the constitution into the yardstick for the establishment of new laws. It is for this reason that he put through legislation which in effect instituted the principle of equality of rights for children born out of wedlock, even in the matter of inheritance. (Thus it was that a constitutional obligation which had appeared as far back as 1919 in the Weimar constitution and which was renewed in the Basic Law of the Federal Republic was actually put into practical effect after more than half a century.) And for this reason he considerably recast the criminal code. All that remained within its ambit were actions that were unquestionably injurious to society at large and against which society must therefore seek and obtain protection. "In a free democracy it should not be the case that everything which offends against the moral code should be subject to punishment under the law." This approach led to substantial limitations upon the law especially in the area of moral conduct. Since Heinemann's reforms, adultery, homosexual relations between consenting adults and sodomy are no longer matters for action under the law. Whether they are morally right or wrong is a question outside the competence of the criminal court judge. What the citizen does within the privacy of his own four walls should be of no concern to the courts. The criminal code is concerned only with guaranteeing the protection of the public.

So politics for Gustav Heinemann is a secular affair. The sense of Christian responsibility which is the underlying motivation of the politician should not dictate the kinds of conclusions he arrives at when dealing with specific individual issues. And anyway, Christians can differ among themselves on such matters. It is possible, and often essential, for them to compromise.

Heinemann's Christian conviction is also a source of his ability to compromise in political questions. The man who gave up his ministerial office on grounds of conscience is very wary of using the term conscience at all in political matters. It is known that it would take grounds like the atomic armament of the Federal army or the reintroduction of the death penalty to make him step down from the highest office in the land.

But matters like that are not the everyday order of decisions which a political man has to make. In questions like levels of taxation, the raising of pensions, changes in the law on rented accommodation or reforms in this or that area, Heinemann regards compromise not as a necessary evil, but as a condition for political success.

As Minister of Justice in the grand coalition he was frequently urged by his friends not to put his name to a particular reform if it did not succeed in fully realising the ideal which lay behind it. Heinemann contradicted this view by stating that it was better by far to bring reality to a compromise which was within the bounds of possibility than to renounce the attainable for the sake of noble but remote ideals. In the words of Max Weber, which is is fond of quoting, politics is rather like drilling holes in hard planks of wood, not just in the hope of producing an ideal piece of work, but with a keen eye for what can be achieved in practical terms. So the Christian conviction of the politician cannot simply be gauged by measuring it against the attitudes of the average Christian. In Heinemann's case, it makes its presence felt in a difference area altogether. And that is where the ultimate motivations and innermost impulses for his political actions lie.

If Heinemann speaks about the motivations underlying his political attitudes, about the well-springs of his realism, then it is true to say that his Christian convictions are finding their expression. Christian virtues such as penitence, humility, and trust come into play and in a strange way are compounded together with the will for national survival in order to produce a political conception.

Penitence: Heinemann's signature to the Stuttgart Declaration of Guilt was not simply a matter of participating in an important communiqué from the church, but a public admission of his own inadequacies. What Heinemann has made of his life can only be understood if this ability to call into question, to revise his views, to change direction, is fully recognised. As a man of thirty, he faced the challenge of the Christian message and became a man of the church. When he was forty-six, he had to recognise that merely being a member of a religious denomination and attending church were not enough, and so be became an active politician. At the age of fifty-one, he had a brilliant career with the CDU in prospect, but gave up ministerial office on grounds of conscience. When fifty-eight he wound up the failed experiment of the All-German People's Party and went over to the SPD.

A man who is thus capable of calling himself into question is likely to be more than a little astonished at how difficult others find it to face the demand of questioning themselves, a beloved tradition, an ingrained way of thinking, or a hardened prejudice.

The Stuttgart declaration, which stated that, because of the Germans, "untold suffering has been brought upon many nations and many lands", had its political consequences for Heinemann. For this reason Heinemann never became party to the illusion that no German accounts remained unsettled from the lost war. Hitler's Germany had instigated the Second World War and the loss of the territories in the east and the division of Germany were a consequence of this war which Germany herself had sparked off — Heinemann had never for one moment cherished any illusions on this score. This is why, in his speeches made during the period of the cold war, he constantly warns his audiences against suppressing the German past, encourages them to examine themselves instead of indulging in a fruitless reckoning up of the supposed balance of good and bad on both sides, and warns them not to be too hasty in acquiring for themselves a good conscience in the new friend and foe relationships of the cold war.

But Heinemann shows no trace of that remarkable German notion that in the context of international relations the concept of justice can exist "in its own right," or "as a principle as such," totally divorced from the historical context, or that it is possible to authenticate legal claims. A backward glance at Germany's past greatness should not be blinkered against the way in which that greatness was thrown to the winds.

Legal titles can become invalidated. Simply adding up supposed claims in ⷑⷖⷑⷖ ⷑⷖⷑⷖ ⷑⷖⷑⷖ ⷑⷖⷑⷖ ⷑⷖ ⷑⷖ ⷑⷖ ⷑⷖⷑⷖ ⷑⷖⷑⷖⷑⷖⷑⷖ ⷑⷖⷑⷖ ⷑⷖⷑⷖ how Heinemann faces up to the question of guilt and brings the concept of penitence into the political arena.

Nor is trust a current expression in the political vocabulary. Mistrust is usually held to be a better form of protection against the tricks the opposition gets up to, and trust is regarded as a luxury to be reserved for close personal friendships. As the idiom has it, politics is a game of poker and anyone playing with his cards visible is at a distinct disadvantage from the outset. But that is only if you confuse trust with blindness and gullibility. Heinemann is neither blind nor gullible. But he is aware of the fact that a lack of trust in home politics can in the long term lead to a poisoning of the political atmosphere and the polarisation of individual factions; in foreign affairs it produces confrontation instead of co-operation, thus undermining the political foundations of a secure peace:

> The mutual mistrust of the two power blocs locked in their world-wide struggle is the biggest obstacle to any peaceful outcome. Thus we are making our own contribution towards peace, if we never

44

permit ourselves to become caught up in a web of mistrust, but, turning our minds against the past, seek with uplifted hearts a way across the barriers between us ... Only if we venture to have trust ourselves can we demand trust from others. It is not a case of peace at any price, or war at no price — but rather unceasing willingness to come to an understanding.

Humility: an old German misapprehension, whose ghost still stalks through encyclopaedias and leading articles, has it that politics is nothing more or less than a struggle for power. Heinemann did not deny that politics was concerned with a struggle for power, but in relation to specific goals. In internal affairs it means the development of a free constitutional democracy with a social conscience. And in foreign relations it signifies security through the medium of a political balance of interests, not through the threat of force. In both of these areas the Christian virtue of humility has a role to play, even though Heinemann hardly uses the term himself. (One of the characteristics of humility is that it is not the subject of constant references.) It does not contradict the will for survival, but imposes limitations upon it: the individual should not permit his own standpoint to assume absolute significance, nor should he overestimate his own possibilities, nor impute the purity of his opponent's motives, nor again fasten on some negative image of the enemy which comes ready to hand — such are the effects of humility on politics.

Heinemann's incapacity for intrigue and hatred also stem from the same cause. In the period of his campaign against Adenauer's German policy he had to endure a great deal of slander and many personal slights. He was suspected of being a Communist in disguise, or a fellow traveller. He was not slow to defend himself against such accusations, even in the courts. But he never paid like with like. As he stressed time and again in articles and public pronouncements, even the opponents of rearmament should be able to feel that the Federal government recognised that they too sought peace in their own way. Heinemann would not allow anyone to cast doubt on the sincerity of Adenauer's intentions. This was the way Heinemann conducted himself with a political opponent — whereas Adenauer called him and his friends "fools of the first water" or "traitors".

This inability to feel hatred, to slander, or to conduct himself like a demagogue does not mean that he is irenical by nature. Heinemann is no passive peace-lover; on the contrary, he is always spoiling for a fight, impatient, and even has the occasional outburst of rudeness or anger. But he does not permit himself hatred, because hatred is indefensible in the Christian. His political opponent does not become an enemy. And the same applies to an opponent outside politics; he is not reduced to the level of someone committing ill for its own sake. In Heinemann's eyes, evil does not become incarnate within any one individual, nor in a group, nor yet in a political system. Those who think in terms of white and black are on occasion not averse to deliberately overlooking their own imperfections. Both faults — turning the enemy into a devil and refusing to see any blemishes in one's own position — Heinemann regards as denying what he terms the Biblical realism of man. "We must face the truth about man, that is, we must recognise man exactly as he is, as a creature inextricably caught up in a web of evil." All men are sinners, all men are imperfect, not just one's political opponent.

Anyone who thinks along these lines is proof against the professional disease of the politician, which, in the words of Erhard Eppler, is not falsehood, but vanity. True, Heinemann is self-assured, but he is certainly not vain. He knows what he stands for. And above all, he knows what he wants. But he is indifferent to his personal impact upon others. It would not occur to him to say all the right and easy words in order to win over his hearers. He seeks to convince them through the power of his arguments, not to blind them by pathos or flattery. He wants to be accepted for what he is, and he takes others as they are: as human beings with their preferences and weaknesses. Helmut Gollwitzer once said of him that "he is too much of a Christian to be an idealist, and too prosaic first to idealise his friends and then cast them disappointedly aside."

But his is not the coolness of an Adenauer or a Bismarck, nor is it founded on the power of circumstance or success. Cynicism is a feeling foreign to Heinemann. His own prosaic turn of mind derives from the fact that he is constantly aware of the gap between what ought to be and what can be achieved.

It could be said that what makes Heinemann stand out is his sceptical humanity. His scepticism prevents him from expecting more from himself and others than can be achieved. His humanity prevents his bluntness from spilling over into cynicism.

God is active and present in worldly affairs. Gustav Heinemann believes this, and counts on it. Because he believes it, "compulsion" becomes a term for the atheist. In politics there are power groupings, obstacles, mistakes — but no such thing as compulsion. In his earlier days, Heinemann was too inclined to link his belief in God's worldly involvement all too directly with political decisions. But anyone with a measure of perception was able to recognise that even then Heinemann was arguing politically, with a greater measure of realism and rational analysis than his opponents were prepared to admit.

The attraction of the way in which Heinemann conducts an argument, according to Rudolf Augstein, lies in the fact "that he is able to bring together incontrovertible moral integrity and impressive rational argument." The reader of the documents relating to Heinemann's campaign against Adenauer's foreign and German policy will find Augstein's assertion substantiated. On the surface it is a battle about hard-headed political decisions: integration with the West and rearmament at the cost of reunification, or reunification at the cost of military neutrality. Those were the alternatives which seemed to present themselves at the beginning of the fifties. And in this battle Heinemann expressed his arguments in a very straightforward manner:

> If you want reunficiation you must renounce the idea of integration with the West, because to attach yourself to the West means

detaching yourself from the East ... The only thing which will enable us to make progress without war is a treaty which would be signed not only by the Western powers, but also by Russia ... How is Russia supposed to look favourably upon a reunited Germany if that reunited Germany is to become a member of the Western alliance against the Soviet Union? ... We are concerned with very concrete political issues. It is proper that this should be so, for I take the view that an idealistic aspiration towards peace, however powerful, is not sufficient by itself alone. To establish and maintain peace is a task for clear heads and cool minds ... Military armament can form part of a political security system, but it is neither the principal nor the sole determining factor. In the first instance political security signifies a continuous state of balance of power and interests on the basis of large-scale co-operation in the spheres of equal rights and common effort ... The controversial issues, including German reunification, are still with us. But from now on the only way of bringing about their solution is by the employment of a new political approach not based upon force.

These are not the words of a politician with his head in the clouds trying to overcome the confrontation between the great powers by faith-healing. In the fifties it was regarded as scandalous that at the height of the cold war anyone should propose a "newpolitical approach not based upon force." Nowadays we understand this kind of language a lot better, since Willy Brandt as Federal Chancellor put into practice under different circumstances what Heinemann had previously preached as a political outsider. The policy of non-aggression nowadays has all-party support.

---

1. In 1950 Gustav Heinemann left Adenauer's cabinet because of differences over the German defence contribution. His resignation document was signed by Federal President Heuss and countersigned by Federal Chancellor Adenauer.

2./3. In 1953 Gustav Heinemann and some political associates founded the All-German People's Party (GVP). This letter from Heinemann to fellow party-member Erhard Eppler dates from this period.

4. On 21 October 1969 Federal President Heinemann signed the document appointing Willy Brandt to the office of Federal Chancellor.

Im Namen der

Bundesrepublik Deutschland

entlasse ich

den Bundesminister Dr. Dr. Gustav Heinemann

auf seinen Antrag aus seinem Amt als Bundesminister

des Innern.

Bonn, den 11. Oktober 1950

Der Bundespräsident

Theodor Heuss

Der Bundeskanzler

Adenauer

GESAMTDEUTSCHE VOLKSPARTEI
DAS PRÄSIDIUM

ESSEN, DEN 30. Juli 1953
AN DER REICHSBANK 14
TELEFON 31639

Herrn

Dr. Eppler

Tübingen

=========

Keplerstr. 20

Lieber Herr Eppler!

Sie werden am 2. August wahrscheinlich den schwersten
Stand haben, wie ich aus vielerlei Briefen aus dem
[Südwesten] erfahre. In den letzthätigen Verhandlungen mit
dem BdD haben wir die GVP-Position in vielerlei Hinsicht
wesentlich verbessert: Insbesondere soll jeder Kandidat
vor Aufstellung eine politische Erklärung unterschreiben,
die sehr viel von dem Widerspruch auffangen wird. Herr
Bodensteiner wird in Freudenstadt sein. Am 3. August
wird in Düsseldorf abschliessend geklärt, ob die Mannheimer
Vereinbarung beiderseits anerkannt bleibt. Es müssten also
vorsorglich die auf der Liste erscheinenden BdD-Kandidaten
nur mit der Massgabe aufgestellt werden, dass sie im
Falle der Nichtdurchführung des Mannheimer Abkommens
ausscheiden und die Nachfolgenden aufrücken.
Ich überlasse es Ihnen, ob Sie sich selbst *in Düsseldorf* für Ihren
Landesverband beteiligen wollen. Persönlich würde ich es
begrüssen.
Völlig widerspruchsvoll ist das Verhalten von Prof. Noack,
er rebelliert gegen das Abkommen und will gleichzeitig
Spitzenkandidat bei Ihnen sein. Falls Ihr Parteitag es
wünscht, bin ich bereit, auf Ihrer Liste zu kandidieren,
wobei Sie dann freilich damit rechnen müssen, dass ich im
Falle der Wahl dort annehme, weil Nordrhein-Westfalen
nicht alle vier beiderseitigen Parteihäuptlinge allein
tragen will. Hier soll die Liste geführt werden von
Heinemann - Wirth - Wessel - Elfes, wobei Frau Wessel und

einer von den beiden anderen Genannten gegebenenfalls
hier annehmen würden.

Mit freundlichen Grüssen,

Ihr

(Dr. Heinemann)

PS. Soeben erfahre ich durch Ihre Frau von Ihrem Unglücks
fall und bin darüber sehr bestürzt, sowohl um Ihretwillen
als auch um der Aufgabe willen, die für den 2. August
auf Ihnen liegen sollte. Nun wünsche ich Ihnen zunächst
Genesung. Lassen Sie sich durch nichts bewegen oder aufregen.
Gottes Weltregiment bleibt, auch wenn Mitspieler ausscheren.
Ich wäre dankbar, wenn Ihre Frau mir gelegentlich Näheres
über Ihr Befinden mitteilen möchte.

Mit herzlichem Gruss von uns allen hier,

Ihr

Im Namen der

Bundesrepublik Deutschland

ernenne ich

auf Grund des Artikels 63 Absatz 2 des Grundgesetzes
für die Bundesrepublik Deutschland

Herrn

Willy Brandt

zum Bundeskanzler

Bonn, den   21. Oktober 1969

Der Bundespräsident

In the fifties Adenauer and his associates were talking in terms of liberating eastern Europe as far as the Urals. It remains for the historians to decide whether Adenauer himself really believed in this policy of strength. Whether Heinemann's proposal of a militarily neutral Germany united on the basis of free elections and extending as far as the Oder-Neisse line in accordance with the Soviet notes of early 1952 would have been attainable, will never be known, because the seriousness of the Soviet offer has never been put to the test.

In any event, Heinemann recognised long before his opponents that military force can no longer be employed to impose political solutions because no practical alternative to peace exists any more. He first voiced this view, not when he was President of the Federal Republic, but way back in the early fifties. At that time people were keen to brand him as a wildly impractical Christian dreamer, an idealistic firebrand. He was dubbed an apostle of Gandhi, and this was held to be a most apposite insult. At the time, the illusory politics of strength was regarded as realistic and Heinemann's realistic concept of a balance of interests was considered an illusion. It was thought possible to work out policies in central Europe without reference to the security interests of the Soviet Union. Only a few people, as Paul Sethe remarked at the time, were prepared to number Heinemann among those "independent spirits" who "set clearheaded consideration of the nature of foreign policy" against the pipe dream of reunification through intimidation of the Soviet Union.

If Heinemann is reminded nowadays of those arguments of the fifties, he talks about them without bitterness. It is not his style to lament lost opportunities. The fact that much of what he was trying to bring about then is now being supported even by his former political opponents Heinemann regards more as an irony of history than belated recognition. As he has often said, politics is concerned more with immediate issues than with fundamental principles.

This detached view of the business of politics explains Heinemann's independent approach to political parties. It is true that politics is a team affair, and the lone campaigner is a comic spectacle. But in Heinemann's view political parties are indispensable, because in a representative democracy they offer the opportunity for the citizen to play an active role in shaping policies and influencing opinion, so that the voter can have a real choice between competing alternatives. Parties are, however, not associations for the preservation of a particular outlook on life, but practical alliances formed for the purpose of pursuing political objectives. In the context of such common aims, solidarity with political allies is essential. But when an individual can no longer support the aims of a particular party, he is free to leave it.

Heinemann feels no inhibitions about talking about the fact that in the course of his life he has changed parties more than once. As a student he belonged to the German Democratic student group. In 1930 he was associated with a small group of Protestant republicans, the Christian Service for the People. In 1933 he voted for the SPD, because that party seemed to him then to offer the sole possible way of averting the impending disaster. It never once crossed his mind to consider joining the NSDAP. In 1945 he was one of the co-founders of the CDU. In 1952, after he had parted company with the Christian Democrats, he founded the All-German People's Party (GVP), and after this party came to grief, he threw in his lot with the SPD in 1957. In a country, in which joining a political party is rather like taking marriage vows, Heinemann's pragmatic approach to the parties has caused much offence. Countries with a longer democratic tradition would have made a lot less fuss about Heinemann's actions. Winston Churchill is but one prominent example.

But it is unjust of many parliamentary delegates who cross the floor in the course of a parliament because of the dictates of their conscience or on opportunist grounds to point to Heinemann as the precedent they have followed. Heinemann has never transferred from one party to another in this fashion, taking his mandate along with him as a dowry. He left the CDU two years after he withdrew from ministerial office, when he had spent a long time in opposition outside parliament. And he only joined the SPD after his own party, the GVP, had voted with a large majority in favour of disbandment.

A substantial proportion of the GVP membership followed Heinemann into the SPD, among them his closest associate Dieter Posser, who is now Minister of Justice for North Rhine-Westphalia, and Johannes Rau who became leader of the SPD in the Düsseldorf Land parliament and subsequently Federal Minister of Science. Erhard Eppler, the Federal Minister for Economic Co-operation, had entered the SPD in 1955.

When Heinemann became a member of the Social Democratic party in 1957, many regarded this committed Protestant and former industrialist as a foreign body in the traditional socialist party. Old party hands felt unable to accept him as a Social Democrat by adoption. In the end, Heinemann did not work his way slowly up the ladder from the local association to the heights of Federal office, but swiftly rose to the top: after just one year's membership he became one of the party leaders. Heinemann regarded the term "comrade" as an outmoded hangover from the days of class struggle. Things like that all led the long-serving members of the party to regard this late entrant with a certain degree of suspicion, traces of which can still be detected even today. Heinemann found it perhaps even more surprising that the Social Democrats unanimously elected him to the Presidency in 1969 than the fact of his victory over Gerhard Schröder.

When he entered office, Heinemann asked for "critical accompaniment." That is an unusual request in a country in which the relationship between power and the spirit, between politics and the intellectual, has rarely been a happy one. The memory is still fresh of a Federal Chancellor in office calling writers "yapping dogs." And the majority of the population did not find the comment outrageous. According to a German tradition which goes back to the attitudes of the autocratic state, criticism must be positive if it is to be tolerated at all. This mistrust of the critical spirit and this anti-intellectual stance are attitudes Heinemann has never shared.

Whether he himself is to be regarded as an intellectual is a secondary issue. If an intellectual is to be characterised as someone who reveals a sensitive curiosity for the philosophical and literary productions of his time, then Heinemann is clearly no intellectual. He only has a slight knowledge of contemporary literature. He has read a lot of Heinrich Böll and Günter Grass, but others only sporadically. He prefers critical discussions with writers to actually reading their novels. He himself has no connections with fiction writing. He prefers "things of flesh and substance." So he mostly reads jurisprudence and historical works, and naturally a lot of theology. He read Golo Mann's Wallenstein at one sitting. (When he was talking about this, he employed a culinary metaphor: "That's the only way of quaffing a draught like that!")

Heinemann has not always been so averse to literature. On his own admission, he composed many pieces of poetry when he was at grammar school. And at the age of seventeen he actually wrote a full-length drama: a tragedy in five acts with the title "Konradin, the Last of the Hohenstaufens," a prose work with ballads interspersed in the action. Two years ago, it came to light among some old papers, and to the amazement of its author it was given its première at the Villa Hammerschmidt on the occasion of his seventy-second birthday. At a later stage Heinemann must evidently have lost his literary proclivities somewhere along the way.

But if you define an intellectual as a man of independent and original thought who expresses himself clearly and employs watertight arguments, then Heinemann may well be numbered among them. What is much more important than such definitions, however, is how such enlightened thinking works out in political practice. All too frequently criticism remains without practical effect, because reforms which the politicians recognise to be necessary are not carried through for fear of offending the voters. When Minister of Justice, Heinemann was frequently enough accused of not keeping in step in his reforms with the mood of wide areas of the population. Heinemann did not accept the validity of this argument. He accepted that the politician should, of course, seek to convince as many people as possible, but he should not be expected to wait patiently until deep-rooted prejudices die a natural death in the population. On the contrary, the state should play an active part in removing prejudice from the population through the agency of its legislation.

Heinemann regards all Utopian projections of the future with a due measure of scepticism. He is well aware of the fact that the continued maintenance of status quo does not necessarily offer a real future, and for this reason he understands the revolutionary impatience of the youthful generation better than most of his contemporaries. He has always made it clear that the tasks of the future are not to be solved by adopting a state of mind which will admit of no experimentation. But he also knows that the Kingdom of Heaven is not realised on earth. The notion that a change in the system of ownership would be sufficient to create a world free of hatred, wickedness and hostility Heinemann regards as pure heresy. As he is fond of saying, the nearest we can get to the ideal is the "relative Utopia" of a better world.

In his inaugural speech as President he said,

> The secret of the great and revolutionary advances is likewise one of finding the one small step which is the key strategic move in that it induces further steps to be taken in the direction of a better world. That is why there is little purpose in despising the imperfections of our present reality nor of seeking to bring down the absolute into the everyday. Instead of doing either, let us rather seek to change conditions step by step by means of criticism and collaboration.

Criticism, readiness to compromise, fairness and tolerance in political conflict, confidence in man's rationality, but scepticism towards idyllic Utopias — in all these respects Heinemann appears as the representative of a tradition quite different from the Christian heritage, namely that of the Enlightenment. He himself would probably note this with some considerable surprise. Heinemann regards the term "Enlightenment" as referring to a developmental stage which he left behind him when he embraced the Christian faith after years of "all manner of reason and Enlightenment." But he is using the word in a very personal meaning which only makes sense if it is related to his own past experiences. When he turned to Christianity at the age of thirty he lost none of the family spirit of the forty-eight revolution. And the liberalism of the assembly at St. Paul's church was itself nothing other than a belated attempt to give practical political effect to the ideas of the Enlightenment.

Criticism, or critique, an expression to which Heinemann returns to time and again, is the key word of the European Enlightenment. Immanuel Kant, who sought to release human society from its self-imposed passive subservience, included the word "critique" in the title of each of his three principal works. Only those who do not let others speak for them, who speak on their own behalf, not just repeating the ideas of others, can lay just claim to the title of maturity. Criticism is to be directed against everything that justifies its continued existence purely on the grounds that it exists already. And justice was to become "the distillation of those conditions under which the arbitrariness of one individual can be reconciled with the arbitrariness of another according to the general principles of freedom." Whether or not Heinemann has read his Kant, his life and work certainly bear the marks of the Kantian heritage.

The concept of a philosophically neutral state in which secular and ecclesiastical authorities are strictly segregated is one which Heinemann has consistently supported, and it too derives from Enlightenment thought. At the end of the religious wars in England recognition of the fact that people with different religious loyalties can only live together on the basis of practical mutual tolerance led to the passing of an Act of parliament which for the first time gave a state guarantee (albeit a limited one) of freedom of conscience. Heinemann has often referred with admiration to this English heritage. It marks the beginning of the history of human rights backed by constitutional guarantees which was to culminate a century later in the proclamation of human rights in the Virginia constitution of 1776. The Basic

Law of the Federal Republic, which in Heinemann's estimation bestows the dignity and rank of statehood upon the Republic, forms part of this tradition with its guarantees of the right of free development of personality, of the equality of all men before the law, of freedom of religious faith and practice, and the right of freedom of expression.

Heinemann's critique of the German tradition of an autocratic state is also an example of the Enlightenment at work. The first duty of the citizen, in Heinemann's opinion, is not to hold his peace, but to be restless, to be active and critical, for the citizen is not a subject, but in a democracy he is sovereign. If this self-assurance is lacking in the citizen, the best of constitutions can be of little value. This is why Heinemann endeavours, whenever possible, to enhance this quality in the citizen. In his assaults on the authoritarian state mentality, there is more than a trace of the Enlightenment aspiration that all men are free and independent by nature and as free and equal men they should therefore be able to conduct their own community affairs.

Heinemann's patriotism also bears traces of Enlightenment modes of thought. He has been committed to German unity like few others. In the fifties he campaigned for reunification. Of course, he had always been aware that "nations are not divinely ordained to live together under the panoply of statehood." But he was reluctant to surrender the hope that Germany might recover her unity within the context of a single state which her neighbours would have no cause to fear.

Heinemann is a patriot. He has no inhibitions about employing the term "fatherland," because he makes no attempt to conceal the fact that his fatherland has been a difficult parent. His brand of patriotism has none of that stuffy arrogance which fails to distinguish between love of the fatherland and rabid nationalism. Gustav Heinemann's dream of a German fatherland involves Germany as a community of freedom and justice, and on the international level, a good neighbour living in peace. In the parlance of the Enlightenment that is called "patriotism with an international face."

Whilst in Western Europe generally the ideas of the Enlightenment led to democratic revolutions, Germany, in a bitter phrase of O. H. von der Gablentz, funked the Enlightenment. It was not until seventy years had passed since the American revolution and over half a century since the French revolution that a German response to the Enlightenment seemed to flicker for a while. This was in those few short weeks at the beginning of 1848, when the dream of a German revolution was dreamed and thrown away in St. Paul's church in Frankfurt. It is not surprising that Heinemann associates himself with this tradition of 1848.

These two traditions — a forty-eight cast of mind handed down through his family, and Christian faith born of the experience of manhood — together make up the picture of Gustav Heinemann the politician.

The way in which the enlightened liberal and the Christian traditions are blended in Heinemann's personality can be demonstrated by a turn of phrase which Heinemann has used both in the context of the gospels and of the Basic Law, namely "a supreme offer. Of the bible he says: God accompanies us along the false paths we take with the supreme offer of reconciliation through His son." And in the context of the constitution: "Our free society within a philosophically neutral state is a supreme offer." This is more or less how he has expressed it on countless occasions.

This use of the same term is no coincidence, because both the gospels and the Basic Law have in his view a common concern for the dignity of man. The very first article of the Basic Law makes reference to the inviolability of the dignity of man. It is to be an obligation backed by the whole power of the state to respect and preserve it. As is the case with other democratic constitutions of the last couple of centuries, this notion of the dignity of man can be traced back to the doctrine of the Enlightenment that all men possess inborn, inviolable and inalienable basic rights.

For Heinemann, human dignity goes much deeper than that. Even though it is a concept not to be found expressed as such in the Bible, Heinemann sees in the relationship between God and man the true basis of human dignity, as the Bible shows: "Dignity of man! It has been given to us by God the creator, who has called each and every one of us by name and said to us, You are mine."

However the idea of human dignity is interpreted, it stands at the meeting point of the Christian and the enlightened liberal traditions:

> It is my conviction that Christianity has the special and particular task, in this constitutional application of the dignity of man, of recognising a measure of its own preaching on the nature of man as a person; this will enable Christianity to contribute to the full practical realisation of the social order we have established.

In this sentence Gustav Heinemann, the black, red and gold Protestant, reveals himself in full.

In the last hundred years of German history that is a rare enough combination. As a rule, Protestants have not been black, red and gold liberal democrats, but black, white and red German nationalist autocrats. Liberals have only seldom been men of the church. And it seemed that it would continue to be the case in the Federal Republic that a man of such views would be compelled to act the role of an outsider. But it is a most hopeful sign for German democracy that a former outsider like Heinemann is now the leading representative of the state. For Heinemann does not owe his rise to the highest office in the land to characteristics that are normally regarded as indispensable to the politician. Sociologists would probably say of him that he is not a figure with a clearly-defined "persona." He is neither a strong patriarch like Adenauer, nor kind and good-humoured like "Papa" Heuss, nor is he a man exuding security and clouds of cigar smoke like Ludwig Erhard. Heinemann is not a charismatic figure, but monosyllabic, and sometimes blunt. He has a profound aversion to chasing after popularity in any shape or form. The effectiveness of his speeches has nothing to do with histrionics or stylistic flair. It depends on normal seriousness, intellectual rigour, and simple language which can be readily understood. It never occurs to him to tell people only what he thinks they want to hear.

But even this lack of a feeling for popularity has its positive side.

Heinemann's whole life, even with its mistakes, stands for the principle that moral convictions and political realism are not mutually exclusive propositions, that morality is not a private affair which the politician would do well to remove from his mind as swiftly as possible when he enters public life, and that realpolitik does not have to be synonymous with a reckless power game.

That is the basis of his credibility. And it is also the basis for the respectful sympathy with which the younger generation regards him. In the turbulent Easter days of 1968, when young people went out on to the streets in a mood of rebellion after the attempt on Rudi Dutschke's life, and the democratic system seemed seriously threatened, Heinemann alone possessed the authority to speak out strongly with the voice of compromise. His authority did not derive from the office he held — he was neither the President nor the Chancellor, only a member of the large cabinet in the grand coalition. His authority derived solely from the credibility of a man speaking as he did. It is well worth recalling the words he used at the time:

> The shattering events and steadily rising disturbances of the present time make it encumbent upon all of us to stand back and reflect. Anyone pointing an indiscriminate accusing finger at the actual or supposed instigators or wire-pullers should not let it escape his attention that in the hand with the outstretched index finger there are also three other fingers pointing back at himself. By this I mean that we all have to ask ourselves what we might have done in the past to cause anti-Communism to get to such a pitch that murder is attempted and that demonstrators have so forgotten themselves as to indulge in acts of vandalism and even arson.
>
> Both the assailant, who made the attempt on the life of Rudi Dutschke, and the eleven thousand or so students who have been involved in demonstrations outside newspaper buildings, are young people. Doesn't this mean that we, the older generation, have lost contact with sections of our young people or have at least lost our credibility in their eyes? Does it not mean that we must take criticism seriously, even when it originates from the younger generation?

Improvements in this and other areas can only be successful if there is no further provocation from either side. Emotional outbursts are two a penny, but they are not particularly helpful — they simply increase confusion. Nothing is so much needed now as self-control — even in the public bars or wherever else the events of recent days are being discussed.

Our freedom is given shape and substance by the laws which we have given ourselves. It is a matter for the police and the judiciary to ensure that these laws are respected and recognised. There is no reason to doubt that the police and judiciary are doing their duty.

But what is even more important is for us to help one another to conduct ourselves in a democratic manner which will permit police and judiciary to exercise their function.

One of our basic rights is of course the right to demonstrate in order to mobilise public opinion. The younger generation also has a claim to have their wishes and proposals heard and taken seriously. But acts of violence are plainly wrong as well as being foolish. The lesson is an old one: riotous behaviour and acts of violence have exactly the opposite effect on public opinion to that intended by those involved. Politically motivated students should also recognise this fact and conduct themselves with restraint.

Our Basic Law is a supreme offer. For the first time in our history it seeks to affirm the validity of the dignity of man in a peaceful, democratic and socially conscious state, within which there is ample room for a multiplicity of points of view, which should be clarified by means of open discussion.

It is our common task to find common ground on the basis of our constitution and to put its articles into practical effect. The turbulent situation in which we find ourselves must be exploited to our common advantage.

In retrospect, Gustav Heinemann once called this speech on television his speech for the candidacy of the office of Federal President. When he gave it, no one thought he would ever be a candidate for that office, least of all Heinemann himself. Eleven months later the Federal parliament elected him to the presidency.

The Figure-Head of State

At the beginning of May 1972 editorials were appearing in some papers expressing the view that the "hour of the President" had now come. The week before, the opposition leader Rainer Barzel had lost a constructive vote of no confidence, and Chancellor Willy Brandt lost his parliamentary majority on the following day when the vote was taken on the Chancellor's budget. In this situation of parliamentary stalemate it was the duty of the Federal President, according to these commentators, to resolve the deadlock. Only the Federal President was capable of acting, they maintained, and moreover the Basic Law was claimed by some to offer a much greater freedom of action in a crisis situation to the head of state than was generally assumed to be the case.

The commentators were wrong. The hour of the Federal President had not yet come. It is true that neither the Chancellor nor the leader of the opposition had a majority in parliament. It is also true that there was a great deal of talk about new elections. Erhard Eppler, the Minister of Development, proposed that the Federal President should take the role of honest broker, call the party leaders together and get them to agree publicly on new elections, and then Barzel too would not be able to hold off any longer. But Eppler's proposal only highlighted the dilemma without contributing to its solution. For there is nothing in the constitution about an agreement between the Federal President and the leaders of the parties as a means of paving the way to new elections. The opposition would also have had to make concessions, not an easy thing for them to do immediately after failing to carry through a vote of no confidence.

The Basic Law only admits new elections when the Chancellor has lost a vote of confidence or resigns; but in both cases the opposition can prevent new elections taking place if they can elect a new Federal Chancellor in the Federal parliament. And at the end of the crisis week in Bonn, Rainer Barzel was resolved to have another go at toppling the Chancellor, this time with the help of those for whom a premature end to the parliamentary term would mean a loss of allowances and pension rights. At any rate, this was how Chancellor Willy Brandt read the situation and for this reason he was prepared to take a defeat on the budget vote rather than be faced with the possibility of new elections by losing a vote of confidence. Since the Chancellor was not prepared to open the way to elections, the Federal President had his hands tied. Even in a situation which was demonstrably stalemated he could do little more than express his point of view. It was up to the leader of the government to take the decisions.

This Bonn crisis week began for Gustav Heinemann on the Sunday evening, 23 April, at seven o'clock in the President's living room in Bellevue castle in Berlin. He had dined somewhat earlier than usual so that he could watch the results of the Baden Württemberg Land elections on the television. With him were Frau Heinemann, her sister Gertrud Staewen, the Heinemann's youngest daughter, Barbara Wichelhaus, his old fried Helmut Gollwitzer and Frau Gollwitzer, his personal adviser Popitz, and the present author. It was clear from the first results that the CDU would gain a working absolute majority. Some of us watching reacted with disappointment and resignation. Heinemann remained impassive. He was especially interested in the crucial position of the Free Democrats. If they were able to hang on to their share of the votes in the Stuttgart Land parliament no repercussions on the Bonn coalition would be likely. By about 8 o'clock it became clear that the Liberals had with their 8.9 % achieved a result which promised consolidation in Bonn. That was decisive; Heinemann did not watch the rest of the election report from Stuttgart.

The FDP had won in Baden-Württemberg, but in Bonn at the same time they lost a parliamentary deputy. Twenty minutes before the polls closed Wilhelm Helms, who came from Bissenhausen in Lower Saxony, telegrammed his resignation from the FDP. Willy Brandt's parliamentary majority was dealt another body blow.

When Gustav Heinemann returned to Bonn at midday on the Monday, Rainer Barzel had already made up his mind to bring about the fall of the Chancellor. At five past six in the evening Olaf von Wrangel, parliamentary manager of the CDU/CSU party and their permanent liaison officer with the Federal President, rang up Heinemann's Secretary of State Dietrich Spangenberg and informed him that the party leadership had endorsed Barzel's decision. If Heinemann considered it necessary to have talks with the opposition leader, Barzel would place himself at the President's disposal. Spangenberg immediately informed the Federal President of Wrangel's call. Heinemann decided to receive Barzel on the following day, but first he wanted to talk to Brandt and Scheel.

Willy Brandt appeared on the same evening, at a quarter past nine. He looked exhausted. His vigorous campaigning in Baden-Württemberg had not borne fruit, and his hopes that the treaties with the East would have a favourable impact on the Land parliamentary elections had not materialised. The treaties, which were the centrepiece of his foreign policy, seemed now imperilled because a farmer from Bissenhausen, who had once even been a member of the conservative German Party, realised too late that he had transferred his allegiance to the wrong pary. But Willy Brandt was neither despairing, wretched nor resigned on that Monday evening; his mood was rather one of "positive fatalism" (Konrad Ahlers), a state of mind that was to help him more than once in the days that followed to bear up under the strain of threatened defeat. It had come to his notice, Brandt told the Federal President, that, apart from Helms, the opposition had supposedly persuaded a few more people to cross the floor to the FDP. He could not verify this, but now the battle was on in earnest.

At nine o'clock on the following morning the President's closest staff met as usual in Heinemann's office: Secretary of State Spangenberg, his deputy Professor Caspari, press adviser Müller-Gerbes and his two personal advisers Markscheffel and Popitz. By then Heinemann had already had his daily turn in the Hallenbad, read the morning papers and worked through some files at his desk. He showed no sign of the tension which everyone involved feels at such times of crisis. His staff stood waiting at the round conference table until Heinemann, coming across from his desk, asked them to be seated. The appointments for the day were talked over, and a couple of necessary alterations were made. A meeting with Foreign Minister Scheel was added for 11.45 am, and a ministerial caller who had been fixed for 3.30 pm was put off to make way for Rainer Barzel to see the Federal President. Then details were discussed as on every ordinary working day, for example, the question as to whether the publisher Axel Springer should be officially congratulated on his sixtieth birthday and, if so, in what form. Everything is dealt with on the spot or instructions given as to how it should be handled. The discussion is always clipped, friendly and businesslike. Heinemann cannot tolerate longwindedness or forgetfulness. Everything must be well prepared, decided, or ready for decision. Heinemann's observations are terse: "All right", "Yes, I know", "You're doing that? Carry on ..." In between there is time for a laugh, a thoughtful question, even a joke.

Shortly after half past nine Dr. Paul Friedrich Martin came from the Federal news agency with the press report. Normally the topics in this survey are wide-ranging, from everyday occurrences in Bonn to the outstanding events of international politics. On this day, however, the interest of the commentators was concentrated almost exclusively on Barzel's vote of no confidence. Whilst Dr. Martin was giving his report, Heinemann was going through his speech for his visit to the army in Coblenz on the following day. He was already familiar with most of the press commentaries. (Later Dr. Martin, who had previously given the press reports to Heuss and Lübke, confirmed that Heinemann was always far better informed than either of his predecessors.)

In the meantime, Secretary of State Spangenberg had been trying to get Foreign Minister Scheel on the telephone. He was informed by the Minister's

With his children Barbara Wichelhaus, Christa Delius,
Uta Ranke-Heinemann and Peter Heinemann

With his grandson Oliver Heinemann

The morning conference with (from left to right) Professor Caspari, the Federal President, Secretary of State Spangenberg, Heinemann's personal adviser Markscheffel, press adviser Müller-Gerbes, and Dr. Martin from the Federal press and information office, who attends daily with the press digest office that Scheel was currently with the Foreign affairs committee. But even there Spangenberg was unable to contact him directly, but passed on the information that Heinemann wished to speak to Scheel in the Federal President's office at half past eleven. At five to ten Spangenberg was rung back and told that Scheel would come at the appointed time. Ten minutes later Spangenberg informed the CDU member of parliament von Wrangel that the Federal President would be free to see Barzel for discussions at half past three in the afternoon.

At eleven Heinemann received the new German Ambassador to Tunisia, Dr. Heinz Naupert, who was making his obligatory formal visit to the Federal President before his departure for Tunis. Scheel arrived thirty minutes later. Anyone seeing him who was not aware of the fact that he had considerable worries could be excused for thinking that Scheel had just returned from a victorious battle. He looked fresh, optimistic, almost good-humoured, at least like someone for whom nothing would go wrong. He assured the Federal President that the FDP parliamentary party would not fall apart, that the constructive vote of no confidence was by no means won for Barzel. At this time there was already talk about the prospect of Kienbaum and Kühlmann-Stumm joining Helms and voting for Barzel, and that would mean the fall of the Chancellor if the CDU parliamentary party voted solidly behind Barzel. At midday Heinemann received a government delegation from Haiti, just another of those many courtesy visits which do not mean a great deal but which have to take place. Then the Federal President took his lunchtime break.

Shortly before three Heinemann was back at his desk looking through files, signing letters, reading the draft of a speech, carrying out the everyday work of the President. Rainer Barzel was due to appear at half past three. He drove up to the Federal President's office building nine minutes late. His black Mercedes 300 still bore private plates, and the vehicle was not flying the pennant of the leader of the government. Barzel, bronzed as ever, had a friendly greeting for everyone who crossed his path, and took great pains to conceal his confidence in victory behind a dignified exterior. Like all who call on the President, he entered his name in the visitors' book, which lies open outside the office of the President on the first floor of the building. On the page which bears the date 25 April 1972 the names of Ambassador Naupert (like a good German official, he had not neglected to preface his name with his title of doctor), Foreign Minister Scheel and the members of the Haiti delegation had already been entered. There would be room on the page for two more signatures. But Rainer Barzel did not make use of the space. Instead, on the right-hand page, which was still blank, he signed his name in his elongated, energetic hand so assertively in the middle of the page as if to say: this page belongs to the new Federal Chancellor and to no one else.

The conversation with Heinemann lasted precisely half an hour. Heinemann asked his guest if he was certain of a majority in the vote on Thursday and whether he was confident of lasting out the rest of the parliamentary term with a tight working majority. Barzel answered both questions in the affirmative and gave the reasons behind his decision to make a bid for power: the Baden-Württemberg election result was, he argued, a clear vote against Willy Brandt and his Bonn coalition; there was no longer a majority in parliament in favour of the treaties with the East; and in such a situation he, Barzel, could not refuse to listen to the voice of the voters. Barzel left the Federal President at nine minutes past six.

The leading Bonn politicians continued to have a succession of further meetings (late that evening the top men in the coalition were still sitting in the Palais Schaumburg and discussing how they were going to keep hold of the two waverers, Kienbaum and Kühlmann-Stumm); but for Heinemann the political part of his working day was already at an end with the visit from Barzel. Early in the evening he and his wife participated in the prize-giving ceremony in Rolandseck station for the winners of the Olympic painting competition organised by German newspapers.

On the following day the tension in Bonn increased. On the agenda of the Federal parliament stood the debate on Section 04 of the 1972 budget, the

Federal Chancellor's estimates. Discussion time on the Chancellor's budget is traditionally used for general debates on government policy. On this occasion it was a matter of survival for the government, and for the opposition of proving that the coalition was at an end and that they were in a position to take over the reins of government. The duel between Chancellor and aspiring Chancellor resulted in a clear points victory for Willy Brandt. For the first time that week he went on to the offensive and delivered a speech whose effect was felt far beyond the debating chamber. Millions of people in the Federal Republic were following the tense hours in Bonn on their television sets.

Gustav Heinemann was not one of the viewers. On this particular day he was not in Bonn at all, but in Coblenz visiting a Federal army leadership school. This visit had been planned weeks before. And the hectic situation in Bonn gave Heinemann no reason to call it off. The ball was very much in the court of the party politicians. Heinemann could only have stood on the sidelines in Bonn, as becomes his office. The only difference made to his visit to Coblenz was that Defence Minister Helmut Schmidt was unable to accompany the Federal President, because he could not be spared from the budget debate.

As usual, Heinemann turned up too early for the army helicopter which was waiting for him in the park of the nearby Palais Schaumburg. The machine was in the air ten minutes before the appointed take-off time. Press adviser Müller-Gerbes caught it by the skin of his teeth. During the flight Heinemann was serious; it was clear that he was absorbed in thought. It was too noisy in the helicopter to ask him what he was turning over in his mind. There is no doubt that he would have given much to be present if that really was going to be the decisive day in parliament. But his duties as head of state were keeping him far away from the political storm-centre.

There were only three indications in the course of the day of what was at stake in Bonn. At a quarter to twelve Heinemann's press adviser rushed to the telephone. Rumour from Bonn had it that a huge demonstration march was on its way to the parliament as an expression of sympathy for Willy Brandt. But the report turned out to be premature. Demonstrations for the Chancellor were not to take place until the evening. At midday Heinemann gave a programmatic speech on the duties of the Federal armed forces to the entire complement of the Army School. Only the opening sentences departed from the prepared manuscript: "In disturbed times like the present every man should continue on his way in peace. Let us do so here." That is all Heinemann had to say about what was going on in Bonn, and then he addressed himself to his subject. In the midday break, the press men did their best to persuade the Federal President to comment on the constructive vote of no confidence. Their efforts were in vain. Heinemann would express no opinion on the matter.

For the rest, the day followed its allotted course. At nine thirty Heinemann was briefed on the history and objectives of the School. This was followed by a visit to three of the courses currently taking place, and it was at midday that Heinemann addressed the whole School. In the afternoon Heinemann was the guest of the Federal army supply command.

Just before six in the evening the President's helicopter touched down in Bonn. The battle of words between government and opposition was still being waged in parliament. The CDU seemed to be certain that they would succeed in bringing about the fall of the Chancellor. In the evening the President of the parliament von Hassel requested the Federal President's office to draw up the declaration of Barzel's appointment in good time for Thursday. The opposition leader had already worked out the protocol for his assumption of office: the Federal President was to deliver over the documents of appointment to the new government; the oath-taking ceremony was set for four o'clock; and Rainer Barzel intended to set up shop in the Palais Schaumburg at five. Even the members of the Cabinet had been decided upon; the members of the Barzel government had already had their likenesses taken by a Bonn official photographer against a blue background. The FDP leadership had another attempt at winning over their wavering

76

supporters to vote against Barzel. Scheel and Mischnik took on Kienbaum, and Ertl and Genscher sought out Kühlmann-Stumm.

But meanwhile, in the market square in Bonn and in the streets of other towns and cities something was taking place, the like of which had not been seen in the Federal Republic since the demonstrations against the state of emergency laws. The people went out on to the streets to demonstrate against a threatened decision of the Bonn parliament. There were 10,000 in Hamburg, 12,000 in Frankfurt, and 15,000 in Bonn. They demanded what the "Hamburger Morgenpost" had printed in banner headlines on its special edition: "Willy Brandt must stay Chancellor."

The two FDP members of parliament, on whom the fate of the socialist and liberal coalition seemed to depend, were not impressed by these expressions of sympathy for the Chancellor. On the following morning Kienbaum and Kühlmann-Stumm declared their total commitment to Barzel in a meeting of the FDP parliamentary delegates. The SPD got to know of this through the parliamentary secretary of state Karl Moersch: "You can give up hoping; they've made up their minds this morning in the party meeting." The race seemed lost.

Heinemann was ignorant of all this. Between nine and ten he had his closest staff with him again. Again the order events for of the day had to be altered. A choir which wanted to serenade the Federal President was going to have to step down. But the television appearance recalling the Care Pact action by the Americans, which was due to be recorded at half past eleven, was kept in the programme. The finance committee of the Federal parliament was invited to the Villa Hammerschmidt for dinner and discussions. The engagement was not called off. It was decided to await the outcome of the decision in Bonn.

Then they turned to matters of detail, as on any normal day. The press report by Dr. Martin stressed particularly the upsurge of support for Willy Brandt, the excellent way he had played his part in the budget debate in parliament, and the evening demonstrations. A few papers also expressed their views about the possible role of the Federal President if Barzel failed to swing the vote of no confidence his way and Brandt linked the vote on the Chancellor's budget on the following day with the issue of confidence. There was nothing new for Heinemann in these press commentaries. He would make his decision when the time was ripe. But he expected his office would have worked out the various contingencies in good time and to have sorted out the important questions under constitutional law concerning the function of the President in such circumstances.

Shortly before ten the meeting broke up, a few minutes before the decisive sitting was to begin in parliament. Secretary of State Spangenberg reminded them to watch the television. Only Heinemann did not seem inclined to follow the summons: "I have no desire to listen to all that."

Five minutes later, however, he switched the set on. Alone in his office, he saw, not the aspiring Chancellor Barzel, nor even the original choice Walter Hallstein, but former Chancellor Kurt Georg Kiesinger lead the no confidence debate, saw Willy Brandt giving a speech, which sounded like a last testament, saw Walter Scheel, pugnacious as never before, castigate the renegades in his party, saw Herbert Wehner with his sharp tongue unmask Franz Josef Strauss as the man who was really stage managing the fall of the Chancellor, and saw Richard von Weizsäcker give parliament a lesson in the art of losing (a speech which may well have been ringing in the ears of his fellow party members later on).

At half past eleven Heinemann recorded his television broadcast. Then he hurried back to continue watching, accompanied by his personal adviser and the author. In the meantime, the members of parliament had been summoned to the secret ballot, and speculation was running wild in the lobbies. Even at this stage Heinemann remained calm on the surface, only expressing his annoyance at the inflated language of the television reporter. In between times he read files and signed letters. At sixteen minutes past one the result was announced. The SPD members embraced one another. The figures were not yet known. In the lobbies there was talk of a tie with 248 votes to each side. That would mean defeat for Barzel, but would not give Brandt victory. For the first time, Heinemann revealed signs of impatience. He lit a cigarette, but still sounded in good spirits: "Come on, let's have the figures."

At twenty-two minutes past one the President of parliament, von Hassel, announced the voting figures. Rainer Barzel had only 247 votes, two less than he needed to become Chancellor. The coalition party members leaped from their seats, shouting and applauding. Barzel did not even try to conceal his disappointment. He remained in his place, shaking his head. Once again he had made his move too early. Willy Brandt, who had been scarcely able to conceal his emotion when he came back into the debating chamber, sat down again in the seat reserved for the Federal Chancellor which Rainer Barzel had failed to take from him. His features were mask-like. Heinemann commented on the result in a brief sentence which recalled his own election as Federel President: "It really was a change of power." Then he went to lunch, saying "I hope things continue well."

The tension died away. Heinemann's staff unwound, and press officer Müller-Gerbes poured out a round of drinks. Only Secretary of State Spangenberg, whose Mecklenburg breeding did not permit him to indulge in spontaneous expressions of jubilation, held on to his reserve. He was the first to point out that Barzel's defeat did not mean that the battle was over as far as the coalition was concerned. It was true that the fall of the Chancellor had been averted, but at that moment no one knew if there would be a majority in parliament for the Chancellor's budget or for the treaties with the East. Spangenberg had to be back at two in the Palais Schaumburg, where the Cabinet was discussing the situation after the vote. Was Willy Brandt to attempt to survive the rest of the parliamentary term in the face of an opposition which needed only two votes to gain a majority? Ought he to exploit the upsurge of sympathy which the public had expressed for him after Barzel's defeat by holding early elections and make the vote on the budget an issue of confidence? At a quarter to four Spangenberg reported to the Federal President on the Cabinet meeting. So far no decision had been taken.

That meant for the President that he was not needed in Bonn for the rest of that afternoon. He could take no part in the coalition's consultations, although it was this selfsame coalition which had brought him into office. So Heinemann went off to visit his youngest daughter, Barbara Wichelhaus, in Frechen near Cologne. For the evening he had invited his personal adviser and the author to a game of skat.

Shortly after four, Spangenberg received two delegates from the SPD parliamentary party for a discussion about new elections. At half past six he talked on the same subject to the Minister Horst Ehmke in the Palais Schaumburg. Ehmke asked Spangenberg to obtain an expression of view from the Federal President for the Cabinet meeting at nine o'clock. The Federal government wished to know whether, if Brandt asked for a vote of confidence the next day and lost, Heinemann would dissolve parliament immediately or give the opposition one more chance at a constructive vote of no confidence before dissolving parliament.

At a quarter to eight Spangenberg reported to the Federal President on his conversation with Ehmke. He put before Heinemann a draft statement of intent which he had had drawn up two days previously by the Federal President's office. There was nothing in the constitution, argued Spangenberg on the basis of this analysis, to prevent an immediate dissolution of parliament. Interpreters of the Basic Law agreed that in the event of a parliamentary crisis the head of state could take emergency action. It had been demonstrated on that day at sixteen minutes past one that the opposition leader could not command a majority in parliament. So if the Chancellor were to lose his majority, Spangenberg argued, the President would be free to emerge from the political sidelines and act by dissolving parliament. Heinemann listened to this line of argument, but still reserved judgement. The responsibility for dissolving parliament was one of such gravity that he felt unable to commit himself in advance.

Just before nine Spangenberg returned to the Cabinet, and Heinemann called his two skat partners to their game in the Villa Hammerschmidt. He played expertly and boldly, never taking long to make up his mind. He would far rather lose an interesting hand than play for safety. When the evening came to an end just before midnight he had won hands down. In the course of the game, at about half past ten, Spangenberg came round once again to report on the cabinet meeting. The government had decided not to ask for a vote of confidence on the following day. Chancellor Brandt wanted no new elections until after the treaties with the East had been ratified. The decision had almost taken itself. But it did not give the impression of being the result of a strategy well worked out in advance. The current situation could have been foreseen days ago, but it is clear that neither the coalition leaders nor the Chancellor's office had worked out the tactical, let alone the strategic position.

During a pause in the skat game Heinemann talked about the loneliness of his office. He did so without complaining. The head of state cannot become involved in the party decisions in a tense situation like this. But that evening he would have been happier to be there discussing things with the party leaders or going over the excitement of the day again with old political comrades in the "Rheinlust", the regular bar of the SPD. But his office does not permit him to take such liberties. Instead, he had to stay in the Villa Hammerschmidt and play skat. (While he was doing this, Frau Heinemann was watching the Apollo 15 landing on the television. The return of the Apollo astronauts from the moon, which a little while ago had had everyone on the edge of their seats, had turned into a side-issue on this day of extreme political tension.)

Friday 28 May 1972: at nine o'clock the usual morning meeting of Heinemann's staff took place in his office. The SPD parliamentary party had already endorsed the Cabinet decision of the preceding evening and had expressed itself against a vote of confidence. So the vote on the Chancellor's budget on the parliamentary agenda for the day would definitely not lead to new elections. But the vote would still decide whether Brandt had a parliamentary majority of at least one vote with which he could, if need be, continue to hold power until the end of the parliamentary term, or whether a state of absolute balance would be achieved. That would mean for Barzel that he would have recovered some of the ground he had lost by not getting the no confidence vote through, and for Brandt's government it would mean the beginning of a period of incapacity.

On this particular morning Heinemann had no fixed engagements. He worked at his desk and watched the result of the voting on the television: 247 for, 247 against — a state of equilibrium, of equal forces neutralising each other, had indeed been achieved.

Late that afternoon the leaders of the coalition and the opposition met in the Palais Schaumburg in order to discuss possible ways out of the impasse, particularly in view of the fact that the vote on the treaties with the East was fixed for the coming week. At the end of a meeting lasting four and a half hours, Barzel was no longer able to prevent the possibility emerging of the opposition agreeing to a common formula by means of which the Eastern treaties could be assured a safe passage through parliament. Gustav Heinemann had already left the Federal capital early in the afternoon. At four he was in the social centre of the Evangelical church of Wesphalia in Villigs near Dortmund taking part in a brains trust.

The "hour of the President" still had not arrived at the end of a week of crisis in Bonn. For as long as Willy Brandt did not put the confidence vote and hence could not be defeated, Gustav Heinemann was not in a position to dissolve parliament and announce new elections. As the events of the week had shown, it was of course possible for the Federal President to talk to the leading politicians whenever he desired. The opposition leader, who was trying to topple the Chancellor, placed his reasons for doing so before Heinemann. The Chancellor and the Foreign Minister, the leaders of the two coalition parties, appeared before the President when he summoned them. And Heinemann was given up to the minute information on all the important political happenings: his Secretary of State attended the Cabinet meetings ex officio and for the opposition von Wrangel, their parliamentary executive met the President to keep him advised of the situation. Heinemann had to be

82

sure how he was to conduct himself in the event of a vote of confidence failing. But the decision as to whether new elections should be called or not was not and is not a matter for the head of state, but for the leader of the government. Even in a situation of evident stalemate, in which neither the Chancellor nor the leader of the opposition can command a parliamentary majority, the Federal President has no powers of his own which would entitle him to act.

In the months that followed, a public debate arose on the issue of how Heinemann would act in the situation where a vote of confidence failed to gain a majority. Where this happens, the Federal President becomes the central figure, and the subsequent course of events is in his hands. According to Article 68 of the Basic Law, which deals with the issue of confidence, Heinemann has three courses of action open to him. He can refuse the Chancellor's request for the dissolution of parliament. Or, alternatively, he can accede to that request. In that event he has to decide whether to allow the full interval of twenty-one days permitted by the constitution to elapse before the dissolution or not. This is a decision which can have far-reaching consequences. If the President waits for twenty-one days, that gives the opposition the opportunity to attempt to bring about the fall of the Chancellor again by means of another constructive vote of no confidence. But if the President dissolves parliament immediately, then he clearly deprives the opposition of this opportunity.

Franz Josef Strauss, who grasps at any opportunity to attack Heinemann in public, was already making precautionary accusing noises to the effect that such a course of action on the part of the Federal President would amount to nothing less than a "coup d'état from above." On 4 July 1972 Heinemann received the opposition leader Rainer Barzel and told him what his attitude was. In his view, the current stalemate position in the Federal parliament made it essential that the decision should be placed in the hands of the electorate. All the parties represented in parliament had voiced themselves in favour of elections. So there was no longer any reason to delay any further the dissolution which everyone sought after the refusal to put the vote of confidence. In a television interview on 6 July Heinemann repeated what he had told the opposition leader two days before:

> If the constitution permits dissolution within a period of twenty-one days, the actual moment of dissolution can just as well come at the end of the period as at the beginning. The situation at present is that it has been known for weeks that we should be moving in the direction of a dissolution of parliament, and all the parties are in favour of elections. So I see no good reason at the present moment why, after a vote of confidence has been refused, there should be any more delays.

Heinemann had deliberately chosen his words with care: he could see "at the present moment" no reason for unnecessarily delaying the dissolution of parliament; and he went on to say that he had not yet reached a final decision, and moreover in the place of the opposition he would not give up in advance the right laid down by the constitution to a second vote of no confidence. This caution was well-founded. If the "hour of the President" really were to strike, Heinemann must take good care not to act in such a manner that he might be suspected of party political bias. If he deprived the opposition of a second bite at the no confidence vote by dissolving parliament immediately, then there must not be the least shadow of doubt about his actions being conditioned solely by concern for the proper working of the parliamentary system and not by sympathy for one party or coalition of parties.

The real crux of this crisis summer was that the dissolution of parliament would not be resolved until the autumn, six months after the stalemate situation had begun in parliament. The week at the end of April when the stalemate was setting in brought to light a loophole in the constitution. Up until then the division of responsibilities among head of state, government and parliament seemed clear. As long as the government had a majority in parliament which permitted them to retain power, the Federal President stands on the political sidelines. But in the event of government crisis the President comes out into the open. The most important political task of the head of state is the resolution of government crises. For this purpose the Federal President has certain powers in reserve. But, in order to prevent any long-term extension of these powers, they are restricted in their application to three clearly defined situations. The Federal President is permitted to take the centre of the stage when, in elections for the Chancellor, the leading candidate does not have an absolute majority at the third ballot; when a Chancellor loses a vote of confidence and requests the dissolution of parliament; and when — this third case is somewhat complicated — a Chancellor, despite a lost vote of confidence remains in office and parliament votes out a bill which the government has declared to be urgent in nature.

Up until now, none of these three contingencies, for which the Basic Law has made provision, has actually arisen in the history of the Federal Republic. The fourth eventuality, which actually occurred, was not foreseen by the Parliamentary Council which drafted the constitution: namely, stalemate in the Federal parliament. The Federal President in such a situation ought be in a position to put the decision in the hands of the electorate by dissolving parliament — if not on his own authority, then at the initiative of the Chancellor or by a decision in parliament with a specific majority. Instead, the dissolution of parliament can only come about as the result of an issue of confidence, which even those moving the resolution want to see defeated — a somewhat cock-eyed situation. This is why in his television interview of 6 July 1972 Heinemann indicated that when things had calmed down the legislators should take a long cool look at the question of whether the dissolution of parliament could not be rendered less difficult.

But even a modification to the Basic Law of this nature would bring about no fundamental changes: the Presidency is not the centre of power. It is the Federal Chancellor who holds all the power.

There is no more disputing the fact that this is the one and only way in which the Basic Law regards the balance of power since Konrad Adenauer early in 1959 toyed with the notion of exchanging the office of Chancellor for that of President, and then turned the idea down flat. He had hoped that, as Federal President, he would be able to continue to hold the reins of political

decision. But he convinced himself of the fact that the constitution does no'
give the head of state the degree of political scope for action which he
intended to exploit in that office. If he wanted to determine the course of
political events for the future, he was going to have to remain Chancellor.

There are historical reasons why the drafters of the Basic Law did not
want the President to be a powerful figure. The sixty-five men, who from the
autumn of 1948 until early 1949 were busy drawing up a constitution for
the Federal Republic, had gained their political experience in the Weimar
Republic. It was taken for granted among them that the excessive amount of
power accorded to the Reich President played a substantial role in the
collapse of Weimar democracy. And that must not be allowed to happen
again.

The President of the Weimar Republic was indeed a powerful man. He
was directly elected by the people and hence his democratic credentials were
even stronger than those of the party leaders. The Reich President could
name a Chancellor of his choice (who in normal times needed the confidence
of a parliamentary majority), and could also dismiss him from office. He
could institute a plebiscite if parliament passed a law which he did not like,
and he could also dissolve parliament. He headed the high command of the
armed forces and became ruler in a state of emergency. Under the notorious
Article 48 of the Weimar constitution he was able to suspend basic rights,
issue emergency decrees without seeking the approval of parliament, and
employ armed forces for the re-establishment of public security.

Despite this enormous power, it was virtually impossible to remove him
from office. It is true that the parliament had the right to propose a referendum for the dismissal of the President if the motion was passed with a two
thirds majority. But in view of the state of the political parties in the Weimar
parliament, this was tantamount to making the President irremovable.
A multi-party parliament which always found it difficult to achieve simple
majorities for the everyday decisions of ordinary politics was simply just
not capable of mustering a two thirds majority. And in fact this means of
removing the President was never seriously considered.

The Weimar Republic was certainly not the only system to founder because of weaknesses in its constitution. But the Parliamentary Council was convinced that the Weimar constitution played the major part in the downfall of the Republic, and the intention was to produce a much better constitution. The drafters of the Basic Law were worried about two things in particular: fear that the democratic masses could be unduly manipulated and fear of a crisis situation. The new state was to be a democracy, but strictly a representative one. For this reason, all those parts of the Weimar constitution which referred to plebiscites were excised. But above all else, the Federal Republic was to be stable, not torn apart by crises like the Weimar Republic. This is why the dual system of President and parliament was dispensed with in the Basic Law, since it had worked out so disastrously for the Weimar Republic. The Federal Chancellor was to be the sole focal point of power, and he alone was to determine the guidelines of policy. In order to make it more difficult to topple a Chancellor, Carlo Schmid devised the constructive vote of no confidence. The five per cent clause was introduced to prevent a fragmentation of the party system. And parties that conflicted with the constitution were to be banned.

The head of state was shorn of his power. In contrast to Weimar, the President of the Bonn Republic was no longer to be directly elected by the people, nor was he to be able to appeal directly to the people over the heads of parliament in matters of legislation. The Federal President is no longer in charge in a state of emergency. He is deprived of supreme command of the armed forces. He is not in a position to choose one of his own men as Chancellor, nor can he dismiss a Chancellor from office on his own authority. The dissolution of parliament depends on two strictly defined exceptional situations. The term of office of the President is no longer seven, but five years, and he can only serve a maximum of two successive terms. He is not present at Cabinet meetings, and he certainly is not in the chair. As a rule, he is elected from the parliamentary ranks, but he does not enter the chamber between the time of his assumption of office and his departure from office except on occasions outside the normal run of parliamentary busness, for example, a memorial ceremony on the death of a predecessor.

Whenever the Federal President acts in the name of the state, it is not he who bears political responsibility but the Chancellor or the appropriate Minister. The Federal President is the representative of the Federal Republic under international law, he concludes treaties with foreign states in the name of the Federal Republic, he receives and gives accreditation to ambassadors. But the political responsibility for the treaties lies with the Federal government, and it also determines the acceptance and dispatching of ambassadors. The Federal President gives the assent to the laws which parliament has approved, and for this purpose he has a limited right of scrutiny. But he is not the guardian of the constitution: that is the task of the Federal constitutional court. The Federal President appoints and dismisses Ministers, but in order to do so he requires the countersignature of the politically responsible Chancellor or Minister. The President carries out the right to grant pardons on behalf of the Republic, but the authority for sentencing mainly lies with the Länder rather than the Republic, and there is no death penalty. The Federal President awards the state honours, but the lists are drawn up principally on the basis of proposals from officials of the Republic, the Länder, and the local authorities.

The drafters of the Basic Law managed to create a state with a powerless figurehead, but they had more than just good historical grounds for allowing the entire political responsibility to fall on the shoulders of the Chancellor rather than the President. They were also modelling themselves on a fine working example: the British constitutional monarchy.

In Britain, a distinction is drawn between the "dignified" and the "efficient" parts of the constitution. The monarch forms part of the "dignified" elements of the constitution, and he or she permanently holds the highest position in the state. If the institutions of the parliamentary system of government operate without interruption, then the monarch is left with only a symbolical function. He or she embodies the unity of the nation but has no powers to

With former Federal President Dr. Heinrich Lübke

With Willy Brandt and Walter Scheel: announcement of the socialist-liberal
coalition

With Leo Bauer

◁ With Professor Helmut Gollwitzer

With Federal Chancellor Willy Brandt (New Year reception)

With Secretary of State Egon Bahr

Hilda Heinemann

make any decisions nor any political responsibility. The only roles of the monarch are "to be consulted, to encourage and to warn."

The monarch only assumes a political role when the balance of parties in the Commons makes it impossible for the government to function. In this situation the monarch has certain reserve powers. He or she becomes an "efficient" part of the constitution for the duration of the crisis. The monarch seeks to bring about a return to normality by working towards the formation of a new majority government. Party political neutrality is a prior condition for the monarch's authority under these conditions. The strength of the monarchy lies not in its power, but in the respect which it commands.

The office of Federal President has been fashioned on this model. Like the British monarch, the Federal President belongs to the "dignified" rather than the "efficient" part of the constitution. Only when a government crisis arises does he have reserve powers like his British model. The Federal President is the living symbol for the Republic, the unity of the state, the validity of its fundamental values and the binding nature of the rules laid down for the resolution of political conflicts.

When he signs the treaties which the Federal Republic concludes with other states, he is embodying the power of the Federal Republic as a state vis à vis other states. By giving the assent to the laws passed by the Federal parliament, he is documenting the fact that they must be respected by all, also by those who opposed these laws when they were still bills before parliament. By appointing the individuals who are to be entrusted with political leadership or high office in the state, he is symbolising the dignity of the democratic system.

Only a man who is not obligated to one particular part of a system can be held to be representative of the entire system. As Dolf Sternberger puts it, the Federal President is at one and the same time the "President of the opposition." Consequently he must keep his distance from all parties, particularly the one from whose ranks he has emerged. It speaks for itself that he resigns all party positions after his election. He is permitted neither to be a member of the Federal nor of any Land parliaments. He is equally forbidden to hold any other remunerated office, to follow any other trade or calling apart from that of President. In addition, he may not be a board member of any industrial undertaking. His material independence is secured by means of a substantial income.

His obligation to be neutral prevents the Federal President from taking a public stand on the party political issues of the day. When he makes any kind of political statement — for example, in his Christmas broadcast on radio and television, at the New Year's reception or during state visits — he must remain aloof from all current political conflict.

The office of Federal President demands from its holder the art of reserve and discretion, but even in normal times he is not limited to representative and symbolical acts. He is not just performing a decorative function. The Federal President participates in the everyday business of politics by virtue of certain discretionary powers in the appointment of senior officials, officers and judges of the state, and in giving the assent to laws. In addition, he has a limited right to involve himself in the formation of governments.

The Basic Law is short and to the point in the context of the role of the President in giving the assent to laws: "The laws which have come into being according to the provisions of the Basic Law will be given the assent by the Federal President after their countersignature and will be announced in the Federal Gazette." (Article 82) There is no express reference to discretionary powers. But the Federal President does have to satisfy himself that the laws have actually come into being "according to the provisions of the Basic Law." That is the source of his discretionary powers.

If a law is constitutional both in the way in which it has come into being and in content, then the Federal President has no choice but to put his signature to it. So he cannot refuse to sign either on grounds of content or on political grounds. But where there are well-founded doubts as to the constitutional validity of the law, he is authorised to refuse his signature.

Up until the present time, every President has become involved in conflicts of this kind. Gustav Heinemann has refused his signature in one case.

This was a law relating to the protection of the term "architect" as the designation for a specific profession. The Federal parliament and Federal Council had carried the bill in July 1969, that is, when the grand coalition was still in being. On 19 December 1969 Federal Chancellor Brandt sent the bill, which he had already endorsed, for the Federal President's assent. In a covering note he drew the President's attention to the fact that the Ministers of Justice and Home Affairs had certain constitutional reservations about the bill. Heinemann instituted a legal enquiry in his office and asked for two further legal reports from the Justice and Home Affairs ministries. As a result of these enquiries he decided to withold assent from the bill, and informed the Presidents of the Federal parliament and the Federal Council and the Chancellor of his decision on 23 April 1970: "After a thorough examination of the constitutional situation I do not find myself in a position to give my assent to the architect's law and publish it in the Gazette." In its judgement on the engineers law in July 1969 the Federal constitutional court had, the President continued, ruled that the Republic has no legislative competence to determine who should bear a particular professional title. The grounds for this decision which led to the judgement by the constitutional court with relation to the engineers law equally held good for the architects bill and this established it as unconstitutional. Heinemann drew attention to the fact that the legislators had the option of challenging his negative decision before the constitutional court. The Federal parliament did not exercise this option, and so the architects bill did not become law.

The Federal President has comparable powers of scrutiny when it comes to the appointment of Ministers, senior civil servants, Federal judges and the military. In this respect too, the political responsibility lies with the Federal Chancellor or the appropriate Minister, and the Federal President is not permitted to exploit this right of scrutiny for his own political ends. He is not able to impose personal decisions, but he can prevent them by refusing to sign the relevant documents of appointment.

If the Federal President has serious grounds for objection to the technical or personal qualifications of a candidate, he will attempt to dissuade the Federal government from their choice. Such matters have to be handled discreetly to prevent them from turning into public issues of prestige either for the President or the government.

There is one instance of the appointment of a senior civil servant under Heinemann sparking off a public debate. Early in 1972, Karl Schiller had proposed his brother-in-law, Professor Machens, for the post of President of the Federal Institute for soil research in Hanover. The Cabinet had been informed of the family relationship between Minister and candidate for the post when it put forward Schiller's proposal for decision. When it was Heinemann's turn to sign the papers of appointment, he announced that he had reservations. He summoned Schiller and sought to persuade him to choose another candidate. Schiller asked for twenty-four hours' grace to think the matter over, and then sent his Secretary of State Schöllhorn to see the Federal President. Schöllhorn repeated the assurances that Schiller had given: namely, that there were no doubts in the Cabinet about the competence of the candidate, and that a brilliant expert should not be disadvantaged in his promotion prospects just because he happened to be related by marriage to a Minister. Heinemann signed. Only later was there considerable public disquiet when the boycott against Machens began in the Federal institute in Hannover. Heinemann had actedly perfectly correctly, announced his reservations, and in the end put his faith in the decision taken by the government. But the public discussion of the Machens affair also had its unfortunate repercussions against Heinemann, who found himself unjustly accused of having actively encouraged nepotism.

There have been occasional disputes in relation to the Federal President's right of scrutiny in the case of candidates for ministerial posts. Theodor Heuss is said to have refrained from naming Thomas Dehler as Minister of Justice, and Adenauer withdrew his proposal. Heinrich Lübke frequently spoke out against certain candidates, but he never let things come to the point of a trial of strength between himself and the government. This kind of problem has so far not arisen for Heinemann. He acted in an advisory capacity in the formation of the 1969 government, and there were no causes for conflict.

According to Article 63 of the Basic Law, the Federal President has the right to advise when it comes to the election of a Federal Chancellor: "The Federal Chancellor is elected by the Federal parliament without a debate on the advice of the Federal President." But the meaning of this Article is not that the Federal President can recommend one of his own men to parliament. What he must do, rather, is to hold discussions with the party leaders in order to discover which candidate has the best chance of obtaining the required absolute majority at the first ballot. If the majority is clear, the involvement of the President is restricted to one of ensuring that the constitution of the government being formed conforms to the will of that majority.

This was what happened when the 1969 government was formed. After the Free Democrats had declared that they would form a government together with the Social Democrats, a majority was assured for Willy Brandt. Gustav Heinemann put his name forward for election.

If Willy Brandt had not been elected on that occasion, and if in the next fourteen days no other candidate had gained an absolute majority in the Federal parliament, and if, at the third ballot, there was only a simple majority for the leading candidate and not an absolute majority, then Heinemann's role would have been decisive. It would then have been up to him to decide whether he would accept a minority government, or whether he would ask the electorate to vote again, by dissolving parliament.

Because the Federal President has to take on such a weighty responsibility in times of crisis, this excludes the possibility of a popular outsider with no political experience being elected. In the sixties views in favour of an outsider were occasionally being voiced in public. It was considered that the office of head of state was purely decorative in nature and could therefore be filled by a representative would had no party political connections, by a "Professor Hindenburg," as Herbert Wehner expressed these unpolitical aspirations. This would not only mean ignoring the fact that the head of state can take on a central role in times of crisis. Even the normal everyday work of the President can only be carried out by experienced politician. Dealings with the ambassadors of foreign states, the wide variety of contacts with politicians of all parties, scrutiny of the laws and proposed candidates for high office — a political outsider would have his work cut out trying to perform all these duties. The more thoroughly a Federal President knows the workings of parliament and the executive on the basis of his own experience, the better he is equipped for his office.

The Federal President works with the help of a body of officials which forms the Federal President's office. It is the function of this office to keep the President informed of all political events at home and abroad, and of what is happening on the economic, social and cultural scene, to advise him on the conduct of his office, to plan his journeys and all public appearances, and to carry out his instructions or transmit them further. In comparison with other groups of Federal officials, the staff of the Federal President's office is small. In 1972 it consisted of 101 people in all, of whom twenty held senior appointments.

The office is led by a Secretary of State, whom the Federal President himself selects and appoints. So the Federal President is not even the head of his own office. His Secretary of State is at one and the same time in charge of the other employees and the closest adviser of the Federal President. His function as adviser can only be properly carried out if he can obtain a direct insight into the work and decisions of the Federal government. For this reason, he has the right to attend all Cabinet sessions and all Cabinet committee meetings. This right is laid down in the standing orders of the Federal government. Even in the event of a dispute between the government and the President the head of the Federal President's office cannot be excluded from Cabinet meetings.

The standing orders further lay down that the Secretary of State should enjoy unrestricted access to the papers to be placed before Cabinet meetings.

This prevents him from being confronted in a Cabinet session with proposals or motions of which he has had no prior knowledge, and which he has not been able to discuss with the President. So, although the President is not involved with the actual decision-making processes of the Cabinet, he does have the opportunity of putting his own views across through the agency of his Secretary of State.

At first, Gustav Heinemann had tried to obtain a Secretary of State from the ranks of the CDU/CSU. He wanted to do so in order to underline the non-party nature of his office. But the two candidates whom he asked — Paul Mikat and Heinrich Köppler — both refused. Then Heinemann called upon the West Berlin Senator Dietrich Spangenberg. This man, a native of Mecklenburg, is a convinced Social Democrat of the Willy Brandt school and had had a meteoric career in the Berlin administration. His first love is the army, whose troops he has visited on several occasions as Secretary of State. Spangenberg is an energetic head of the President's office, but he is far more of a politician than a bureaucrat. His relationship with Heinemann is one of friendly loyalty. Their years of working together have brought about an understanding between the two men, which makes long-winded discussions of a problem rarely necessary. Like Heinemann, Spangenberg is a taciturn man, but at times his language is much more blunt than that of his superior.

The fact that Heinemann, in contrast to his predecessors in office, selected as his Secretary of State a home politician rather than someone with Foreign Office experience is a strong indication of where he considers that his most important duties lie. At the beginning of his period of office the state visits to Germany's neighbours directed public attention more to the foreign political aspects of his work, but his particular interest is none the less concerned with the possibilities of his office to influence internal policies. Heinemann regards the noblest task of the head of state as being one of taking the sting out of the relationship between individual and the state, of encouraging the citizen to play an active role in politics, and of arousing his awareness for the social and political changes which are necessary. True, the actual power which he has at his disposal as head of state is severely limited. But lack of power is not necessarily synonymous with impotence. A Federal President who enjoys the confidence of the leading politicians of all parties has considerable possibilities for influencing the political decision-making processes. A Federal President who succeeds in gaining the respect and approbation of the population at large can play a significant part in stimulating public awareness. If a President knows how to exploit these opportunities, then he can aspire to that true authority which no legalistic power can force into being.

"Just like at Home"

In other European countries, the heads of state reside in royal palaces, even in cases where for many long years the highest position in the land has been held, not by a monarch, but a president who is a commoner: the French President lives in the Elysée palace; his Italian counterpart resides in the Palazzo Quirinale; and the Austrian Federal President's residence is the Hofburg in Vienna, the former palace of the Austrian Emperor. The official residence of the German head of state, by contrast, is the villa of a former industrialist.

If you go from the University of Bonn along Adenauerallee in the direction of the government quarter, you will pass by a stretch of land rather like a park just before the Bundeskanzlerplatz; here, set well back, there stands a white, rather old-fashioned building, a cross between a small castle and a dwelling house. If it were not for the Federal flag flying from the roof and the soldier of the Federal frontier guard on duty at the iron garden gate, you would scarcely think that this could be the official residence of a head of state.

Previously this was where rich industrialists lived, among them a Rudolf Hammerschmidt, who gave his name to the villa. He was the third occupant and chose Bonn as his place of residence after he, like the previous occupant, Leopold König, had amassed a considerable fortune in Czarist Russia. In the last years of the nineteenth century the expanding university town of Bonn, with its attractive setting below the Siebengebirge, at the point where the Rhine valley broadens out into the plain, became a favourite refuge for wealthy men in retirement. Villas standing in their own spacious grounds were constructed on the former wine slopes to the south of the town. The Palais Schaumburg, which stands near the Villa Hammerschmidt, and which

105

today is the official residence of the Federal Chancellor, was also once the private home of an industrialist. The Federal Republic purchased the villa and park from Hammerschmidt's heirs for 750,000 DM, a price which sounds incredible by today's standards. The villa was destined to be the official residence of the Federal President.

Theodor Heuss freed the building from the cake-icing ornamentation of the late nineteenth century and had the interior reconstructed for reception purposes. The division of the rooms has undergone little essential modification since then. The visitor enters the villa by way of the park. He crosses a couple of steps covered in red carpet and passes into the entrance hall. It is a square room, sparsely furnished, holding a magnificent Baroque writing table, on which the Federal President's visitors' book is laid out, two antique commodes, and nothing more. The terrace room abuts on to the entrance hall whose most important piece of furniture is a rarely-played Bechstein grand. This room gives access to the covered terrace and thence down a flight of outside steps to the rear part of the park, which stretches out towards the Rhine. On both sides of the terrace room are two long narrow rooms: to the left, the dining room, which can accommodate thirty-six guests and to the right the gallery, in which the representatives of foreign states present their papers of accreditation. The pillared room, so called because of the two rather unattractive pillars which cannot be done away with because they are load-bearing, is the only room which provides seating accommodation for a largish number of people. It is here that the Federal President conducts interviews with his guests, with heads of state, ambassadors, with politicians and other groups of visitors. There cannot be too many visitors at any one time; there are only a score of seats in the room. The furniture is a rather ill-assorted collection: modest modern chairs stand alongside an assortment of individual pieces from the Baroque, Empire and Biedermeier periods. One treasure is the so-called "ladies' room." The wife of the first Federal President furnished this little room with Louis XIV furniture, which it is true shows some signs of wear, but it is the one room in

106

the Villa Hammerschmidt with a uniform style. It is there that the exchange of gifts takes place on the occasion of state visits; and here too Queen Elizabeth withdrew between official engagements during her state visit. The floors of the reception rooms are covered with carpets from virtually every classical carpet-producing country of the Orient. The most valuable are gifts of the Shah of Persia. Some of the pieces of furniture are also valuable, some being state property, others permament loans from the Länder, like the Baroque writing table in the entrance hall, which came originally from Augustusburg castle in Brühl.

The most valuable part of the villa's furnishings is the picture collection: from the eighteenth century Canaletto's "Moat Garden in Dresden," and a work by the Cologne Baroque painter Anton de Peters; from the nineteenth century five paintings by Carl Spitzweg and one by Hans Thoma. The classics of the twentieth century are represented by a few famous names. In the dining room hangs the most valuable of all the paintings, Kandinsky's "The Cow" painted in 1910 and valued at one and a half million marks, and also works by Alexei von Javlenski, Paul Klee, Ernst-Wilhelm Nay, Willy Baumeister and Fritz Winter. The finest work in the pillared room is Emil Nolde's "Rough Sea with scudding Clouds" from 1948. In the gallery there is a splendid wall of Grieshabers: six large coloured woodcuts, entitled "Treeblossom."

Hilda Heinemann has been responsible for the acquisition of the majority of these paintings, in the form of loans from artists and collectors. She also ensures that contemporary art is on view in the Villa Hammerschmidt. In a two-month cycle, she sets up exhibitions of works by young sculptors and painters chosen by herself. More than twenty artists have had their works put one show in the Federal President's house, and over forty thousand visitors have seen them.

On the first floor of the villa are the Heinemanns' living quarters and the personal office of the Federal President's wife. Heinemann's office is not in the villa itself, but a few yards away on the first floor of the Federal

President's secretariat, a simple two-storey building on the edge of the magnificent park. It was built in 1950 and is now far too small. A large proportion of those who work in the secretariat have their offices in former dwelling houses in the vicinity of the Presidential offices. There are plans for a new building, but as yet no money is forthcoming.

As a retirement home for an industrialist, the Villa Hammerschmidt was certainly a splendid residence; but as the official residence of the head of one of the richest countries in the world it is a modest building indeed. Six rooms for reception purposes, none of them bigger than the public rooms of a medium-sized hotel, are hardly extravagant. When Gustav Heinemann took over the villa from Heinrich Lübke, the heating only worked sporadically, the kitchen facilities of the house were severely restricted, and the exterior badly needed redecorating. It took three months to renovate the place thoroughly: the kitchens were provided with modern equipment, the first storey was fitted out as a flat. In the palm house, which had been built on to the villa and had in days gone by held a collection of tropical plants, modern suites for the Federal President's guests were constructed.

But now as before the Federal President cannot accommodate the head of a foreign country under his own roof. Up until recently he has had to make some arrangement, such as renting the former Chancellor's bungalow in the park of the Palais Schaumburg or the presidential suite of a Bonn hotel. More recently the Baroque castle of Gymnich near Bonn has been placed at his disposal. And he still cannot play host to more than thirty-six guests in his own house. (There have been occasions on which twice that number have eaten in the Villa Hammerschmidt, but that meant setting up a second table in the gallery, giving rise to problems of protocol: who is to sit in the same room as the President, and who is to be seated in the second dining room?) And it is still impossible for more than twenty at a time to take part in discussions in the Villa Hammerschmidt.

On every occasion on which the Federal President has more guests than can be squeezed into his official residence, he has to hire accommodation elsewhere. For smallish receptions the Godesberg fortress is used. For the

108

larger functions the Beethoven Hall in Bonn is called into service. State receptions are held in Augustusburg castle in Brühl, which is more than a dozen miles away from Bonn. The Land of North Rhine-Westphalia is the owner in Brühl. The castle cannot be heated, and so it is only useable in summer. Thus it is that the head of the Federal Republic of Germany is only able to receive a state visit in the summer months.

In Berlin, the conditions are more favourable for the President when he is acting out his role as representative of the Federal Republic. He has at his command there his second official residence, Bellevue castle. Situated near the zoological gardens and lying on the banks of the Spree, it was originally a princely country seat to the west of the fortified city. The castle was built in 1784 by the architect Johann Michael Philip Daniel Boumann for Prince August Ferdinand of Prussia, the youngest brother of Frederick the Great. It is an early construction in the classical style, a building of rustic severity characteristic of the majority of Prussian castles around Berlin. The castle is set in a large park, laid out in a style which marks the transition from the French to the English fashion for landscaping.

The castle suffered severe damage during the Second World War. When it was rebuilt in the fifties the exterior was reproduced according to Boumann's original plans, but the layout of the rooms inside was altered in accordance with the building's new role. Only the so-called "Langhans" room on the upper storey of the main building was reconstructed in its original form at the request of Theodor Heuss. It is in fact a room with walls at right angles to one another which appears to be elliptical because of a cunning arrangement of eight blue marble pillars. Its walls are richly decorated with paintings and reliefs. As well as the "Langhans" room, four salons, and one large and one small dining room are used for reception purposes. In the large dining room up to two hundred guests can be accommodated, and the commercial scale kitchen in a side wing of the castle is more than capable of feeding that number. On the ground floor of the main building is situated the office of the President and a number of other offices for members of his staff.

Theodor Heuss was able to take symbolic possession of Bellevue castle shortly before the end of his term of office. It was only fully occupied by Heinrich Lübke. "Occupied" is putting it a little bit too strongly. Four or five times a year the Federal President passes a couple of days in Berlin; Heuss kept to this pattern, so did Lübke, and now Heinemann is following suit. Once a year the castle and park are swarming with people, invited by the Federal President to his summer party. But for eleven months out of the twelve the castle stands empty, a silent witness to the fact that it is not Berlin, but Bonn, which is the capital of the Federal Republic. Berlin was not one of the options open when the Federal Republic went in search of a capital. The sole metropolis that Germany had ever had (although it only lasted three quarters of a century between Bismarck's foundation of the old Reich and the fall of Hitler) had been carved up among the four occupation powers. The choice might have fallen on one of the old Land capitals, particularly on Frankfurt, the city of Goethe, whose history and geographical location made it seem well worthy of the status of capital of the new Republic; and Stuttgart or Cologne were also possible choices. But the decision was made in favour of Bonn — or rather, Konrad Adenauer made the decision in favour of Bonn. His personal wish coincided with the prevalent conviction of the time that Bonn would be as temporary as the state whose capital it now became.

The Federal Republic has long since ceased to be regarded as a temporary arrangement, as has Bonn. But Bonn will not be made into the centre of the Republic. This town, whose cultural life has no greater pretensions than that of the average provincial town, in which no regional newspaper is published and where not one single broadcasting station has its headquarters, differs from other towns of the same size mainly because land prices are higher than the average and because an exceptionally large proportion of the population is made up of civil servants. It is true that the population has now risen to 300,000 since a few nearby townships and villages have been brought under the same local authority, but that has not turned Bonn into a city. The industrial centres lie in Düsseldorf, Frankfurt and Hamburg. The great theatres and orchestras are to be found in the Land capitals, but not in Bonn.

The presence of the international diplomatic corps in Bonn has made little recognisable difference to the life-style of the capital. Social life is usually a matter of private gatherings, and if the Chancellor or the Federal press agency put on a large function, the big names in show business and the arts have to be flown in from outside.

Up until now, there has never been a military parade in Bonn. If it ever occurred to someone to put on a parade, there would be nowhere to hold it. The attractive market square in Bonn is more suited to the sale of produce than to military demonstrations, and the Bundeskanzlerplatz, which takes its name from the nearby offices of the Chancellor, is not a square, but a junction for through traffic.

There is nothing else like it anywhere in the world, nowhere else where a country of considerable economic strength and no mean political signifi-cance has a sleepy university town as its capital city. True, Bonn was thought of as a provisional capital. But it is not only the politicians who have come to accept that what was thought of as temporary is now to be seen as per-manent — the general public has accepted the view too. It all happened quietly, without great passion, without a painful coming to terms with the inevitable, without any throwing off unattainable dreams. The Germans do not dream of a capital city, even Berlin is not regarded as such any more.

In reality, Bonn is a secret symbol for the relationship of the post-war German to politics and the state. It has not come about in the Federal Republic that the city stands for the state, that the centre of political power is also the focal point of culture and science, of the economic and social worlds, and this lack is scarcely missed. The Germans rest content with the fact that Bonn is the place where politics goes on. The splendour of the state is not something the Germans feel any need of; it brings back unhappy memories for them.

A large but not very functional skyscraper block for members of parliament has been built, and in the open fields between Bonn and Bad Godesberg a new government quarter is coming into being. But these changes are not heralding a new attitude towards the state. These buildings are simply needed because the old ones are not big enough. Unornamented buildings constructed with a specific purpose in mind will appear here, not architecture of exemplary proportions fashioned to symbolise the state.

When the members of parliament building was constructed, the speaker of the Federal parliament at the time, Eugen Gerstenmeier, vetoed the introduction of hot water taps in the washbasins in the parliamentarians' rooms. He could not see the taxpayers accepting such extravagance on the part of their representatives. The episode typifies the atmosphere of Bonn. The state should not be characterless, but neither should it be extravagant, rather efficient and unobtrusive. Above all else it must maintain a watchful eye over its expenditure on upkeep. The politicians and the electorate are of one mind on this score.

So Bonn as a Federal capital is not just a solution faute de mieux, and the Villa Hammerschmidt as official residence of the head of state is no understatement. What may be regarded by outsiders as provincialism is regarded in Germany as modesty. At times even the reasonable sums expended on the capital have been regarded as excessive by the Germans. When Heinemann was having a covered swimming pool built for him in the park of the Villa Hammerschmidt, there were a few disgruntled mutterings.

---

1. Gustav Heinemann's signature to the Act ratifying the treaty with the Soviet Union.

2./3. The Federal President receives foreign ambassadors and dispatches German ambassadors. This is the letter of accreditation for the new German ambassador to Swasiland.

4. The Federal President gives over fifty longer or shorter speeches in the course of a year. This is the manuscript of a speech with hand-written alterations.

112

Gesetz
zu dem Vertrag vom 12. August 1970
zwischen der Bundesrepublik Deutschland
und der Union der Sozialistischen Sowjetrepubliken

Vom 23. Mai 1972

Der Bundestag hat das folgende Gesetz beschlossen:

Artikel 1

Dem in Moskau am 12. August 1970 unterzeichneten Vertrag zwischen der Bundesrepublik Deutschland und der Union der Sozialistischen Sowjetrepubliken mit dem dazugehörigen Brief der Regierung der Bundesrepublik Deutschland zur deutschen Einheit an die Regierung der Union der Sozialistischen Sowjetrepubliken vom 12. August 1970 sowie dem Notenwechsel zwischen der Regierung der Bundesrepublik Deutschland und den Regierungen Frankreichs, des Vereinigten Königreichs und der Vereinigten Staaten vom 7. und 11. August 1970 wird zugestimmt. Der Vertrag, der Brief und der Notenwechsel werden nachstehend veröffentlicht.

Artikel 2

(1) Dieses Gesetz tritt am Tage nach seiner Verkündung in Kraft.

(2) Der Tag, an dem der Vertrag nach seinem Artikel 5 in Kraft tritt, ist im Bundesgesetzblatt bekanntzugeben.

Die verfassungsmäßigen Rechte des Bundesrates sind gewahrt.

Das vorstehende Gesetz wird hiermit verkündet.

Bonn, den 23. Mai 1972

Der Bundespräsident

Der Bundeskanzler

Der Bundesminister des Auswärtigen

Gustav W. Heinemann
Präsident der Bundesrepublik Deutschland

an

Seine Majestät

~~Sobhuza II~~

König von Swasiland

Eure Majestät, Grosser und Guter Freund!

Von dem Wunsch geleitet, das durch die Abberufung des Herrn
Bernhard Heibach erledigte Amt des Botschafters der
Bundesrepublik Deutschland in Mbabane wieder zu
besetzen, habe ich beschlossen, dieses Amt Herrn

Alexander Graf York von Wartenburg
zu übertragen.
Seine bewährten Eigenschaften berechtigen mich zu der Erwartung,
daß er in der ihm übertragenen ehrenvollen Stellung bestrebt sein
wird, sich Eurer Majestät Anerkennung zu erwerben.

Graf York von Wartenburg wird die Ehre
haben, Eurer Majestät dieses Schreiben, das ihn in der Eigenschaft
eines außerordentlichen und bevollmächtigten Botschafters der
Bundesrepublik Deutschland beglaubigen soll, zu überreichen.

Ich bitte, ihn mit Wohlwollen zu empfangen und ihm in allem,
was er in meinem Namen oder im Auftrage der Regierung der
Bundesrepublik Deutschland vorzutragen berufen sein wird,
vollen Glauben beizumessen.

Zugleich benutze ich diesen Anlaß, um meine besten Wünsche für
Eurer Majestät persönliches Wohlergehen und das Blühen und Gedeihen
des Königreiches Swasiland zum Ausdruck zu bringen. Ich verbinde
hiermit die Versicherung meiner vollkommenen Hochachtung.

Ihr guter Freund

Der Bundesminister
des Auswärtigen

Scheel

Haus des Bundespräsidenten

Bonn, den 10. August 1972

Herr Präsident,

~~meine~~ Sehr geehrte Damen und Herren!

Wenn ich Ihnen den Terminkalender des Bundespräsidenten in seiner

manchmal ~~erstaunlichen~~ *grausamen* Vielfalt vorblättern würde, könnten Sie mit

Recht sagen, daß der Bundespräsident entweder ein Spezialist auf *ert allgemein—*

allen Gebieten ~~zu sein habe~~ oder aber ein Hochstapler. *sei* Wenn Sie mich

fragen: Ich halte beides ~~für~~ *Auslegungen meines Terminkalenders* Übertreibungen.

Zwar bin ich ~~nicht~~ *kein* Physiker, auch ~~nicht~~ *kein* Naturwissenschaftler. Dies

könnte ~~ich zum~~ *ein* Anlaß ~~nehmen~~, darauf hinzuweisen, daß ich ~~eigentlich~~

überhaupt gar nicht geeignet bin, hier vor ~~Ihnen~~ heute ~~eine Rede zu halten~~ *etwas zu sagen*.

Das wäre ~~ein~~ *aber nur* relativ billiger Versuch, mich aus der Verantwortung

zu ziehen. *Es gibt aber einen allgemeinpolitischen Gesichtspunkt zur naturwissenschaftlichen Forschungsarbeit, der mich veranlasst, dem* ~~...~~

~~Die Probleme, um die es bei aller Diskussion über die gesellschafts-~~
~~politische Verantwortung des Naturwissenschaftlers geht, sind zu~~

~~umfassend und berühren uns alle unmittelbar zu sehr, als daß hier~~

~~ein rethorisch eleganter Trick am Platze wäre.~~

Dies Zettel

Es müßte ~~jedem Politiker~~ *uns allen* auffallen, daß man die Naturwissenschaftler

unter den Bundestagsabgeordneten praktisch an zwei Händen abzählen

kann. Es müßte auch zu denken geben, daß im Bundeskabinett nur ein

Heinemann the Federal Minister of Justice used to indulge in his sport every morning in a public pool. But the President's position and security considerations prevent him from following suit now.

The head of state is not exempted from the principle of keeping upkeep costs low. It may be that the Federal President is the first citizen in the state, but the emphasis is firmly on the word citizen. He must not be allowed to live frugally, but neither must his life be too luxurious. The Villa Hammerschmidt meets these requirements. One of the many visitors looking round the Federal President's house is reported to have called out in astonishment: "But they've got Ingrain here just like at home!" It is not recorded whether this exclamation was an expression of applause or disapproval. It might be safely assumed that it was the former that predominated, for the President is not living in a palace but just a better than average citizen's house.

Gustav Heinemann fully agrees with this view of the President as a citizen. He has always lived on a modest scale. It is true that as an industrialist in the Ruhr he earned a great deal, but he has never been a big spender. The Heinemanns did not own a car. Gustav Heinemann did not even have a driving licence. When he returned from a trip abroad in 1964, his wife surprised him with the news that she had passed her driving test. But even this did not make them purchase a car.

Nor has Heinemann ever dreamed the German dream of a home of his own. The Heinemanns have for the past thirty-six years lived in the same house in Schinkelstrasse in Essen. Schinkelstrasse is a quiet, tree-lined side road not far from the old part of Essen with roomy but not very elegant houses built in the twenties. The main difference between number twenty-four and the other houses is that the facing is a slightly darker shade of grey. All that betrays the fact that this is the home of the Federal Republic of Germany is a recent small extension built on for the police detective.

The house is welcoming and bright enough inside; its furnishings are of a solid, comfortable elegance. The pictures on the walls, which include lithographs by Chagall and Picasso, betray the artistic leanings of the lady of the house. Heinemann's library is worthy of attention. It includes political literature from Tocqueville to Willy Brandt and Rainer Barzel as well as a valuable collection of original material from the early days of the Social Democrats; there are also a large number of historical and biographical works and a comprehensive section of theological writings. That Heinemann has an interest in bibliography is revealed by the many old editions he possesses, among them first editions of Melanchton and Erasmus of Rotterdam, J. J. Moser, Schiller and Jean Paul, the four-volume original edition of Prussian provincial law dating from 1794, and as a curiosity, which Heinemann proudly shows to his guests, "The Electorate of Brandenburg Court Midwife, that is: a most necessary Guide in Cases of difficult and awkward Births, by Justine Sigmundin, née Dittrichi, published in Cölln an der Spree 1690," a lavishly illustrated document of practical good sense from the early days of gynaecology.

Heinemann is especially fond of his garden, which although not particularly large is quiet and well-tended. Whenever appointments in Bonn permit, the Heinemanns spend the weekend in their Essen home. The Federal criminal investigation department has installed a comprehensive security system, but the alarms are well hidden and otherwise everything is as it was before. In this house their four children grew up, and now that they have married, they return with their own children so that they can visit their grandparents. Frau Heinemann has spent the majority of her life in the house; in all the years during which Gustav Heinemann had a simple one-roomed flat in Bonn when he was a member of parliament, and later a Minister, she remained behind in Essen. It was not until after her husband had been elected President that she joined him in Bonn.

Anyone who has been accustomed to a modest way of life does not become a spendthrift overnight. And Heinemann has not altered his lifestyle. Now and then, his office causes him to be the focus of a glittering company, and these days he has to wear evening dress more often, something he avoided when he could in the past. But he will not tolerate excess. For example, his rank entitles him to a Mercedes 600 for official purposes, but he regards this as unnecessary and is quite content to follow his predecessor and keep to a 300 model. If a 600 is needed, for foreign state guests, for example, then a hire car with a chauffeur is obtained from the Mercedes works in Sindelfingen.

"Ingrain just like at home" — Heinemann is fully in agreement with the sentiments underlying this exclamation. For if a renunciation of unnecessary exclusivity and a thrifty deployment of limited funds can help to bridge the gap between state and citizen, then Heinemann has succeeded in one of the principal tasks which he has set himself in the conduct of his office. He regards bringing state and citizen closer together as one of the prime objectives of his role as President.

The changes which he has advanced in the context of state protocol also reflect this concern. It took a long and difficult battle with the competent authorities to put them through, a battle which he only half won in the end. "We need men with self-assurance, men who act and conduct themselves like citizens. In my new office I at least shall do all I can to contribute to this process," Heinemann said after his election. And it is this way of doing things that he is after when it comes to protocol. In his view, it ill becomes a republic to hark back to the vanities of a tradition that belongs in an old monarchistic period.

Views like this found little favour among those who controlled such matters. They defended the customs of protocol not only on the grounds that they have become a valuable element in the rules of the game of international diplomacy since the Congress of Vienna, but also because protocol itself helps to give the state some of the aura it needs to acquire in the eyes of its citizens if it is to exercise some influence as a republic.

Heinemann does not dispute the fact that rules of protocol are necessary in order to facilitate diplomatic communication between states and in order to create a dignified framework for state business. But he finds it hard to submit to the plethora of rules and directions that dog the heels of the President. As far as dealings with foreign statesmen and potentates is concerned, Heinemann has bowed to the inevitable with reasonably good grace. There is no real avoiding military ceremonial at the welcoming and departure ceremonies of foreign heads of state, evening dress and decorations at state dinners, copious security arrangements and minutely detailed advance planning of the events. But if he had his way, the number of large-scale evening meals would be cut from two to one; Heinemann finds it rather a waste to talk twice in rapid succession to the same people in the same surroundings about the same subjects. He would also be glad to dispense with the traditional presentation of the diplomatic corps during state visits. But the diplomats cling tenaciously to sacred privileges, and so Heinemann soon gave up trying to put through his wishes in that direction.

But he has altered the ceremony of accreditation of ambassadors. It used to be the case that the ambassador who was making his first visit to the President should deliver a speech, the contents of which had to be notified to the President in advance. The President would then reply with a speech which was similarly prepared in advance. These addresses are no more. Instead the ambassador hands over his accreditation documents in the course of a brief ceremony in the gallery of the Villa Hammerschmidt. Afterwards Heinemann and his guest withdraw into the pillared room for a conversation. In this way he gets to know the new diplomat personally and the time is employed much more gainfully. The small military attachment of the Bonn guards batallion, which parades in honour of the ambassador, has remained. To do away with them would have offended against international custom.

It is easier to bring about changes in protocol in the context of ocassions at which only Germans are present, For example, military guards used to parade whenever the Prime Minister of one of the Länder or a member of the Federal government came to visit the head of state. Heinemann saw no valid reason for the expense, so he did away with it. The rules governing dress were also made less strenuous. At New Year's receptions in the Villa

Hammerschmidt cutaway jackets with a black waistcoat were the rule; Heinemann was content with an ordinary dark suit. On the occasion of state receptions in Brühl castle nothing but full evening dress used to be acceptable, but nowadays a plain dinner jacket is accepted for those who do not possess full evening dress. As far as Heinemann is concerned, rules about clothing are purely superficial. Naturally, any function should be properly conducted, but Heinemann does away with everything he regards as excessive. "On my invitation cards," he promised jokingly after his election, "the following will be printed: Suit desirable, but optional."

The biggest changes Heinemann has made concern the New Year's receptions. Certain rules had come to be accepted on the occasion of these receptions. In the course of proceedings which dragged on for over two and a half hours, Heinemann's predecessors used to receive the following: members of the President's secretariat, Bonn municipal politicians, representatives of the press, the Federal officers for the Länder, the Chancellor of the Order Pour le Mérite, the Presidents of the Federal Treasury and of the five supreme Federal courts, the heads of government of the Länder, the Chairman of the Federal parliament, and last but not least the Chancellor with the members of his cabinet. (By tradition, the diplomatic corps is not received in the Villa Hammerschmidt, but in the Beethoven hall.)

Heinemann considered that public servants loomed too large in this list. He felt the lack of representatives of organised social groups; and, in addition, he wanted to be able to receive ordinary citizens in his house on the occasion of the New Year's reception. For this reason the quota of state dignitaries was sharply cut back; in Heinemann's New Year's receptions the Länder are now no longer represented twice over, but only by the head of government or by the Land representative to the Federal Republic. Instead of the Presidents of all five Federal courts, the head of the constitutional court and one other court are invited. Their place is taken by representatives of the trade unions, of the employers' associations, and the churches. But Heinemann's greatest concern is to be able to greet among his New Year's guests a group of ordinary citizens, a cross-section of the population. On the guest list for 1971, for example, there were seven building workers, two of whom were foreign workers, five nursing sisters, four youth workers, two young academics, a lady pharmacist and the lady owner of a hat shop as representative of the self-employed, a bank manager and a union secretary, a prison official and a probation officer as well as two representatives of voluntary aid organisations.

A comparison between the new list of guests and the previous lists makes Heinemann's intentions clear. The state is not just composed of officials, judges, soldiers and politicians. We, the citizens, are the state. And since the New Year's reception is the sole large-scale opportunity in the year for the Federal President to welcome into his house representatives of the entire state, he insists that he should not just be surrounded by representatives of the people, but also the people themselves who elected these representatives. It is naturally impossible for him to invite more than a handful, and the means of selection is not by any means representative. But the important thing for him is the gesture: in the Federal Republic the citizen is sovereign.

Heinemann places the greatest value upon inviting as often as possible members of all levels of society. The object of these invitations is only rarely of a formal social nature, when, for example, he invites the Prime Ministers of the Länder and their wives to meet him, or the German Nobel Prize winners. Once he also invited the police detectives who look after his safety to a social evening. But such occurrences are the exception. Heinemann has no great interest in socialising on behalf of the state, at functions to which only the privileged have access. Instead, he invites such people along to political discussions.

His evening discussions have a dual purpose. On the one hand, they give the participants the opportunity of conducting an off the cuff exchange of views on more or less neutral ground. For this reason the press are not invited to such gatherings. Those taking part must be confident that nothing of what they say will become public knowledge. On the other side of the coin, Heinemann makes use of these evening discussions in order to obtain for himself first-hand information. He calls them his "on-going further education course." On occasion Heinemann is able, as a result of the information that he obtains, to make suggestions to the appropriate Federal parliament committee, to a Ministry or to some other official body. On one occasion an evening conversation in the Federal President's house had direct political consequences. The legal committee of the Federal parliament who were Heinemann's guests came to an agreement in the course of the discussion that they should, in the reform of sections relating to pornography, insert a paragraph on the journalistic representation of brutality.

The membership of these evening groups has been as varied as the subjects discussed. Heinemann has invited judges and public prosecutors, businessmen and representatives of the self-employed, university professors and youth representatives, the press council, writers and caricaturists, as well as members of the Federal parliament committees. There have been discussions on particularly delicate issues of public debate: the reform of the penal code, the problem of drug-taking, the position of unmarried mothers in our society.

The President's secretariat calls upon the help of the appropriate Ministries when deciding upon the composition of these discussion groups. For example, the proposal for the composition of the group on the drug problem came from the Ministry of the Family, Youth and Health. It was an odd assortment: the Ministers Strobel, Jahn and Genscher took part, as did the President of the Federal office of criminal law, Ministerial officials, university professors, psychiatrists and toxicologists, city youth care officers and senior school teachers, and also the young people themselves who are active participants in the struggle against the hold of drugs.

The guests for these evening discussions groups, who at the most number around thirty, congregate in the villa between seven and half past. They are greeted by the Federal President and Frau Heinemann, and drinks are served in the gallery. At half past seven precisely the President announces dinner in the dining room. The order of seating is reproduced on a small diagram, so that everyone can find his place without difficulty. As a rule, the meal consists of three courses, with which white and red wines are served, followed by champagne.

After the second course, the President delivers a short speech of introduction to his guests, in the course of which he usually departs from his prepared text. These evening meals are quite informal; there is none of the awkwardness and nervousness that might be associated with sitting at the same table as the head of state. But Heinemann does not linger over the meal; he is a quick eater, and the pleasures of the table mean less to him than the conversation that is to follow. It is said that Heinemann has been known to leave the table before the last guest has finished his sweet.

After the meal there comes a stroll to the former Chancellor's bungalow, which stands in the park of the neighbouring Palais Schaumburg. This is the only place with a room large enough to hold a discussion group of between thirty and forty people. Before the company settles down, coffee is served, and later there is a choice of drinks. The discussion is not led by Heinemann himself, but by one of the guests who has been asked in advance to take this role. Heinemann normally says little; he is more concerned to listen. Occasionally he offers encouragement, corrects a point, or answers a question. If the discussion takes an interesting line, it can go on for a long while, sometimes into the small hours. If Heinemann finds it tedious it can happen that he brings proceedings to a close as early as ten o'clock.

The participants in these evening functions are not the only guests of the Villa Hammerschmidt. Of course, not everyone can walk into the home of the President just like that. This is the province of the Federal frontier guard, who patrol the gardens, and the Bonn security division of the Federal criminal investigation department, which is responsible for the personal safety of the Federal President. But controls are reduced to the absolute minimum. To the extent that security considerations permit, the President conducts an open house.

The citizens of the Federal Republic take the fullest advantage of this. Every year, something in the region of 20,000 visit the Villa Hammerschmidt: school classes and firms, people living in a constituency who have been invited to Bonn to meet their member of parliament, representatives of cities and local communities which Heinemann has visited and who are now returning the compliment. These groups of visitors are guided through the Villa Hammerschmidt by an adviser from the President's secretariat.

Whenever Heinemann's appointment permit, he greets the guests himself, as he did for example in the case of a group from Oberviechtach who made their visit in March 1972. He had spent three days in this little Bavarian town in the summer of 1970. These were very special days for this small community in the economically depressed region on the Czechoslovakian border. And since the Federal President is always accompanied by journalists on his journeyings, Oberviechtach received its measure of public attention, which in turn had a noticeable effect on the tourist trade. As an expression of gratitude, a delegation from the town came to Bonn, bringing their band in local costume, the mayor and the local member of parliament. The band serenaded the President on the garden terrace. Heinemann thanked them smilingly for their return visit. The mayor replied respectfully, but swiftly came to the point: the visit of the Oberviechtach delegation to Bonn, he admitted honestly, was directed more at the tourist trade than the person of the President. Since Heinemann's stay in Oberviechtach the number of visitors had doubled, and in 1971 the total number of overnight stays had topped the 100,000 mark for the first time. The community was anxious to maintain this level, continued the mayor, and for this reason he would be glad if, for publicity purposes, a couple of pictures could be taken of this visit by the Oberviechtach delegation to the President. Heinemann did not take unkindly to such directness; on the contrary. He encouraged his guests to direct their efforts to doubling their tourist figures. He posed willingly among the town band to have the photograph taken. He asked the bass tuba player to perform a virtuoso solo. The mayor handed the President a commemorative medal; and in exchange the mayor got his photos, so everyone was happy.

Heinemann delights in such opportunities for direct contact with the man in the street. There is no programme planned down to the last minute to interrupt the conversation, no crush of press photographers to make the scene into a state event, no waiting throng to receive the imperious wave, a gesture he has not learned even to this day. In this setting, in his own house, he acts in a relaxed manner, swiftly making contact with simple people, a thing he often is not able to do in other contexts.

It is not easy for him to make direct contact with the citizen when he is out and about on official visits as head of state to an industrial concern or a school. It can happen that he walks straight past a group of children, who have been waiting for the great moment of his visit for weeks, scarcely noticing them, or that a planned conversation with a group of workers does not get under way, because Heinemann passes impatiently on.

The reason is not, of course, that the "little man" is not important to him. He means far more to him than the leading figures in the state; no President has taken as much interest as Heinemann in the problems of the little man. But during official functions his reserve easily overcomes his good intentions. Especially when a large number of people have gathered together in the presence of himself as head of state he finds it very difficult to be friendly and demonstrative.

In Paderborn, for example, where he made an official visit early in 1972, a few hundred people who had previously only seen the President on television, waited patiently for him behind a rope barrier in the market place. He had been a good hour in the town hall for the official reception by the council and local dignitaries. Then he finally appeared, accompanied by the mayor and his Bonn assistants. There was applause and a few friendly shouts. Heinemann seemed scarcely to notice them. Only when he was on the bottom step outside the town hall did he make up his mind to reply to this greeting. But he did not pause to reward the waiting crowd with a friendly gesture. It did not enter his head to walk round the half circle which the crowd had formed, shaking hands and allowing himself to be feted a little. Instead, he raised his right hand, almost hesitantly, no higher than shoulder level, let it fall abruptly, and disappeared into the waiting car.

Heinemann would be only too pleased to strip the office of President of all the stiff ceremonial which he is convinced only erects unnecessary barriers between the citizen and the state. But his good intentions sometimes clash with the reserve of his public appearances which themselves make the gap wider. Once, twenty years ago, Heinemann said that one can be master of a situation only within four walls. He lacks the outgoing approach which would make him enormously popular, like the first Federal President. But nor would it occur to him to deliberately stylise his public persona, in contrast to Theodor Heuss. It is something he simply could not do. He has little gift for ceremonial, he can just endure state jollifications, and he lacks the vanity necessary for adopting a paternalistic pose.

But this lack of demonstrativeness does not appear to have done much to damage the approval of his fellow citizens. Public opinion polls in May 1972 established that 80 % of the population are satisfied with the way he is conducting himself in office, a percentage which is far above anything obtained by any other politician in Bonn. It may be that Heinemann's office, which removes him from party conflict, helps him a little, but it does not explain the full measure of this support for him. People respect the credibility of Heinemann who is able to win people over without pandering to them.

Heinemann is of little use to the tabloid press and the illustrated weeklies, which entertain their readers with court reports on crowned and uncrowned heads. He wants to be neither a state actor nor a substitute monarch aloof from the lowly concerns of the common people, but for his appointed time in office the first citizen of his country.

The "Federal Wailing Wall"

On 2 December 1968 Georg Schirling, who had had both legs amputated at the thigh, wrote a letter to the authorities in his home town of Essen. He asked if it might be possible to have a parking space reserved for his use outside his home. The kerbside in front of the house was usually occupied by parked vehicles, and as a result he often had to make his way on his crutches for quite considerable distances when he came home from work of an evening. He found it particularly difficult to reach his house safely in wet and icy weather.

Three months later the Essen authorities sent him a reply. According to this letter, "it was regrettably not possible within the terms of traffic regulations to lay down the necessary road markings for such a purpose." The local authority "was only in a position to impose limitations upon traffic movement under the provisions of the traffic regulations when such limitations proved necessary for general road safety purposes or to facilitate the free flow of traffic. Personal requests," the official continued, "even when advanced on the basis of a severe illness or disability such as yours, can regrettably therefore not be taken into consideration."

Georg Schirling repeated his request on several occasions, but without success. On 14 October 1970 he wrote to the Federal President and sought his aid. Heinemann immediately called the Essen authorities on the telephone. He was informed that the traffic laws only permitted exceptions to be made when the public interest was involved. The private difficulties of an individual citizen were not, it was said, of public interest. Heinemann was not satisfied with this reply. He insisted that some means or other of helping the man should be found. That produced results: a sign was erected outside the house bearing a notice to the effect that the parking place should be left clear for a severely disabled person.

So Georg Schirling received assistance, but he was just one among many hundreds of handicapped people. Similar cases followed, in Brunswick, in Munich, and elsewhere. Heinemann approached the appropriate civic authorities and asked that the request should be treated in a non-bureaucratic fashion and met with success. In April 1971 a severely disabled person in Nuremberg, who had tried in vain to obtain a parking concession from the authorities, wrote a letter of thanks to Heinemann: "You did not act according to rules and regulations as the others did, but you helped someone when the need was there. For the rest of my life I shall remember to whom I owe this debt of gratitude."

Heinemann was not content to let the matter rest with individual cases. At the end of 1970 he wrote a letter to Georg Leber, Federal Minister of Transport. He described the Essen case and then went on:

> I should like to make use of the opportunity this individual case has presented me with to press you most urgently to examine whether a change in the traffic laws will be able to bring about a more general solution. I take the view that the handicapped in our productivity-conscious society frequently do not receive their fair measure of justice, and that in a consitutional state based on social justice they are the very people to whom we owe a particular responsibility.

Leber took up the proposal, but initially he came across difficulties. For a year the problem was discussed by experts in the Ministry of Transport and with the Land authorities. The outcome was that they did not consider it possible to alter the legal position to the advantage of the handicapped person. Then Heinemann called Leber to a personal meeting and urged him to make an effort to improve the legal situation. At the end of the meeting, Leber gave it to be understood that he would find a solution.

At the beginning of February 1972, the Federal Ministry of Transport sent to the Federal President's office the discussion draft of a law for the revision of traffic regulations. This draft contained, under the heading "Objectives," the following: "The legal possibilities must be established for enabling parking spaces to be placed at the disposal of severely disabled persons in the vicinity of their place of residence." The letter accompanying the draft stated that "this draft is shortly to be discussed with the Federal agencies, the Länder and the motoring associations. I shall be happy to keep you informed of the progress of the discussions." Heinemann's persistence had paid off.

Another example: in the small township of Hessisch-Lichtenau, between Kassel and Eschwege, the Home Mission of the Evangelical church maintains an orthopaedic clinic, which forms part of a rehabilitation centre for handicapped senior schoolchildren. 62 % of the pupils are only able to get about with the aid of wheel-chairs. In the autumn of 1970 the director of this institution, Pastor Hartmann, heard that the Federal postal service was planning to build a new post office in Hessisch-Lichtenau. He wrote a letter to the postal authorities in Frankfurt asking them to consider the needs of the handicapped in the construction of the building. The most important point to be observed was the avoidance of narrow doorways. In addition an entrance at pavement level would be advantageous, because it would not be possible for the handicapped to negotiate steps with their wheel-chairs. Pastor Hartmann added that he would be glad to act in an advisory capacity during the planning stages.

A few weeks later, in the residence of the Federal President, an "ideas competition for promoting help to the handicapped" was inaugurated. It had come about at the initiative of the Federal Minister of Labour, Walter Arendt. Pastor Hartmann, who had been invited to Bonn to take part in the ceremony, made use of the opportunity to place his problem before the Federal President. At that time he had still received no reply from the postal authorities. Heinemann asked the competent adviser in his office, a senior civil servant by the name of Ottinger, to pursue the matter. Ottinger wrote to Frankfurt, underlined Heinemann's interest in the plans for Hessisch-

Lichtenau and asked for information about what developments had taken place in the matter so that he could pass this on to the President. Just a fortnight later he received from the authorities in Frankfurt a copy of a letter to Pastor Hartmann, in which the post office assured him that they would be only too glad to take up Hartmann's proffered advice in respect of the new building.

The pastor expressed his gratitude in a letter to the President:

> I have never in the past had occasion to write a letter of thanks of this kind. But then there has never been a head of state who has been so committed to helping those in our midst who are seriously underprivileged.

Commitment towards helping the under privileged: that is a key phrase for Gustav Heinemann's conduct in office. Even in his inaugural speech before the Federal parliament he referred to this matter:

> On the occasion of my election large numbers of letters have come to me from people from all occupations and at all levels of society in which high expectations — far too high expectations — are placed on my assumption of office. I take these expectations seriously. In so far as they relate to personal matters, they represent calls for help in the manifold difficulties of everyday life, from those in need and sickness, those with housing problems, those in trouble with the law, those who suffer loneliness or injustice. Such needs are evidently far greater than our prosperous society is generally prepared to concede.

What Heinemann suspected in his inaugural speech has turned out to be an everyday experience for him. The needs are manifold and great and the Federal President is daily confronted with ever new problems. Heinemann has said about this aspect of his work that he often feels as if he is a kind of "Federal Wailing Wall." Apart from the normal official post, Heinemann receives something of the order of two hundred letters a day, which concern individual emergencies, problems which those involved can find no way out of: housing difficulties, training questions, pension problems, legal issues, requests for a job or a financial loan. Among these letters are also to be

The Federal President receives a group of young people

Meeting to found the German Society for Peace and Strategic Studies in the Federal President's house

Visiting the factory of AEG-Telefunken in Berlin

found the occasional inventor who hopes that, with the help of the President, he will be able to achieve the success he is seeking. Many of the letter-writers see in Gustav Heinemann a kind of substitute Kaiser, who can simply publish a decree altering the verdicts of state agencies: reversing official decisions, changing judgements in the courts, granting free pardons, finding work or accommodation, giving financial assistance. Most of these are outside the President's power. The right to grant pardons normally does not lie with him but with the individual Land governments. Judgements of the court can only be reversed by a higher court; and the financial means at the disposal of the President for the support of individuals is extremely limited.

But the post is not the only source of the problems which are brought to Heinemann's attention. There is scarcely an official discussion in the Federal President's office in which a problem of some kind is not brought forward, whether the leaders of the taxpayers' association are visiting Heinemann, or representatives of some business undertaking, university teachers or a small informal group concerned with the problems of drug dependents. And every time that Heinemann undertakes a journey, his notebook is filled with problems which he is supposed to help to solve.

Sometimes it is just enough for the Federal President to listen when someone is relieving his feelings. Heinemann is a good listener. He concentrates his entire attention on the person who is speaking to him, interposes brief questions, on occasion tries to give a sense of perspective to the problems being discussed, but at other times seeks to offer encouragement. In Berlin, for example, he received the "Governing Body of the Performing Arts", a federation of four organisations concerned with amateur theatre. They complained about the fact that acting was becoming an almost exclusively professional business, that there were too few full-time supporters for their activities, that there was a lack of money and interest on the part of officialdom, and that there was no Federal academy for the amateur theatre. Heinemann expressed his preparedness to ensure that they were given access to the appropriate authorities. More than that he could not do. But the most important fact is that the amateur actors were received by the Federal President in person. The fact that the head of state took an interest in their problems gave them the moral support they so badly needed.

During the same stay in Berlin, Heinemann received the local councillors for the district of Wilmersdorf, the Land leaders of the freedom league "Imperial Banner black red and gold," stout-hearted old men who forty years before had done their best to defend the Weimar Republic from its radical enemies on the right and left, and who were now lamenting the fact that there were none to follow them, and finally a group of young helpers of both sexes engaged in social work. A motley assembly of callers, but after a couple of minutes the conversation in each case invariably turns to anxieties and requests which they wish to draw to the attention of the head of state.

An adviser from the President's office is present at each of these conversations noting down the representations of the visitors and ensuring that the problems which are drawn to the President's attention are taken further. Every now and then an individual or an organisation will try to enlist the Federal President's aid in avoiding the legal decisions of a competent court. Propositions of that nature are turned down flat. But that kind of thing does not often occur. Whenever anything can be done, Heinemann does his utmost to ensure that it is done.

Paderborn is a good example. During Heinemann's one-day visit on 9 March 1972, a discussion took place in the late afternoon with politicians, economists and other representatives of the town and the surrounding areas. The main problem of the eastern part of Westphalia, Heinemann was told, was the inadequacy of the transport system. Paderborn is not connected to the inter-city express service, the Autobahn links are below standard, and, most important, the nearest commercial airport is too far away. But it is not possible for eastern Westphalia to have an airport of its own, because the airspace in that part of the world is reserved for military purposes. On these issues Heinemann subsequently wrote to the Ministers Leber and Schmidt.

He also passed on a request that concerned the German Affairs Ministry, namely, that practically the entire fish population in the Weser had died out in the past few years because the DDR had been polluting the river with potash waste. The Ministry has already let it be known that this question is on the agenda for future negotiations with the DDR. And finally in Paderborn, Heinemann was told by a representative of the Red Cross that there are instances of Germans, who want to emigrate from Poland, being deprived of their jobs there if West German relatives take the initiative and propose the emigration. Heinemann was asked to take steps to persuade Polish officials to desist from exerting this kind of pressure. The request led to a correspondence between the Federal President's office and the German Red Cross.

"You are well known as a man with a feeling for the problems of ordinary people, who is prepared to act in unorthodox fashion," one of his visitors in Paderborn said. Gustav Heinemann is indeed well known for this. In the first six months in office he received more letters requesting help than either of his predecessors were sent in a full year. And there has been no let-up since in the numbers. There is a sharp upward surge whenever Heinemann makes a public speech about underprivileged groups in society. The adviser in the Federal President's office who deals with these requests has been struck by the fact that, since Heinemann entered office, the members of fringe groups have plucked up a great deal more courage in writing about their problems to the President: foreign workers and the homeless, drug dependents and prisoners, and particularly those who are physically or mentally handicapped.

Heinemann places great value on being informed of these requests. In many cases he takes the decision himself. What is most important is that each case should be considered individually. Even in instances where no help is possible, the person concerned receives a personal letter from the Federal President's office on his particular case. Heinemann will not permit individual cases of need to be dealt with according to a ready-made formula.

The President can help most by opening doors. A letter from the President's office to a section of the administration, a telephone call to a mayor, a conversation with a Minister — initiatives like this are generally enough to ensure that a citizen in need receives help more swiftly than if he had sought to approach the autorities entirely off his own bat. Usually a letter is sent to the appropriate local authority who are closest to the facts of the matter, rather than to the central Land offices, which would take some time to act through all the official channels. This cutting through red tape is, of course, only possible in cases where swift and direct help is required, not for decisions of principle which have to be considered by a higher authority. The Federal President is not in a position to issue directives. He is dependent on the willingness of others in authority to co-operate, and they are prepared to do so. Although the authorities to whom Heinemann writes sometimes find it irksome to have their affairs meddled in from above, swift and friendly action is usually forthcoming. The Federal President's office operates all the more readily when it makes some contribution to the expenses incurred.

For such purposes the President has an official social fund at his disposal of 400,000 DM per year. That is not a great sum of money in view of the huge number of cases worthy of support which he has to deal with. So the contributions which the Federal President's office is able to pay out in the form of aid can only be of the order of 100 DM to 300 DM. In addition, all payments from this fund, which comes from taxes, must conform to the provisions of the Federal auditors.

In order to be able to offer assistance even in those cases which either fall outside terms of the official provisions or where these provisions are inadequate, Gustav Heinemann has followed the precedent of his predecessor Heinrich Lübke by setting up a private social fund, which he did on the occasion of his seventieth birthday, on 23 July 1969. The fund is maintained partly from his monthly pension which he continues to receive from his old firm Rhine Steel in the form of an earmarked gift, and also from his fees for television and radio appearances. Some firms have donated substantial sums to Heinemann's private social fund, and gifts large and small come in from private individuals. One big advantage of this fund is that in individual cases it is possible to pay out much larger sums than could have been provided from the official fund. Heinemann himself takes the decision on every case.

More important than direct material support is the indirect aid that the Federal President's office is able to give. One example is the President's position as honorary godfather of a seventh child, which he undertakes in accordance with an old custom. There is, in addition to the honorary documents, a financial donation of DM 100. The Federal President's office takes the opportunity to enquire of the competent housing authority about the living conditions and financial circumstances of the family concerned. If the housing is inadequate, efforts are made to help, either by means of an additional loan of DM 6,000 for the purchase of a house or by the local authority in whose area the family is living placing at the disposal of the family a plot of building land.

Heinemann has released the conditions of this position of honorary godfather from outmoded moral notions. Previously all seven children had to be of the same parents and the reputation of the family had to be unblemished. Heinemann has done away with both these preconditions. If, for example, the widowed father of four children marries again, and the marriage produces three further children, then the family is still entitled to enjoy the privileges of the President's honorary sponsorship. Even more important is the fact that illegitimate children are no longer discriminated against. Now they too are eligible to become the President's honorary godchildren. Heinemann's chief concern is for the children, not for their parentage.

If all these areas in which the President offers help and assistance are taken together, an impressive picture emerges. But measured against the real scale of need, the Federal President's ability to offer aid is none the less modest in proportion. And besides, this aid is given without the public being much aware of what is happening. But Heinemann's concern is the public. This is the nature of his office. Being a "Federal Wailing Wall" also means for Heinemann drawing the attention of the public to the needs of minority groups. This is done partly through his speeches, partly by means of visits to the places of need. He calls this his "searchlight role."

When Minister of Justice, Heinemann was able to introduce changes in the sentencing laws. But as head of state he is obliged to restrict his activities to drawing public attention to the problem by himself visiting a prison. Such visits do not remain private affairs. The journalists who accompany the Federal President ensure that they receive full publicity. Heinemann exploits this kind of opportunity as often as he can. He visits homes for the disabled, rehabilitation centres, prisons, and hostels for foreign workers, centres for the homeless and old people's homes. And now and again he will appear unannounced and without a large retinue. On his way from Bonn to Essen one weekend, for example, he visited a Cologne hostel for foreign workers because he wanted to obtain a plain unvarnished picture of their living conditions. The foreign workers took the strange man for the owner of the building. Heinemann's unexpected visit soon become public knowledge. He later heard by letter that, as a result of his Cologne visit, the city authorities had been showing a markedly increased preparedness to help the foreign workers solve their problems.

Even more than visits to the underprivileged, Heinemann's public speeches succeed in drawing attention to the situation of minorities. In Brotherhood Week in 1970 he was asked if he would address a ceremony in Cologne. His speech was far from formal; instead he was blunt, challenging and to the point. He spoke about the fact that, since the French revolution, freedom and equality had been able to make much greater advances among man than the notion of brotherhood, because brotherhood cannot be laid down by law. Even the guarantees afforded by the basic rights in the Federal consititution would not necessarily prevent social minorities from becoming outcasts in the eyes of public — and private — opinion. This made the need

142

all the more pressing for preparing the way for a greater degree of positive sympathy and understanding for those among the population who by nature or opinion differ from the majority. And then Heinemann became specific:

> How, for example, do we tend to talk about foreign workers in Germany? Are we prepared to regard them on human and social terms as our equal partners in the work towards prosperity? How do we regard children born out of wedlock, and what is our view of the mothers of such children? Who is prepared to take the side of released prisoners and set an example in ensuring their rehabilitation into society? How deep-rooted are the prejudices in our society against people whose skin is a different colour, or who follow a different religious or political creed? These are matters that must be taken into account if we are asked the meaning of the word brotherhood. It is not a matter of statements of principle, but of our personal conduct. Let us ask ourselves what we are doing to destroy prejudice and expose jealousies. Do we allow ourselves to be borne along by the tide of public and private opinion, or do we have the courage to denounce mental inertia and smugness wherever they are to be found in the community?

Nor does Heinemann use his Christmas speeches as occasions for non-committal formality. In the very first paragraph of his Christmas speech for 1970, which was broadcast as customary by all the radio and television stations, he drew his audience's attention to minority groups: "Only a small proportion of foreign workers have been able to return to their homes and families for Christmas. This is a time of even greater despondency for many in our prisons." Then he spoke about the meaning of the Christmas story and about the fact that "God's gifts are also challenges to us." There were many things, Heinemann went on, which we should be reminded of at Christmas time, particularly since some members of our society are far worse off than others. In order to demonstrate how little consideration our society gives to the disadvantaged, Heinemann pointed to the handicapped.

> There are many more handicapped people than is generally thought to be the case. Every year 60,000 children are born who will not be able to keep pace with the demands of our productivity-

143

based society. In total, there are almost half a million children of primary and middle school age who are handicapped, disadvantaged in some way in contrast to other children. Any family can be affected by this problem ... All in all, four million of our fellow citizens suffer from some form of serious physical, mental or emotional handicap.

A survey taken recently shows that nine out of ten of the population are not sure how they should conduct themselves towards the handicapped. Fifty per cent would not like to live under the same roof as a handicapped person. A little while ago a local community in the Federal Republic caused a sensation by the violence of their opposition to the proposal that a home for mentally handicapped children should be established in their midst.

Heinemann is here referring to the Lower Bavarian village of Anmühle, where on 17 October 1970 the inhabitants set fire to the outbuildings of a church in protest against the planned construction of a home for mentally handicapped children. He continued:

Regrettably, this is not an isolated instance. People not only want to cast the handicapped out of their minds, they also want to avoid having to be confronted with their presence.

In this area, we must undertake a thorough re-examination of our attitudes. Our society, which depends so heavily on competition and success, can only be a humane system if it grants to the handicapped minorities full respect, full citizenship, and the greatest possible measure of integration.

This is not the kind of exhortation normally to be expected from a head of state. He relentlessly singles out those areas which the majority would rather close their minds to. He fights against the idea of dividing society into the righteous and the damned. He names prejudices and jealousies by name, speaks in terms of a lack of emotional commitment and of the courage to oppose. Many citizens do not like hearing this sort of thing, especially not at Christmas. They would rather hear words of praise than of challenge, rather have a pat on the back than be asked penetrating questions. The readers' letters in the newspapers cast more light on this than the political

With Secretary of State Dietrich Spangenberg, head of the Federal President's office

At his desk at home in Essen ▷

Travelling in the Federal Republic: the President visits Bavaria

commentators. Letters appear now and again stating that the President is supposedly there for everybody. It ill becomes him in his office to be constantly harping on minorities and criticising the attitudes of the majority. It is to be expected of the President that he should concern himself with acting as a mediator in inter-party conflict.

Theodor Heuss set a magnificent example in regard to the effectiveness of the President as an integrating force. In his skilful, paternal and good-humoured way, he smoothed the path to acceptance by the German people of the new Republic which he represented. Gustav Heinemann would not deny that the task of bringing members of society together is one of the fundamental tasks of the Federal President. But he sees the issue in a different light from Theodor Heuss. In his eyes, the German democracy has, after twenty years, reached the age of discretion. So he does not regard integration in terms of creating an atmosphere of political well-being by giving his fellow citizens a series of patronising pats on the back. Heinemann would not accept a division of labour which would make it the task of the political parties to deal with conflict and the task of the head of state to say that all is right with the world. He takes integration to mean drawing the attention of the majority to those who are not integrated into society at large, to the minorities who have been forced out on to the fringes of society, to the handicapped, the convicted, to foreign workers. He makes it his task to be the advocate of the underprivileged, the spokesman of those who are unable to obtain a public hearing for themselves by their own unaided efforts.

Not one of the Articles of the Basic Law refers to this as a duty of the President, nor has tradition established any such precedent. And the duties of the one person who gives Heinemann the greatest measure of support in this area of his work are even less well established; namely, his wife, Hilda Heinemann, whom he refers to now and then as his "honorary secretary of state."

All her adult life, Hilda Heinemann has known no other work than that of housewife and mother. Now, as the first lady of the Republic, she has embarked upon a very wide range of activities. She entered the Villa Hammerschmidt without any paticular programme in mind. All she knew was what she did not want to be in this new office: she had no intention of letting herself be turned into a substitute royal head of state. Duties presented themselves almost of their own accord. Hilda Heinemann is the first wife of a Federal President to have her own adviser and two secretaries. And these ladies have no cause to complain of lack of employment.

At first, Frau Heinemann continued the work which her predecessors had begun, especially that relating to convalescent mothers, which had first been the preoccupation of Elly Heuss-Knapp. But she did not rest content with merely continuing what was already in existence. She furthered special rest cures for mothers living under particularly difficult circumstances, that is to say, mothers with mentally or physically handicapped children, mothers with blind children, for blind and deaf mothers, mentally sick mothers, working mothers with no husband to support them, student mothers, and also the wives of students. The special rest cures enabled these women to have an opportunity for overcoming their isolation and for comparing notes with others in similar difficult circumstances. The most amazing thing about these special rest cures is that no one had thought of establishing them long ago. There was evidently a serious lack of imagination or initiative in this area.

Hilda Heinemann has both imagination and initiative. She needs qualities like this in her non-existent office. The Basic Law does not recognise the first lady of the state. If she so desired, the wife of the President could live almost the same kind of withdrawn life as an ordinary housewife, or rest content with ladies' tea parties and fashion shows. She is only expected to appear at her husband's side at social functions. (At state banquets, when the titles of crowned and uncrowned dignitaries grace the tables, the card indicating the place at table of the wife of the Federal President bears the word "Housewife.") But she can, if she wishes, make good use of the manifold opportunities for public activities which her position makes possible for her. And Frau Heinemann decided upon a public role. The filing system in the office of her personal adviser, Ruth Bahn-Flessburg, gives some idea of her activities: there are sections for social questions, the care of prisoners, youth welfare, educational issues, working women, help on an international scale for children (she has assumed the patronage of the German committee for this work), Amnesty International — the list could be extended almost indefinitely.

As the wife of the Federal President, she too, like her husband, is able to open doors: any request that she passes on to officials must be examined; if she writes a letter, it must be answered. (But Hilda Heinemann too has learned that even this elementary courtesy is not observed on every occasion.) And, like her husband, she is able to draw public attention to human need. That is the principal objective of her many visits to places where handicapped, lonely or suffering people are cared for.

On every journey that the Federal President undertakes, she is only present at a proportion of the official engagements. For the remainder of the time a special programme is prepared. In Paderborn, for example, Hilda Heinemann held discussions with emigrés from Poland and the socially underprivileged of the city, whilst her husband visited a computer firm. In Berlin a visit to the Federal insurance commission was on the President's programme, but at this time Frau Heinemann went on a tour of the day nursery of a society for the care and advancement of foreign children. The next day he was the guest of the Federal monopolies board, whilst she opened a new centre for spastics.

She shows no fear of the press during these public appearances; quite the contrary. Whilst her husband even nowadays finds it difficult to get used to the idea that all his public actions are followed by a pack of photographers, she deliberately exploits the press to her own ends. She quite openly admits that a visit to a workshop for the handicapped or for deaf mutes has little value for her unless journalists report the event. For the handicapped or the deaf mutes do not gain a great deal from the fact that the wife of the Federal President shakes them by the hand. It is in her view much more important that the public should have their attention drawn to the situation of these people.

Hilda Heinemann does not restrict her activities to those cases of need which, to a greater or lesser extent, society is prepared to accept. She has visited houses for "fallen women," toured a Berlin mother and child commune formed by unmarried mothers, and she keeps in touch with voluntary groups concerned with drug dependents. She was also the first wife of a President to visit a women's prison.

In the women's prison of Frankfurt-Preungesheim a project is under way, the like of which is not to be seen anywhere else in the Federal Republic. A children's home is under construction there, in which twenty-five children of women prisoners are to be allowed to grow up with their mothers. The governor of the prison, Frau Dr. Einsele, and the Frankfurt Humanist Union, who have jointly got this project under way, hope that this children's accommodation will achieve a double purpose. On the one hand, the sense of responsibility of convicted women towards their children, who are mostly illegitimate, will be strengthened; at the same time it is hoped that the children will escape the vicious circle that their mothers suffered, of passing from a loveless childhood via a children's home, youth social service and criminal activities, back into prison again. The home is being built facing away from the prison, so that these children will be able to play with other children of the same age from the locality. Hilda Heinemann laid the foundation stone in 1971, and in 1972 work has got under way.

Anyone who conducts herself in such an unprejudiced manner needs not only imagination and initiative, but also a certain independence from social convention. Hilda Heinemann once said to a lady journalist, "I am quite indifferent to what is supposed to be the done thing." Sometimes even her husband is surprised by the unconventionality of her actions. Early in 1972 she visited a home for "fallen women." As she toured the building, she noticed that spy-holes were affixed to the doors of the women's rooms. She found that offensive and proposed that they should be covered up by posters on the inside of the doors. She argued that such a hostel was not a prison, that the women residing there were not convicted persons, that they had the right to receive guests privately in their rooms. When the warden objected that there were certain grounds which made the introduction of posters undesirable, Frau Heinemann urged that the spy-holes be covered up with name-plates. Back home in Essen, Gustav Heinemann listened to her account of the visit with a mixture of pride and amusement, and said admiringly: "You didn't used to think like that." And his wife replied: "Yes, Gustav, you are right. But now I know better than I did then."

Perhaps the most remarkable thing about this remarkable woman is the ease with which she has accommodated herself at a relatively advanced age to situations such as she has never faced before in her life. In this, she is greatly aided by her ability to react spontaneously and by the interest which she takes in people. She is no more ill at ease talking to women on the fringes of society than to crowned heads. She moves freely among the mentally and physically handicapped as if she were in her element. Wherever she is, she always has the right word or gesture ready to hand which will break down social barriers. But for all that, she is by no means naturally gregarious, but rather withdrawn and cool in her friendliness. Her Bremen background keeps her free of gushing effusiveness and from being oppressively maternal. And she is easily put out. Nor is she ashamed of being moved to tears when confronted with human suffering. But she is able to shake herself free from such moods. "We always bear up well in Bremen" is a phrase she is fond of using.

Her commitment to the socially underprivileged has no trace of the condescending benevolence of the wives of American millionaires, who belong to some welfare committee or other, and comfort themselves through their spare-time activities in the knowledge that their own privileges remain

153

untouched. It is not condescension that drives Hilda Heinemann, but the awareness that all too many of her fellow citizens in need of help are simply written off by society. She will have nothing to do with the question as to whether there is any sense in helping the individual before society at large is transformed. She says, "We have no promise that we shall be able to transform this earth into paradise. No, we cannot wait for that to happen. We must act, and help wherever we can, and right now." It might easily be her husband speaking. In such matters, there is no difference between Gustav and Hilda Heinemann. A long life together as convinced Christians has led Hilda Heinemann to participate almost spontaneously in that area of her husband's activities which he calls the "Federal Wailing Wall."

What worries her is the fear that her work for those in need will go no further than appeals and encouragement. Will others be persuaded to act themselves on her example? Such anxieties are particularly acute when it comes to the undertaking which bears her name, known as the "Hilda Heinemann foundation: residential accommodation for the mentally handicapped."

Hilda Heinemann came to found this project by chance. It was the custom that the wife of the Federal President should invite the children of the accredited diplomats in Bonn to the theatre every Christmas, and at the end of the proceedings hand round sweets. Frau Heinemann was well aware of the fact that the children of diplomats did not suffer from a shortage of sweets and the like, and so she broke with this tradition. She wrote a friendly letter to the children, asking them if they would mind if the money which had up to then been paid out for sweets went in future to boys and girls living in children's homes: the handicapped, haemophiliacs, spastics, the deaf and the blind. But these children were not just given the usual toys or sweets. Instead, Frau Heinemann had enquiries made about the kinds of therapeutic aids the children needed. And so it was that one children's home received a set of wall-bars for Christmas, another a donation towards a swimming pool, and a third was presented with hearing aids.

When she handed one of these gifts over in a home for mentally handi-capped children, she was told that the majority of the young people there stayed in a home until their eighteenth birthday. Then, if their families would not take them back, they would have no other choice than a mental hospital or a home for the chronic sick. It is not impossible to raise money for mentally handicapped children, because such unfortunates arouse our active sympathy. But it is well-nigh impossible to obtain funds for mentally handi-capped adults. Thus it is that, despite the efforts of voluntary organisations, the churches and the local communities, the possibilities of helping these people remain very limited indeed.

The Hilda Heinemann foundation sought to fill this gap in the social services. She aided the construction of living quarters for mentally-handi-capped adults, wherever possible in centres of population and in the neigh-bourhood of their place of work. She supported the equipping of workshops and made strenuous efforts to tie in their work to that of industry at large. And she encouraged scientific research directed towards the improvement of the living and working conditions of the mentally handicapped. Of all the fringe groups, society is most anxious to forget about the mentally handi-capped. The mentally handicapped person is feared by "normal people" more than any other group, and "normal people" try to keep well out of their way. So one of the principal aims of the foundation is "information on the gaps in care for the mentally handicapped; on the prejudices that exist; on the possibilities for full development of those afflicted."

The numbers given by the foundation provide some idea of the magnitude of the task. Roughly one child in a hundred and fifty is born mentally handicapped. That amounts to 10,000 children in round figures per year in the Federal Republic alone. In the Federal Republic there are about 100,000 mentally handicapped adults. From 1972 until 1975 something of the order of 10,000 new living units will be needed, each of which will cost 45,000 DM. Such work cannot be financed out of public funds, and the television lotteries do not want to scare away the viewers with the sight of mentally handicapped people. They would prefer the popular causes: "A place in the sun," or "Action for the problem child" — there is no difficulty in extracting money out of the television viewer for such purposes.

And so Frau Heinemann goes begging on behalf of mentally handicapped adults. The terms of the foundation state that it "seeks help, donations and grants from the public purse, the Federal employment agency, the insurance companies, from industry, the large organisations; and finally, from the general public." They continue: "The money should in the main be collected on a regional basis for specific projects, so that those who give money will also be able to see how that money is spent and will be able to make contact with the project when it is built."

If we really did live in a genuine welfare state, it would not be necessary to go out cap in hand on behalf of our handicapped fellow citizens. But, as things are at present, there is no other way of raising the money. And this is why the number of the foundation's credit transfer account is stamped on the rear of every autographed photograph of Hilda Heinemann: Cologne 2424.

"I do not love the State, I love my Wife"

It is said of Theodor Heuss that, at the end of a visit to soldiers on manoeuvre, he took his leave of them with these words: "Now go off and have a nice victory!" This sentence became justly famous. At a time when the need for the existence of the Federal army was still violently disputed, when the traditional German respect for armed might was locked in bitter conflict with the new attitude of "leave me out of it," Heuss contrived to speak about the military with the arch humour of the civilian.

Gustav Heinemann's statement that "I do not love the state, I love my wife" is of the same order. It is first and foremost a straightforward pronouncement about a successful marriage. (Anyone who knows Heinemann also knows that he truly loves his wife). But this utterance also characterises Heinemann's relationship to the state.

This statement could be taken as it was meant, as did many Germans, among them civil servants and officers, who wrote approving letters to Heinemann on the subject; or Willy Brandt, who said at an SPD party meeting that this statement by Heinemann had exercised a beneficial slackening effect on the frequently strained relationships between individual and the state. But it could also be misinterpreted, and this has evidently happened. Heinemann has been accused of having a distorted relationship to the state. Even worse: it has been said that it is no wonder there is such a lack of pride in the state among the population if the head of state himself sets such a bad example by questioning the power of the state, and by not recognising that the state is not just there for the sake of the citizen, but the citizen for the sake of the state.

But reproaches such as these rest on a conception of the state which Heinemann is seeking to overcome, because he regards it as belonging to

157

the pre-democratic era. In his view, the state is not an abstract authority which demands respect in its own right. A state has as little call upon our affections as do political parties, Ministers, courts, offices of the inland revenue, or traffic lights. "The state," Heinemann has said, "is not a higher form of life. It is rather a necessary system vested with power for the realisation of social justice and the preservation of peace and justice. It is the system which society gives itself so that each citizen can receive his due and live in peace." If those conditions are met, that is, if a state does secure for its citizens conditions consistent with the maintenance of human dignity, then the state deserves approbation, active co-operation, even resolute defence against enemies of the state.

But love? Heinemann has this to say:

> I am well aware that love can be felt not only towards our nearest and dearest, but also for other things: for home, nature, a work of art or objects of sentimental value. But I take the view that the relationship between citizens and state should not be coloured by such irrational sentiments. Our links with the state should be based, not on emotion, but reason.

So Heinemann is talking in terms of "links with the state." Such links must not be uncritical and emotional, but should rather be founded upon insight, upon rational examination. It was this very emotional relationship to the state which wrought so much damage in recent German history. In the Weimar Republic it barred the way to approval of a state system which merited support. On the other side of the coin, the Third Reich could never have pursued its fateful progress so smoothly had it not been so certain of the irrational enthusiasm of the majority of its citizens.

There really ought to be no grounds for controversy in the fact that the head of state himself commends his fellow citizens to a sober and clearheaded appraisal of the state in the light of these historical experiences. But none the less Heinemann's conception of the state is the object of much dispute. This is perhaps partly so because the man who is now Federal President became more and more of an outsider in the fifties, as the ruling CDU bound their government ever closer to the state. But there is probably another reason. Heinemann is accustomed to explain his conception of the state in terms of an expression which is open to misapprehension by those who have no grounding in theology: he calls the state "God's contingency plan" ("Gottes Notordnung"). In German part of the phrase also has the meaning "emergency," and sounds as if it had something to do with emergency brakes, or emergency exit, in any event, like something which is used only in times of crisis, and left untouched when things are normal. But Heinemann means something quite different when he talks of the state in terms of "God's contingency plan" — and that is, that states are necessary because man is not capable of living in peaceful coexistence with his fellow men without a system, because freedom is only possible under a secure, organised system of law and order to which all men must subscribe.

For Heinemann is not after a powerless state. All he is saying is that the power of the state is not of itself a good thing. It all depends on the kind of system it is upholding, the kind of life it offers its citizens and the nature of the guarantees there are against abuse of the system. Because Heinemann considered that the constitutional system of the Federal Republic was the best that German history had ever seen, and moreover, as one of the best anywhere in the world today, he sought to ensure that this state should have at its command sufficient power to defend itself, both from internal and outside threats.

Defence against a threat from outside: Heinemann does not challenge the necessity for the Federal armed forces under the given political conditions of the present time, on the contrary, he underlines it — despite all rumours to the contrary. But it is still true that Heinemann's relationship to the Federal armed forces has been the subject of intense public discussion. He has been accused of not having overcome his neutralist illusions of the fifties, of publicly questioning the armed forces, of simply having no understanding of the military requirements of the Federal Republic, which are now demonstrably inevitable. These accusations are a blend of truth and falsehood, and as such give a totally wrong impression.

It is an historical fact that Heinemann regarded the re-armament of the Federal Republic, introduced by Konrad Adenauer in 1950, as a wrong decision on political grounds, and for this reason he resigned his ministerial office. But it is nonsense to maintain that he is still continuing to think in terms of the political options that obtained twenty years or so ago. Heinemann is enough of a realist to recognise that it is a waste of time to argue now over whether the division of Germany could have been prevented if the Federal Republic had not re-armed. The political development of Europe has advanced far beyond the point when that decision was a live issue. It has established new sets of circumstances, and it is on the basis of these that any politician must formulate his views.

In his speech at the leadership training centre in Coblenz, Heinemann made this explicitly clear:

> Today the Federal armed forces represent our vital contribution to the defence system of NATO ... Given these present circumstances, there is no argument about the necessity for the Federal armed forces. And they certainly should not be questioning their own role, as I am supposed to have said once that they should, and as I still am occasionally accused of having said, despite all I have stated to the contrary.

Heinemann is here referring to an interview which he gave to the "Stuttgarter Zeitung" three days after his election as Federal President, which at the time created a considerable stir.

In this interview, Heinemann had stated:

> My view is that all armament must have a political basis. Armament is not a good thing in itself. But, given that all armament and all military service have a political function to perform, then all members of the armed forces should ask themselves this question: Are our political objectives today the same as they were when the armament was initiated? In other words, the Federal armed forces must be prepared in principle to allow their existence to be called into question for the sake of a better political solution.

And Heinemann indicated the form that such a better political solution might take: he was thinking in terms of a European peace system with no

160

NATO and no Warsaw Pact, which would be the one and only possible way of at some time overcoming the division of Germany.

Heinemann had doubtless been unguarded in these statements. It is true that he had not yet taken up office as Federal President, but he had already been elected and had left the government of the grand coalition. His observations could, not too unreasonably, be taken as fundamental criticism of the Federal armed forces.

So in his inaugural speech before the German Federal parliament on 1 July 1969, he referred again to his attitude towards the Federal armed forces. On this occasion he refrained from speaking about hopes for the future of Europe which might render them superfluous. But at the same time he repeated that the necessity for the Federal armed forces depended solely upon their political function.

> The Federal armed forces are not an end in themselves. We know that they are not in a position to impose any political solutions. It is their duty to prevent force being exercised upon us from outside. This is why we are continuing our defensive effort. And this is why we must respect all those who are engaged in this task.

Heinemann is not opposed to the armed forces as such, but as a politician his imagination ranges far beyond the present status quo in Europe. In the ideological sense of the word, he has never been a pacifist, he is too clearheaded for that. He recognises that a world without armies is as unlikely as a world without hatred, envy, or suppression. But Heinemann is a civilian through and through. Nor has he sought to conceal the fact that he sympathises with those who refuse to undertake military service on genuine conscientious grounds. But he is equally resolute in his opposition to any kind of abuse of this basic right. He himself served for a year in the First World War as an eighteen year-old, in the twenty-second field artillery regiment in Münster, where he rose to become the best gun-layer of his unit. Since then he had virtually no contact with the military, not even with the Federal armed forces.

When he entered office as Federal President, Heinemann took his relations with the Federal armed forces particularly seriously. At the beginning of his term of office, he was especially concerned to learn about them. He made use of his first visit to the inspectors of the forces in the autumn of 1969 for thoroughgoing discussions, as a result of which he gained an overall picture of the status of the forces. He was less interested in questions of strategy or armaments, which he left to the experts. He was concerned with the condition of the troops, matters of discipline, conscientious objectors, the social position of the soldier and his status under the law. Heinemann has repeatedly sought to keep himself informed through discussions with the Federal Minister of Defence and his Secretaries of State, with the Inspector General of the Federal armed forces and his deputies, as well as the Deputy in Military Affairs in the Federal parliament.

But Heinemann has not been content with drawing his information from the men at the top. In the first three years of office, he made nine visits to the troops, and that in more than his predecessors in office did in nine years. On five occasions members of the armed forces of all ranks have been his guests in the Villa Hammerschmidt; whether for a reception or for a dinner, Heinemann ensured that there was plenty of time to talk to them. Only the first of his troop visits was on the occasion of a manoeuvre. Subsequently, Heinemann preferred to call upon the troops in their everyday surroundings. He has visited the army four times, the navy twice, and the air force once.

During these visits, Heinemann examines military equipment, attends military instruction and views the living quarters. Lunch is taken with men of all ranks. In the afternoon he holds talks with separate groups, divided according to rank, an hour each with other ranks, NCOs and officers. He places the greatest value on this direct contact with the troops, for it permits him to obtain an unvarnished picture of the life of the soldier, and also arms him with facts for discussions with politicians and journalists, with conscientious objectors and critical young people.

Heinemann's adviser in military questions is navy Captain Werner Gruner, who was seconded from the Ministry of Defence as liaison officer for the

Federal President. His office is situated in a privileged position, alongside that of the Secretary of State on the upper floor of the Federal President's office, where the only other rooms are occupied by the President himself, his personal adviser and Professor Caspari, the deputy head of the office. His contacts are particularly close with Secretary of State Spangenberg, who himself has visited the troops eight times since Heinemann took office and who is involved in a standing exchange of views with the political and military heads of the Defence Ministry.

At the beginning of Heinemann's term of office, Gruner was especially concerned to improve the relations between army and head of state which had been strained by the public discussion that followed the interview with the "Stuttgarter Zeitung". He is convinced that any tensions have now been overcome. Heinemann also shares this view. He himself has stated in public that his relations with the Federal armed forces are good and cordial. This is more than borne out by anyone who has seen him in discussion with soldiers.

Heinemann has constantly stressed that the armed forces are there in the service of politics. The military is, in accordance with the will of the constitution, subordinate to the primacy of politics. (Unlike the Weimar Republic, democracy in the Federal Republic is not founded upon a dangerous alliance with an anti-democratic army.) It is important to note Heinemann's stress upon the word "service." Heinemann does not regard this in the traditional sense, according to which the soldier serves the "state." The soldier is as little a servant as are members of the civil service, judges, teachers or the police force. Quite the contrary: all organs of the state are there to serve the citizen. In a democracy the position of the state has switched from that of master to servant. Serving the state now signifies service to the community as a whole.

For Germans, the notion of the state as servant is not one which is taken for granted in relation to the function of someone holding public office. It is one which is more reminiscent of the Anglo-Saxon notion of "public

163

service" than of the German tradition of respect for representatives of authority, titles, offices, and officials.

Heinemann states his opposition to the tradition of the authoritarian state, whenever the opportunity for doing so presents itself. To police officers in Hamburg he said:

> In our state each and every citizen participates in the sovereignty of the people. This means that it is not possible arbitrarily to restrict his freedom for the sake of the system. Freedom must not be allowed to fall victim to the system; it is rather the system which should serve the freedom of the citizen.

And to officials of the administration in Bonn he addressed these words:

> Such a conception of the state has this effect on the administration: the administration can no longer encroach upon the citizen as it did in the past, but should now be regarded in terms of an organisation operating in the interest of an increasing level of welfare provision for the citizen. So in our society, the official should meet the citizen half way as an equal partner. The citizen is a consumer of the official's services with rights of his own.

And he said to members of the Brandt government in the Villa Hammerschmidt:

> No one among us is the state. And you too have been entrusted only with limited power for a certain span of time. Make good use of this time!

But if the old autocracy on the part of the government is to give place to a stewardship of power over a given period of time, and if the attitude of

---

1. A page from the President's notebook (original size).

2. For the first time in the history of the Federal Republic parliament was prematurely dissolved. At the instigation of the Federal Chancellor, the Federal President signed the dissolution order on September 22, 1972.

3. On the same day the Federal President set the date for new elections.

4. Heinemann is a close friend of the writer Carl Zuckmayer. This is a letter by Zuckmayer to the President.

164

Reisebuch III
Programm Selbige

Rastatt (caspar)
Rede München
19. 8.
M Kommandant

Anordnung
über die Auflösung des 6. Deutschen Bundestages
Vom 22 . September 1972

Gemäß Artikel 68 des Grundgesetzes löse ich hiermit auf Vorschlag des Bundeskanzlers den 6. Deutschen Bundestag auf.

Bonn, den 22 . September 1972

Der Bundespräsident

Der Bundeskanzler

Anordnung
über die Bundestagswahl 1972
Vom 22. September 1972

Auf Grund des § 17 des Bundeswahlgesetzes vom
7. Mai 1956 (Bundesgesetzbl. I S. 383) in der Fassung
der Bekanntmachung vom 3. Juli 1972 (Bundesgesetzbl. I S. 1100) ordne ich an:

Die Wahl zum Bundestag findet

am 19. November 1972

statt.

Bonn, den 22. September 1972

Der Bundespräsident

Der Bundeskanzler

Der Bundesminister des Innern

CARL ZUCKMAYER

23·12·1971

3906 SAAS·FEE·SCHWEIZ

Verehrter Herr Bundespräsident und
lieber Freund,

ich habe mich von Herzen über
Ihren ausführlichen Glückwunsch gefreut,
und ich bin froh und erfreut, dass
Sie nach Amriswil kommen werden.
Unsere guten Gedanken sind bei
Ihnen, Ihrer Frau und den Ihren beim
Weihnachtsfest, das wir hier, noch
bevor der Geburtstagsrummel losgeht,
in den Ihnen bekannten Holzwänden
ganz unter uns begehen.
Mit Segenswünschen zum Neuen Jahr,
für Sie, Ihre Gesundheit, und für
das deutsche Volk

grüße ich Sie,

Ihr treu ergebener
Carl Zuckmayer

the official is to be one of service to the citizen who has his rights, then at the same time the old subject must be replaced by a self-assured, critical citizen who is ready and willing to accept responsibility. Heinemann never tires of speaking on this theme. He does so in Christmas messages and in speeches on German history, to scholars and apprentices, to an ecclesiastical audience and to journalists, to politicians and to female workers in an industrial concern. He campaigns on behalf of civilian courage and solidarity, he encourages his audience to take an active part in society and in political parties, he exhorts them to adopt an attitude of critical vigilance towards officialdom, and underlines the necessity for debate within the context of the parliamentary system for better answers to the political issues of the day.

Because Heinemann conceives of the state in terms of a system which serves the citizen, and because he will have none of its pomp and circumstance, he also seeks within the context of his office as head of state to avoid all display of the splendour of the state for its own sake. This conception of his office has also led to changes in the two areas in which the supremacy of the head of state is particularly in evidence, namely, in patronage and in decorations and marks of distinction.

Heinemann himself has never been particularly fond of medals and honours. Of course, as head of state he is obligated on certain state occasions to bear the insignia of the highest degree of the Federal Republic's order of merit, the special award of the Grand Cross. But to a certain extent this order is part and parcel of his official costume, just as the innumerable foreign orders bestowed upon him form an inevitable part of his high office. Until he entered office as President, Heinemann had succeeded in avoiding any kind of decorations, despite the fact that he had been Land Minister once, Federal Minister on two occasions and for years President of the synod of the Evangelical church in Germany. The sole honours he had accepted before becoming President were the honorary degree of doctor of theology from the University of Bonn in 1967, and a year later the Theodor Heuss Prize which he was awarded in recognition of his "loyalty to principle, his avowed faith, his political steadfastness and his courage as a citizen."

But Heinemann does not transfer his personal aversion to marks of distinction to his office as President which demands of him that he should head orders on behalf of the Republic. He is fully conscious of the motivation which led Theodor Heuss more than twenty years ago to found the order of merit at a time when the Federal Republic was being built up. It is awarded, in the words of the decree on its institution, "for achievements which have served the reconstruction of our native land in the field of politics, or within the context of social, economic or intellectual activity, and is to signify a mark of distinction bestowed upon all those whose work has contributed to the peaceful development of the Federal Republic of Germany." Heinemann readily recognises that it can be beneficial to a young republic to make public expression of its recognition and gratitude to those citizens who merit distinction. Since the vanity of man is ineradicable, the community ought at least to exploit it to advantage.

What troubles Heinemann, however, is that there is no practical means of bringing about justice in the business of bestowing orders. The financial means available for this purpose are comparatively restricted. (France, for example, spends five times as much as the Federal Republic for this purpose.) Heinemann takes the view that if orders have to exist, then it ought to be possible to hand out more of them, not least to reduce the disproportionately large representation by foreigners, almost twenty per cent in 1971. But heads of state and their entourage must be given orders when they make visits to Bonn, just as foreign ambassadors must have them when they leave Bonn. Such are the ways of international protocol.

Nor is Heinemann particularly happy with the way orders are handed out internally. It is true that it is no longer entirely the case that the practice of according honours orders places "a fine veil over the reality of a state dominated by economic power groups," as Wilhelm Hennis once mischeviously observed. And under Heinrich Lübke there was already a move away from the principle of mere honoraria. But, in Heinemann's view, the thirty-seven per cent for public servants is too high, although working judges are no longer honoured for their service as judges, and the percentage of women receiving honours is far too low. When Heinemann took office, a mere nine per cent were women. This figure has now risen to thirteen per cent, a commendable rise, but still not high enough for Heinemann. If he had his way, those bearing ecclesiastical honours should on principle be excluded from state honours. Heinemann has made discreet attempts to get this view accepted, but he has not met with a favourable response. The dignitaries of the church are unwilling to surrender worldly honours, and so Heinemann has to continue according them distinctions, although he can but wonder at their attitude.

The Federal President is not in charge of the overall conduct of the practice of bestowing marks of distinction. The right to make proposals in this respect lies with the heads of the civil service branches, the Presidents of the lower and upper houses of parliament, the Foreign Minister and the Prime Ministers of the Länder. Suggestions also come from the population at large, and in sixty per cent of cases result in the award of an honour. It is up to the President to decide on the proposals put forward, but he cannot alter the lists of names, nor is he really in a position to reject names which fall in with the legal requirements. All that he can do is to try to influence the competent authorities towards making the award of honours on a broader plane, and according them also to citizens who are not in leading positions in official and economic life.

It has been easier for Heinemann to bear witness to his conception of the state when it comes to patronage. Heinemann once wrote out a document under sixteen headings listing the principal functions of his office. Under number three he entered: "Patronages — only for organisations which do something for others."

In contrast to his predecessors, Heinemann only sparingly allows his name to be used as patron. He takes the view that under normal conditions a good cause is quite capable of making its own way in the world and can well manage without patrons. Only meetings, congresses and individual occasions which undertake service to others receive his patronage. But he is unable to adhere exclusively to this principle. His patronage of the Munich Olympic games, for example, was a purely representative act. In this instance he was falling in with international custom which dictates that the head of state of the host country should not only open the games, but also undertake to be their patron.

But this apart, Heinemann has laid down strict conditions for the acceptance of patronage, even at the expense of risking offence to those concerned. In one particular case, there was not only offence, but a long drawn out dispute, in which Federal and Land Ministers became involved. The German rifle association had enjoyed a permanent presidental patronage under Heuss and Lübke, but Heinemann informed them that it was not his intention to continue this tradition. This refusal was taken as an affront by the association, which tried to persuade the President to reverse his decision. There ensued a correspondence between the Federal President's office and the association which went on for weeks, in the course of which the association enlisted the support of prominent names for their cause. Heinemann closed the correspondence with a letter to the vice-president of the association, Fritz Raddatz, in which he explained his attitude and stated the conditions under which he was prepared to allow patronages initiated by his predecessors to remain in effect:

> In my view such conditions would only exist if the long-term purpose of the proposed object of patronage extended beyond the interests of the membership of the association concerned in order to embrace specific services to the community at large. This holds good for the few cases in which I have taken on permanent patronage, for example the German Red Cross, the German Lifeboat Society, the German Youth Hostels Association. In such associations, and in no other case, can it be of value if their public work is given support in principle by the state. In other circumstances, there is no need for a special declaration of goodwill on the part of the state.

Heinemann continued:

> Perhaps, Mr. Raddatz, you are of the opinion that my conception of how permanent patronages are to be bestowed is too narrow. But

it corresponds to my fundamental conception of the office which I hold and which I wish to liberate from all mere formalities.

Keeping his office free of "mere formalities" also meant that Heinemann chose the occasions for his public appearances with great care. This holds particularly good for his tours of the economically depressed areas of the Federal Republic. He has visited the zonal frontier district of southern Lower Saxony and the Swabian Alb, the Saar and the Fichtel Mountains. The visit which attracted the greatest measure of public attention was the one he made to the Bohemian forest in August 1970.

He spent three days there, in the "sparsely inhabited blind spot of the European economic sphere," as the "Grenz-Warte", the local newspaper, described it, a part of the country where in winter one in every four is unemployed, where the per capita income of the population is under half the average for the Federal Republic as a whole, where there are no large industrial concerns, and the road network leaves a great deal to be desired, where fifteen thousand low-acre agricultural undertakings are run by women and the men have to commute to work as far afield as Nuremberg and Munich. Since the Bavarian King Ludwig II visited the area more than a century before, no head of state had shown his face in this poorhouse of the nation. Heinemann brought with him neither gifts nor promises, but a ready ear and a patient notepad. In his words of greeting to the little town of Oberviechtach, he said that he had come in order to acquaint himself with the problems of the population, both as an observer and a listener, and in order to use his visit to direct public attention on to this economically depressed area.

In that part of the world, where "we have to observe the economic miracle from afar", as a group of demonstrating Catholic workers expressed it in a pamphlet, Heinemann succeeded even in putting aside the brusqueness which has otherwise frequently characterised his public appearances. He shook hands wherever they were stretched out towards him. He went for a stroll with the local council chairman through the woods and picnicked on ham, schnaps and beer. And in the beer tent in the tiny village of Gais-

173

thal, where the fire brigade were celebrating their centenary, he surprised the guests by conducting the local brass band.

The CDU, who in Land and Federal elections normally pulled in around seventy per cent of the votes in this area, suspected in Heinemann's visit an attempt to gain electoral support for the SPD in the Land elections which were four months off at the time, and placed Alfons Goppel, the Bavarian Prime Minister and two Ministers of state at Heinemann's side, in order to demonstrate who held the reins of office in that neck of the woods. But Heinemann had not come to muster support at the polls. Even before his tour he had made it clear that he would oppose any attempt to make electoral capital out of his presence, from whatever side it might come. In Oberviechtach he held discussions with forty-five chosen representatives on the economic condition of the area, in Waldmünchen he talked with twenty citizens, and he took note of the wishes both of the politicians and ordinary people.

Subsequently in Bonn, a string of Ministers received letters in which the Federal President passed on the problems which had been put to him. And a year later in Oberviechtach the tourist trade was beginning to feel the effects of the President's visit in terms of hard cash.

But if a Bonn Ministry pays greater attention to a depressed area because of a letter from the Federal President, or if the tourist figures take a turn for the better, these are no more than desirable side-effects of such tours, not their prime objective. Their goal is to give the inhabitants of the less favoured areas of the Federal Republic the feeling that they have not been written off by "the people in Bonn", but that they too are part of the Federal Republic. And Heinemann regards it as much more meaningful objective of his high office to do this than to waste his time in mere representational functions and formalities.

Heinemann is committed to the idea of the Federal Republic, and campaigns for it in Oberviechtach and everywhere else. This is not because the Federal Republic is the state and he is its highest representative, but because

174

he regards the system of the Federal Republic, founded as it is upon human dignity and human rights, as a "supreme offer" to all its citizens.

For the first time in German constitutional history, the constitution does not work outwards from authority, as did constitutions up until 1918, nor from the legislators, as in the case of Weimar, but from the citizen. The greatest value in the Basic Law is placed upon the dignity of man. For the first time the basic rights are not the objective, but the limitations within which the legislator has to operate. These unalterable rights of man set an insurmountable boundary to the power of the state. For the first time the principle is laid down that it is the obligation of the state authorities not just to watch over the security of the law, but to serve the purpose of social justice. For the first time the Basic Law lays it down as an unalterable demand that the state must operate a free democratic system. For the first time the political parties are specifically recognised in the constitution as instruments for moulding the democratic will. And for the first time the Basic Law guarantees no political freedom to anti-democratic parties — the system of the Federal Republic has been described as a militant democracy dedicated to survival.

The Basic Law with its stress upon freedom puts an end to the old tradition of the autocratic state. The system which had prevailed for a hundred and fifty years had come to an end; no longer was the state conceived of as a neutral force above the tensions of society which always resolved conflicts between democracy and the state in favour of the latter and to the detriment of the former. The Basic Law has done away with this notion of the primacy of the state. It no longer allows the state to have pride of place over democracy; now democracy is the state.

But the tradition of the authoritarian state which the Basic Law has now finally overcome still lives on in political discussions. The critics who accuse Heinemann of "an almost artificial detachment from the state" or of a "distorted relationship to the essence of this state," are still in the thrall of that respect for the state in itself, a sentiment which has long since faded in countries with more long-standing democratic traditions. Since Hegel praised the state at the beginning of the nineteenth century as "the realisation of the moral idea" and as "a thing which is rational in and of itself," since Ranke thought he discovered within himself the concept of the state, there has been a rift between the concept of state and an understanding of democracy in the mainstream of German political theory.

Up until the end of the eighteenth century, the older German philosophy of the state still recognised what had been part of the general currency of European thought since Aristotle; namely, that the dignity of the state does not lie within the state itself, but in its obligation to guarantee for its citizens a system in due accordance with the dignity of man. Only when the German concept of the state became detached from the obligation associated with the state did the greater glory of the nation replace the idea of the common good. Only then was the old right of opposition forgotten. Only a state thus deprived of any postive function could have become the tool of nationalist, and later chauvinist and racist objectives with the consent of its citizens.

In regarding the state from the point of view, not of its power to rule, but its obligation to guarantee a free, social and constitutional system, Heinemann is reforging the link with the older European concept of the state which in other western European countries had never been broken. The mistake which Heinemann's conservative critics are making is that they themselves have lost contact with the European tradition. The supposed conservatives are the "modernists" of the nineteenth century.

Leaving aside the question of who were the genuine conservatives — since 20 July 1944, since the failed attempt on Adolf Hitler, there has been no possible legitimate way back to a belief in the state as such. The men of 20 July had recognised that a state which was no longer founded upon binding moral principles could demand neither obedience nor loyalty. As Wilhelm Hennis wrote, their action "led the problematical separate path of German statehood, by following which we had cut ourselves off from the tradition of western Europe, and of the west as a whole, back into this tradition".

176

It is necessary to reflect back on this historical background if we are to come to a better understanding of what Heinemann meant by his statement that he did not love the state. He engages himself on behalf of the spirit of the community and an awareness of the constitution, and it is these things which he seeks to encourage with all the authority of his office. No longer is democracy to be allowed to come off second best in Germany. This is what he said in his inaugural speech: "Not less, but more democracy — that is the demand, that is the great objective which we, and above all the young, must dedicate ourselves towards achieving". The fact that a call for more democracy comes today from the head of state is a hopeful sign in a country which Gustav Heinemann himself has called a "difficult fatherland".

"A difficult Fatherland"

The Germans do not share a common view of their history; there is no agreement on the great deeds of the past, no consensus on who the nation's heroes are. There is no one place held dear in the memory of the Germans as the location symbolising a tradition which they can all respect. The monuments once erected to this purpose, like the Niederwald memorial in Rüdesheim or the hall of freedom in Kehlheim, are for the generations alive today more in the nature of historical curiosities and are far better known to foreign tourists than to the indigenous population. The national day of celebration comes off little better in this respect. The battle of Sedan, which for the generation of our grandfathers still epitomised the memory of past heroism, has long since ceased to be a valid day for patriotic celebration. By taking 17 June, the Federal Republic chose for itself a day of failure and mourning as its national day.

The Germans only seem able to agree about the great evildoers of their past. Everybody is more or less of one mind that Adolf Hitler was a criminal who led Germany on the path to self-destruction. But even the question of the extent to which the Germans themselves were responsible for the Third Reich cannot be answered with any degree of unanimity. Some Germans see National Socialism as a disaster which might have been averted had it not been for the peace treaty imposed at Versailles, the economic crisis and mass unemployment. Others see the Third Reich in terms of the logical consequence of errors which originated far back in German history, but which ultimately culminated in the tragedy of Nazism.

In a country so uncertain in its own mind about its history, a head of state might do well to keep as quiet as he possibly can about the past. In that way no great harm will be done, and even if it does not bring much approbation, it will at least spare him from criticism. Or the Federal President might do his best to suffuse the past with a vaguely rosy glow. This would not meet with much approval on the part of the intellectuals, but it would call forth relieved support from the mass of the population. Or finally, the Federal President could fix his sights on a critical conspectus of German history, shorn of self-justification and self-pity. That would cause trouble. There is only one thing he cannot do, and that is to restore to the people their lost common historical awareness.

Gustav Heinemann determined upon a critical view of history — and there has been no lack of trouble as a result.

The first speech Heinemann gave as President on the subject of the German past was, however, generally applauded. It was an address on the twenty-fifth anniversary of the attempted assassination of Hitler on 20 July 1944, held in Berlin-Plötzensee at the spot where the leaders of the German resistance against Hitler were executed. People applauded Heinemann for having the courage to admit in public that he could not shake himself free from the question as to why he did not offer more resistance in the Third Reich. This personal courage and the particular circumstances of the speech with its recollection of the resistance aroused respect; on this occasion at least, there were no critical objections raised against him.

But if people had listened more closely to his words, it would have struck them that this speech already contained his basic views on German history which were to unleash a storm of disapproval when Heinemann was to repeat them in his speech on the centenary of Bismarck's foundation of the Reich. In the Plötzensee speech, Heinemann had already said that the Third Reich was no accident. He spoke of the long tradition of German education which inculcated subservience to every form of authority and ultimately led to submission to the orders of a criminal. He reminded his audience of the fact that even at the time of the Kaiser's Reich, long before the advent of Hitler, the Germans were already susceptible to the attractions of a particularly violent brand of nationalism. He pointed out that, outside Germany, nationalist attitudes had gone hand in hand with freedom, whereas inside

180

Germany national unity was realised by the old authoritarian state which utterly scorned the free and democratic ideals of its ordinary citizens.

Among the historians, at least those of the younger generation, these views are not disputed. But there is a difference between the recognition of a fact by scholars and its implantation into the public consciousness. This holds true in all fields. But this difference is particularly great and understandable in a country whose recent history has been so ill-starred. Virtually everything which was valid in the past is now revealed to be false: pride in the victory over France, which gave imperial Germany its self-assurance, or again the war fever of 1914, the legend of the stab in the back in 1919, or the adulation of Adolf Hitler who promised new greatness for his country.

It was difficult enough for many Germans to face the fact that the Third Reich should no longer be entered on to the credit side of German history. But then the task of "overcoming the past," as it was called in the fifties and sixties, ought to stop short with this dark episode and not reach further back to before the year 1933. There were to be no lines of contact between the Second Reich of Bismarck and the Third Reich of Hitler. A critical attempt to come to terms with German history became a taboo subject.

And another of the taboos of recent history is the assassination attempt of 20 July 1944, although from a different point of view. Resistance against an inhuman tyranny, an attempt on the life of the Führer to whom one had sworn an oath of loyalty, violent revolution — in Germany, this was a situation which flew in the face of all tradition. It is impossible to imagine what would have happened if the attempt had met with success. Heinemann expressed it candidly in Plötzensee:

> The Hitler myth and the nationalistic illusion would not have been broken if Hitler had died in 1944. What would have happened would have been that the assailants would have been bitterly accused of having deprived us of victory and the glory of the Greater German Reich.

History took a different direction. After the fall of Germany in 1945, there were none of the preconditions for a second "stab in the back" legend to emerge. It became all too evident that the Third Reich was utterly inexcusable. Anyone announcing restrospectively his opposition to Hitler would also have to approve of the resistance, in which the vision of a "better Germany" became visible. In the context of 20 July, historical self-criticism acquired a certain degree of respectability. Thus it was that Gustav Heinemann was able to put into words some unpalatable truths about German history without himself becoming the object of attack.

But when, on the occasion of the centenary of the foundation of the German Reich, he recalled these selfsame truths, there was a storm of disapproval. He was accused of of being one-sided, of presenting a biased account of history based on Social Democrat views, of an excess of moralising, of viciously condemning those sections of the community with a sense of national pride, and of fouling his own nest. The criticisms also became involved in the realm of party political conflict, an area which normally does not venture to criticise the head of state. In Heinemann's speech, Rainer Barzel saw a lack of a clear stand against the political system of the DDR and warned his party that silence in the face of the injustices wrought against our compatriots in the other half of Germany had become institutionalised. Franz Josef Strauss commented on the Federal President's speech in the "Bayern-Kurier", coming to the depressing conclusion that it was "a highly subjective political essay larded with suspect accusations."

Heinemann had offended against a taboo. Instead of excising the Third Reich from the rest of German history as if it were some irksome ulcer and allowing the rest to be shrouded in that gentle twilight zone where guilt and providence, delusion and fate merge indistinguishably together, Heinemann insisted on casting a critical light on the prehistory of the Third Reich as well. Instead of celebrating Bismarck's foundation of the German Reich as the fufilment of that aspiration towards a democratic national state which had inspired the popular assembly of Hambach and the parliament of St. Paul's church, he reminded his audience that the state of 1871 had realised national unity at the expense of democratic freedom, and had forced the sense of nationhood among the Germans into a reluctant alliance with anti-democratic and monarchistic forces. Instead of praising the imperial Reich as the golden age of the Germans, he spoke of the inner divisions of this Reich which were patched over only by a thin veneer of the splendour of the Reich's early expansive years, divisions whose heritage the Weimar Republic also had to bear. Neither the beginning of the First World War nor the military catastrophe which brought it to an end, neither the internal political failure of the imperial Reich nor the collapse of Weimar democracy were spared in Heinemann's review of the German past.

So much pitiless frankness could not help but cause offence. It was all the more painful because Heinemann refrained from setting some positive achievement in contrast to each and every circumstance he criticised, for this, it was held, would have resulted in a rather more balanced account sheet of the past. It is true that he could have referred to Bismarck's social insurance laws which at the time were the most advanced in the world, but at the same time it should be remembered that Bismarck was seeking to purge all Social Democrats as "enemies of the Reich" in his law against the socialists. Heinemann might have drawn attention to Bismarck's skilful foreign policies which gave Germany forty years of peace — but this foreign policy reposed on the humiliation of France and in addition relied too heavily on the statesmanship of one individual. It collapsed when Bismarck's successors tried to continue his world power politics. And Heinemann could have spelled out the fact that the German imperial Reich was able to count upon the support of the great majority of the population — but the price of this support was too great. It was paid for by renunciation of the old middle-class ideals of a free and democratic state, by that blend of the cult of national power and the spirit of subordination so characteristic of the Wilhelminian period, by a cynical conception of realpolitik, in which the sole determinant was power, not justice or morality.

So the criticisms of Heinemann's speech might have been less harsh in tone if he had spoken more freely of the positive aspects of the past. But the critics spoke out loud and clear. For Heinemann's speech was not provocative because of its evaluation of this or that individual event. What outraged his critics was the fact that Heinemann shattered the illusion that it was only through the advent of Hitler that Germany became a "difficult fatherland."

There is no possibility of drawing up a balanced account sheet of the past hundred years, just as it is impossible to talk in terms of a continuing historical tradition, broken only by the Third Reich, which can now be taken up again today. Since we do not have one single unbroken tradition in Germany, but instead several broken traditions, it is not likely that there will be any broad agreement among those alive today about how the past should be regarded. It is possible to forge links with only one tradition — and to do this implies the rejection of others.

Gustav Heinemann does not fight shy of the consequences of this decision. This is the source of the impact of his speeches about the German past, but it also explains why they are so provocative. In his eyes, tradition is not the privileged preserve of conservatives, nor yet of reactionaries. In the course of a speech on tradition and historical awareness in Germany, he said that "it is not a question of whether we accept tradition or not. The alternatives are rather a question of which traditions we should embrace and the way in which we should regard historical events."

Such a conception of tradition brings release from the obligation of having to justify the national history, to seek excuses for past errors and to sweep unpleasant memories under the carpet. Once this obligation to justify the past has lost its hold, the individual becomes free to seek through history for traditions acceptable to a democratic community. Instead of swearing to a unity bought at the price of self-delusion, it is possible to cut against the grain of history in search of those forces which sought to gain power in Germany and for so long were unable to do so — in search of evidence of the spirit of freedom, self-confident citizenship and successful attempts to overcome the subservient mentality. Heinemann is seeking to convince his fellow citizens that there is an undiscovered hoard of such evidence which well merits being brought out into the light of day. But it is not just desirable to do so — it is essential.

State visit in Rumania: the drive through Bucharest with President Nicolai Ceausescu

State visit to the Netherlands: the drive through Amsterdam with Queen Juliana ▷

State visit to Sweden: trip by barge with Prime Minister Olof Palme

Far too little is known about such things. The school history books hardly mention them. Even the people who live in towns and districts where such freedom movements occurred often know nothing of them. The chronicles and church records of such places hardly make reference to struggles against the ruling powers. And where the authorities were victorious, the memory of such uprisings is swiftly obliterated.

Heinemann has devoted much energy towards reawakening these memories. In many places he has inspired people to take his discoveries further. The history of the "saltpetre" rebels in the southern part of the Black Forest is being researched once more; and the institute for civic history in Münster which Heinemann has visited is devoting a greater degree of attention to freedom movements.

In Rastatt, where the Baden uprising of 1849 was bloodily defeated by Prussian troops, Heinemann's proposal of erecting a memorial of some kind for 1974, that is the 125th anniversary, is to be pursued if sufficient funds can be raised for the purpose. Discussions are taking place on a similar plan for Hambach, the town in the Palatinate where, in May 1832, a powerful popular assembly of the national democratic movement gathered with the object of advancing the cause of the sovereignty of the people and German unity within the context of a republican state.

Heinemann has occasionally been accused of having stood German history on its head in his endeavours to revise our view of the past. It is not possible, it is argued, to inflate individual incidents into a tradition of freedom fighting. And besides, the Germans have by no means always found the authorities over them to be oppressive. It is simply is not right and proper for a head of state to indulge in sweeping condemnations of whole centuries of German history.

Objections of this order indicate a failure to recognise Heinemann's true intentions. It is not his purpose to fabricate traditions which have no basis in the facts of German history. What he is seeking to do, however, is to bring into the open events which up until now have not received their due measure of attention. Or more precisely: he is inviting us to view German history through the eyes of a democrat. This is the direction which his interest in the past has followed. If he takes sides, it is the side of the democrat against the meek subordinate, the peace-loving patriot against the bullying nationalist, the moralist against the cynical power-grubber.

It cannot be denied that at times he has made things too easy for his critics. His often-quoted statement that a free and democratic Germany should rewrite its history right down to the schoolbooks is open to misunderstanding, to say the least. It could be taken as a swingeing attack on historical scholarship. Although it is no secret that the German historical fraternity had been ensnared in a far too apologetic attitude right into the sixties, Heinemann naturally refrains from making any incursions into the independence of scholarly research. Schoolbooks are a different matter; they are frequently repositories for long outmoded historical prejudices, nationalistic distortions and accounts which gloss over unfavourable aspects. Heinemann is passionately concerned to correct such prejudices. This is why he has declared his support for the work of the international institute for school textbooks in Brunswick, where they are concerned with such improvements.

In his inaugural speech Heinemann refers to Germany as one of the difficult fatherlands. And for this very reason there must be no shying away from the facts of the historical past. The only way of overcoming the past is by accepting it, the bad along with the good. This applies to the lives of nations just as it does to the lives of individuals. This is why Heinemann insists on critical probing even into the darkest days of the German past, but not just in order to keep old wounds open.

Heinemann's state visits to countries which suffered particularly because of Germany in the last war are also part of this endeavour to confront and so overcome the past.

State visits are generally held to be hangovers of a past age when potentates still had real power. Since the present constitutions of many countries have deprived their heads of state of power, they gladly go off on tours, revelling in the fancy dress parades and the agreeable formalities of protocol

190

which are all bound up with the business of state visits, thereby compensating for the fact that at home they are entirely superfluous in the political life of the country. So heads of state depart on their state visits at the national expense, primarily attracting the attention of the tabloid press and, for quite different reasons, the taxpayers' associations.

Naturally, this cliché image of the head of state is somewhat exaggerated. It is even less than usually true of the German Federal Presidents to date, neither in the case of the very few state visits that Theodor Heuss undertook, nor for the widerspread journeyings of Heinrich Lübke in the third world, which were very much in the interests of the Federal Republic at large.

Gustav Heinemann is utterly resolved to do nothing which might encourage this picture of the state visit as wasteful tourism at public expense. When he entered office he gave notice that he intended to untertake neither lengthy nor frequent visits overseas. Instead, it was his intention to visit his European neighbours in those countries where, despite all the practical co-operation, relationships with the Federal Republic are still in the shadow of the evil memory of National Socialism.

His first state visit was also the most difficult. It was to Holland in the November of 1969. The invitation had arrived in Bonn only a few weeks after Heinemann had entered office. His election to the presidency had met with an exceptionally favourable response in Holland, as indeed it had nearly everywhere else in the world. The Dutch respected this man who had been a declared opponent of the Nazi régime, who was known as an intrepid democrat able to reconcile deep religious conviction and practical down-to-earth tolerance. The fact that this man had in free elections gained the highest office in the Federal Republic enabled the Dutch to make the decision to forget the sufferings of the past, twenty-five years after the end of the war.

The last time a head of state had visited Holland had been in 1907. Since then, no one in The Hague had felt able to issue any further invitation. After the First World War, solidarity with Belgium, which had been overrun by Germany, stood in the way of state visits. After the Second World War the obstacles were even greater. The German invasion of 1940, five years of occupation, the brutal persecution of the Jewish section of the population and the destruction of Dutch towns and cities were still such fresh and painful memories that they inhibited relationships between Holland and the Federal Republic.

Of course, normal political contacts had been established. There were no startling differences of opinion between the two as EEC members. Trade flourished, and the Federal Republic became Holland's most important trading partner. Germans by the tens of thousands spent their holidays in the Netherlands, and Dutch tourists came to the Federal Republic. But beneath the surface of these normalised relations there could still be detected a certain lack of warmth on the part of Holland.

Before Heinemann took office, it would have been inconceivable to invite the head of state of the Federal Republic to the Netherlands in order to put a final end to any strained relationships. But the Dutch were prepared to welcome Heinemann. The conservative Amsterdam "Telegraf" stated shortly before the state visit that "no man can be a better advocate for a close and friendly relationship between neighbours than Gustav Heinemann, a head of state who commands our affection." Rabbi Dr. Soetendorp, the priest of one of the three Jewish parishes in Amsterdam, expressed it even more directly: "We should never have invited any other man to come here with even the merest taint of the Nazi past about him."

When he was in Holland, Heinemann did not seek to elude the past. On the very first day of his visit, he went to the "Hollandse Schouwburg," the memorial in the old Jewish quarter of Amsterdam to the National Socialists' persecution of the Jews. He had expressly asked to be taken there.

The "Schouwburg," which had once been the Jewish theatre of Amsterdam, became in the war years the collection point for 57,000 Dutch Jews who were transported from there to the extermination camps. After 1950 most of the building, which was unsafe, was torn down. Only the front façade remained, behind which is now an open square. On the spot where the stage used to be, there is now a simple memorial: on a stone plinth in the form of a Star of Divid there stands an obelisk. A plate on the wall which closes off the square bears the following inscription in Dutch and Hebrew: "In memory of those who were taken away from this place. 1940—1945." Heinemann was received in the "Hollandse Schouwburg" by the three Rabbis of Amsterdam. On the memorial he placed a wreath of white carnations with an unobtrusive black, red and gold ribbon. The Federal President was accompanied only by Frau Heinemann and the Dutch royal pair. The official retinue remained behind.

A German head of state bowing his head before a memorial to Jewish sufferings: this was a symbolic event of great power, which can be compared to the moment in Warsaw when Willy Brandt spontaneously fell to his knees. Both men, Heinemann and Brandt, are declared anti-Fascists. But when abroad, neither of them has sought to escape the guilt of the past, altough it does not weigh upon them personally. Instead, as representatives of their country, they bore witness to the nightmare memory of those days in the only way which can help towards preventing others from continuing to hold the German people in reproach for the past.

Heinemann had paused before the memorial to the terror in silence. At a state banquet that evening in the royal palace, he put into words what could not have been said in the "Schouwburg", namely that the Germans had not been capable of preventing the coming of Hitler's régime, nor were they able to get rid of it on their own resources. Precise, clear words, free of self-justification as they are of submissiveness. It was this direct, honest way of speaking which met with such a heartfelt response in Holland.

The Federal President's simplicity and directness stood in strong contrast to the pompous display mounted for his benefit. From the moment he stepped out of the special train in Amsterdam in top hat and tails, he was surrounded by the kind of spectacle such as only used to be put on by the old European monarchies. During the initial ceremony there were two guards of honour to be inspected, and the German national anthem was played three times; and he travelled the short distance from the station to the royal castle in an open state carriage drawn by six horses, past lines of 780 soldiers drawn up in his honour.

After having lived through four political systems without medals or honours, Heinemann now wore for the first time in his life the Federal order of merit with distinction and the "Grand Cross of the Order of the Netherlands Lion" bestowed upon him by Queen Juliana. (Heinemann, said his Secretary of State Conrad Ahlers, knew how to honour traditions when they were unbroken.) Heinemann patiently endured a ceremonial which was so vastly different from what he preferred. There were no plans for unrestricted contact with the population, who received him with restrained friendliness, not even in the days that followed. Nor was there a meeting with the rebellious youth of Holland. The protocol followed the conventional pattern: state banquets, visits to dikes, a flower auction, a visit to a German school, and finally, to the Rembrandt exhibition in the state museum.

Only on one occasion did Heinemann succeed in side-stepping convention. But the incident took place away from the public gaze, on the journey back to Amsterdam one evening from a dinner in The Hague. The Dutch royal couple and the Heinemanns had struck up such a friendship that it was decided that they would make the journey back together in the same car. Queen Juliana got into the back of the car with the Heinemanns, Prince Bernhard sent the security man home and sat next to the driver. Heinemann recalls this episode with great pleasure as one of the happiest journeys he had ever experienced.

But this car trip in defiance of protocol did not take place until the last day of the state visit. Meanwhile Heinemann had been confronted with many more reminders of the terrors of the past. Again at his own request, he visited St. Lawrence's church in Rotterdam, which had been reduced to rubble along with the rest of the mediaeval town centre in the course of a German bombing raid on 14 May 1940. After the war it was rebuilt and made into a place for ecumenical gatherings. Later, in Rotterdam city hall, Mayor Thomassen recalled in precisely enunciated German the fears in the face of the Nazi occupiers, the oppression and the destruction of the city. But then he spoke in conciliatory tones about the guiltless younger generation, and, like the mayor of Amsterdam the day before, honoured Heinemann as one of the older generation of Germans who had stood fast in the days of National Socialist arrogance. He made reference to Heinemann's habit of over-punctuality in a sentence which the journalists present saw as a kind of key to the state visit as a whole: "Here in Rotterdam you are not arriving too early!" That statement had a liberating effect. The slight sense of tension which had been detectable until then, behind all the splendid protocol, fell away before this offer of friendship.

Nowhere in Holland did Heinemann receive demonstrations of appro-bation from the public at large. But there was no occasion for them. It was a remarkable enough sign of respect for their German guest that there were no open protests. The heartfelt accord which grew up during the visit would never have developed had Heinemann shied away from confronting the past. After he had undertaken that difficult task, even his speeches about the common tasks of the future did not just sound like fine empty phrases. They confirmed a common intent to leave behind the sufferings of the past and to initiate a new era of long-term trust and collaboration. When the Heine-manns were leaving, Queen Juliana expressed in the simplest terms the reasons why this state visit had also been a political success: "You have made us open our hearts to you."

Subsequently Heinemann also visited Denmark and Norway. There too he made full recognition of the guilt which Germany had brought upon itself in those countries thirty years before. And there too he made positive steps towards reconciliation.

In the Federal Republic, Heinemann's attitude to his own country during these visits abroad did not meet with undivided support. Many people con-sidered he had gone too far in his willingness to settle the debts of the past. When a journalist asked him if he was convinced that his conduct abroad would satisfy all opinion at home, including the conservatives, he replied by turning the question round.

I take the view that even the so-called conservatives should take their share. They all say today that they wanted no part of Hitler's Fascism and that, although they may have become personally caught up in it, they held themselves aloof and still remained good democrats all the time. If that is so, then they too should heartily welcome what I have said abroad.

In this respect, there is no compromising for Heinemann. It is impossible to work towards finally overcoming the sufferings of the past if one is at the same time to pretend that things had not been as bad as they have been made out to be. But if categorial rejection of Fascism does not succeed in uniting people, that is not the fault of the head of state.

Heinemann's interpretation of the German past, which he has expressed in his speeches, does not lay claim to being the sole true vision of German history. It represents no more than an attempt to permit his "difficult fatherland" to arrive at a sense of history which, untrammeled by excuses and self-pity, allies itself with those traditions which a democratic Germany can properly take up for its future benefit.

Productive Restlessness

Heinemann has been consistently concerned to cast a critical light on the past; and his interest in the future is equally great, if not greater. There is scarcely a politician of his generation in the Federal Republic who is so dissatisfied with past achievements and so determined to see changes in the future. Wherever Heinemann speaks in public on a political theme, this foward impetus can always be detected. Rarely does he dwell on the present for more than a couple of sentences; he moves rapidly on to discuss what has not yet been achieved, what ought to be done and what must be accomplished.

Many of Heinemann's contemporaries, who have a more cautious temperament or hold cosy privileges are less anxious to see changes coming about, and have caused him to acquire the reputation of being incapable of saying yes, of finding it difficult to recognise what has been achieved, of being too restless to give due credit to the present.

It is only necessary to read Heinemann's speeches to refute this impression. Heinemann shows pride in what has been accomplished. Economic reconstruction, which brought a devastated country prosperity and worldwide respect within the space of a few short years; the political and economic assimilation of millions of Germans expelled from the former eastern territories of the Reich; the social and political achievements which have brought the worker a substantial measure of social security and a steadily rising standard of living; and, above all, the construction of a stable democratic system — all these are achievements which Heinemann has fully recognised. What he once said in the Friedland frontier transit camp to German immigrants from Poland has general validity: "In many respects, we have just cause to be thankful and satisfied."

But it is still true that Heinemann's impatience is more highly developed than any tendency to rest content with what has already been achieved. But this impatience is attributable neither to scorn of the present nor is it a matter of striking a pose — as if at were just Heinemann's restless temperament which prevented him from taking a cool look at the passage of time. Nor is his impatience directed at reform for reform's sake. Heinemann had already underlined the true reason in his inaugural speech: "One day's achievements count for little even on the day after."

At first sight, that statement sounds like a harmless cliché such as "Young people are always rebellious", or "There's no stopping progress". But Heinemann's intention is not banal at all, he wants make people uncomfortable. The political tasks which must be faced and solved within the course of the next two or three decades — from the development of a democratic welfare state to securing world peace on a political basis, from overcoming poverty among the population of the developing countries in the face of the wealth in the industrialised nations to achieving a more equitable distribution of wealth between north and south, from the struggle against pollution in the environment to humanising an increasingly threatening technological revolution — demand, according to Heinemann, such intense and resolute efforts that there is no time for smug self-satisfaction with achievements to date.

It is not Heinemann's style to permit himself to be impressed by apocalyptic visions of future holocausts. But he is equally well aware of the fact that great spiritual and moral changes must be wrought if these great political challenges are to be faced and overcome. He is also aware that, in a democracy, the politician cannot arbitrarlily advance far ahead of public opinion. This is why he places his office as President in the service of bringing about these changes in attitude. In his view, only one of the principles of the constitution, that relating to the constitutional state, has been fully implemented. The validity of the basic human rights, the division of power, the independence of the courts, the subordination of the administration to the law, and the openness of the processes of law — all these things have been properly developed in the Federal Republic and there are only occasional instances which would call for criticism.

But that does not mean that the demand of the Basic Law for the establishment of a democratic welfare state has by any means been fully met. The constitution is vague enough about what is meant by a "democratic welfare state". There are no concrete standards laid down for the economic and social pattern of the Federal Republic. What has in fact evolved within the framework of the Basic Law is a capitalist economic system, in which state intervention and trade union representation can ensure that there is no arbitrary exploitation of the economically weak by the economically strong.

In a speech to the Federal constitutional court Heinemann drew attention to the fact that "the economic and social order we have evolved is indeed constitutional, but it is by no means the only system permissible under our constitution." This clarification of the position is essential as a counter to those ideological proponents of the existing capitalist system, who have persistently sought to represent the Basic Law as the constitutional guarantee for the neo-liberal economic order and to condemn any social criticism against this system as unconstitutional.

But Heinemann regards revolutionary changes in the status quo as neither possible nor desirable. People are not given by nature to place the common good over private interest in profit. So the need is all the greater for increased social justice within the framework of the existing order. This is why Heinemann constantly returns to the theme of how much yet remains to be done in the fields of the distribution of wealth, co-responsibility and equality of opportunity in education. Heinemann takes the principle of a welfare state particularly seriously because the Basic Law does not define its framework with any great precision.

A striking example of Heinemann's preoccupation came in the speech he gave in May 1971 to the German municipal authorities conference in Munich on the subject of land ownership and urban construction. Heinemann made no reference to the specific circumstances of the debate on reform of the existing property laws. But he did draw attention to the fact that, according to the will of the constitution, the protection of private ownership is by no means an insuperable obstacle to the achievement of urgent reforms:

> When shall we recognise once and for all that Article 14 of the Basic Law does not just guarantee ownership, but also talks about the possibility of determining its nature and limitations by means of the law? When shall we recognise that Article 14 of the Basic Law states that all possessions carry responsibilities and that their use should not conflict with the good of the community? When, finally, will the legislators get round to writing these constitutional obligations into the land laws?

Heinemann's exposition of the constitution causes great discomfort because he is not just highlighting the freedoms and the rights it lays laid down, but also the obligations which it imposes on individual citizens and the legislator. In his speech to the municipalities he not only drew attention to the protection of private property, but also of the obligations of ownership to serve the common good; and equally, when he addressed the German journalists' association, he underlined the fact that the freedom of the press was not only a basic right but also an obligation under the constitution. The proper functioning of the democratic system depends on the elector having the opportunity to judge between the work of government and opposition. Only then can he be in a position to cast his vote in a responsible manner. In order to be capable of drawing proper conclusions he must have a comprehensive and reliable information service independent of the power of the state. This is why the variety and independence of the press is not a democratic luxury, but a necessity laid down by the constitution.

But no free constitution is of itself capable of making the citizen accept political responsibility. The freedom of the individual also permits him the possibility of withdrawal into his own private world, where he is content to leave political decisions in the hands of others. Heinemann has always made persistent efforts to encourage the citizen to become involved in political life where there is no compulsion for him to do so. He has scarcely given a speech in which he does not make reference to this challenge to become politically involved. He is particularly concerned to draw attention to this challenge of freedom when he is addressing a young audience. The "supreme offer" of the Basic Law does not reside in the fact that everyone can do just as he pleases. It points to the need for the individual to take his share of responsibility for the well-being of the whole state.

Heinemann is, of course, aware that in a representative democracy the opportunities for direct political involvement are limited. Anyone not working for a political party is largely restricted to voting once every four years in the general elections. Heinemann understands the motives which have led to criticism of the representative democratic system among sections of the younger generation. But he does not consider that direct reforms of democracy are practicable in the highly industrialised mass societies. He does not regard the soviet system or the imperative mandate as practical alternatives. It is Heinemann's opinion that the wealth and complexity of the political decisions which have long since caused an undesirable gap to arise between the experts and parliamentarians permits no other system of formulating political will than that of representatives elected for a specific term. At the end of the parliamentary term the decision must once more be placed in the hands of the electorate. And the members of parliament, who between elections enjoy independence from the will of the electorate, must be all the more concerned to establish contact with the public in their constituencies.

Heinemann only considers it possible and desirable to institute reforms in the limited area of local politics. The many initiatives taken by ordinary citizens who have come together for the protection of specific interests in the field of building and accommodation, kindergarten and school problems, traffic questions and the pollution of the environment indicate for Heinemann that democracy is thriving in Germany and are, in addition, a welcome sign of an increased level of self-assurance in the face of officialdom. Individual initiatives of this order are no alternative to the representative electoral procedure which also holds good for local councils. But they constitute a purposeful extension of and at times necessary competition for these councils. In this limited area of local politics the individual citizen can see most clearly that active involvement produces results, that participation in government is possible. For this reason, when speaking to local politicians, Heinemann often stresses that these new manifestations of political will should not be regarded as irksome attempts to interfere. They are an expression of that "productive restlessness" which he himself has constantly sought to encourage.

Heinemann's view of his office as President is such that he has comparatively little to say about international politics. In this regard, he is obliged to exercise even more restraint than when speaking about home affairs. The Basic Law lays it down that the Federal President represents the state authority of the Federal Republic to the outside world, but that does not mean that he is permitted to take any individual initiatives in foreign affairs. That is the prerogative of the Federal government. But even in this area Heinemann has from the outset not rested content with a purely decorative role. This holds good not just for his state visits, but also for his speeches on foreign affairs.

An early example of this is his visit as President to Berlin in July 1969, when the grand coalition was still in power. He could have contented himself with a ritual repetition of those declarations of loyalty and obligation which travellers from Bonn to Berlin have been repeating for years and which have often been misconstrued as a confession of faith. Heinemann did not let things rest with non-committal formulae. Instead, he put before the assembly the concept of a European détente which anticipated the notions underlying Willy Brandt's Ostpolitik. The geographical location and the peculiar political situation of the former Reich capital, Heinemann told the councillors, rendered the city particularly appropriate as a touchstone for a new and better relationship between east and west. Naturally, this would require all sides to have the courage to recognise the realities as they are. The determination of the West Berliners to maintain their links with the Federal Republic is, he continued, by no means irreconcilable with the justified security demands of the east. "Why then should we not seeks for solutions which all of us on all sides can agree to with a clear conscience?"

A few weeks later he made another foreign affairs statement. On 1 September 1969 he gave a broadcast on radio and television on the occasion of the thirtieth anniversary of the outbreak of war. He made use of this look into the past in order to think about the future:

> What we, to our great satisfaction, have achieved with our former "arch-enemy" France remains as an uncompleted task with regard to our eastern neighbours and especially Poland. Poland was the first victim of the onslaught of 1939. . . . Whatever the Polish government may have done in 1939 to give Hitler arguments to support his actions, and however hard the lot of our fellow countrymen was who in 1945 had to suffer the loss of their homes to the east of the Oder and Neisse, nothing must divert our attention from the fact that things cannot remain as they are between Poland and ourselves. Here too the old memories must be buried so deeply that no one will be able to disinter them ever again.

In Europe at large, and particularly in eastern Europe, this speech was very favourably received. It helped to pave the way for the negotiations with Poland which were to follow soon after.

Only on one other occasion has Heinemann overcome the reserve in matters of international politics which he normally maintains. This happened during the memorial ceremony in the Munich Olympic stadium for the victims of the Fürstenfeldbruck massacre. In his speech, Heinemann did not shrink back from asking who was guilty. He placed the responsibility in the first instance on a criminal terrorist organisation which employed hatred and murder to political ends, but he also accused those countries which do nothing to discourage terrorist action. This statement was received with applause, not just inside the stadium, but throughout the world. His words could have caused political complications for the Federal Republic. Heinemann took the risk. In a moment of helpless horror at what had occurred, diplomatic considerations had to take second place to a moral stand.

There are also two institutions, which owe their origin to the initiative of Gustav Heinemann, that are involved with international politics: the "German Forum for Development Policies", and the "German Society for Peace and Conflict Studies".

Heinemann had already referred to the term "peace studies" in his inaugural speech to the Federal parliament. He encouraged the Federal Republic to undertake greater efforts to advance research into both the military relationships between armament, disarmament and securing peace on the one hand and also the social, economic and psychological conditions for peace on the other. He put forward the same proposal more clearly a few weeks later in his address on the thirtieth anniversary of the outbreak of war:

> The actual danger for humanity no longer lies in nature, but within man himself. But man knows less of himself and his abilities to threaten life than he does about his natural environment. The causes of conflict among the nations and the human aggressive drives have been less researched than the laws of atomic structure . . . This is why research . . . is so necessary. We need peace research.

Heinemann's proposal found a wide measure of support among the public at large. It is true that he had his critics, who claimed that peace studies were a fashionable nonsense not to be taken seriously as an academic pursuit and having no bearing on practical politics. But they were in a minority. Federal Chancellor Brandt took up Heinemann's idea and announced in his statement on governmental policy of 28 October 1969 that the Federal government would take active steps to assist in the organisation,

---

1./2./3./4.   The President receives up to a hundred letters every day from citizens of the Federal Republic; this is just a sample.

Lieber Herr Bundespräsident Heinemann!

Ich bin 10 Jahre und gehe auf Neusprachliches Gymnasium in Mönchengladbach. In unserer Klasse sind über 40 Kinder. Ich finde das ist zuviel. Darum wünsche ich mir, daß es Klassen mit nur 20 Kindern bei uns gibt. Ich stelle es mir etwa so wie auf dem Bild vor. Ich hoffe, Sie können da etwas ändern. Danke!

, den 19. August 197

Straße 4

An den

Herrn Bundespräsidenten
der Bundesrepublik Deutschland

53 B o n n (Rhein)

Sehr geehrter Herr Bundespräsident,

Nachdem ich viele Bittgänge gemacht habe, weiß ich mir jetzt keinen Rat mehr
und wende mich deshalb an Sie in der Hoffnung, daß Sie noch eine Möglichkeit
finden, meiner Familie zu helfen.

Meine Familie, d.i. meine 78-jährige Mutter, meine Frau und vier minderjährige
schulpflichtige Kinder -ein Mädchen und drei Jungen-, wird von meiner Frau
und mir versorgt.

Unser Sohn ███████ gehört zu den Geistigbehinderten. E█████ ist jetzt ██████
Jahre alt. Er war zeitweise in der Arbeiterwohlfahrt -Bildungsstätte für
Behinderte-, Siegen. ██████ würde mit dem Schulbus abgeholt und wieder ge-
bracht. Er mußte jedoch diese Schule wieder verlassen, weil ein weiterer
Schulbesuch mit Rücksicht auf die anderen Kinder nicht mehr tragbar erschien;
so jedenfalls teilte man mir mit. E█████ bekommt epileptische Anfälle, bis
zu sechs am Tag wurden in der vorgenannten Bildungsstätte in deren Gutachten
festgestellt, wie in dem gleichen Gutachten mein Sohn auch als aggressiv, jäh-
zornig und unberechenbar beurteilt wird. Leider ist diese Beurteilung richtig,
sie stimmt mit meinen eigenen Erfahrungen überein.

E█████ bekommt plötzlich, für meine Familie grundlos und unvorhersehbar,
Wutanfälle; dabei kann er sehr gefährlich werden, denn dann wirft oder sticht
er mit jedem Gerät, das er gerade fassen kann.

E█████ dürfte keinen Augenblick ohne Aufsicht sein, aber wie soll das meine
Frau bewerkstelligen ? Ich selbst muß meiner Arbeit als Werkzeugschlosser
nachgehen, damit finanziell der Lebensunterhalt der Familie gesichert ist.
Wenn E█████ Geschwister Schulaufgaben erledigen müssen (z.B.), müssen wir
E█████ die Hände auf dem Rücken festbinden. Es ist schon mehrmals vorgekommen,
daß E█████, wenn wir ihn beim Spielen im Garten glaubten, plötzlich doch auf
der Landstraße, die direkt vor unserem Haus ist, vor einem Fahrzeug stand. Wenn
noch nichts sonst geschehen ist, ist es reines Glück. Wir können doch E█████
auch nicht ganztäglich fesseln und festbinden.

Nervlich und körperlich geht die ständige Anspannung insbesondere meiner Frau
über ihre Kräfte, aber auch ich und die Kinder werden überfordert. Wenn erst
noch meine Frau erkranken würde, was sollte ich dann tun ?

Unter dem 4.8.1971 -Aktenzeichen Az.21o/o4- ist vom Kreisschulamt in A█████
(█████████████████) ein Schulpflichtbeschluß ergangen. Hiernach soll E█████
eine Heimsonderschule für Geistigbehinderte besuchen. Wenn E█████ eine solche
Schule besuchen könnte, wäre es ein Segen. Eine Einschulung in eine öffent-
liche Grund- oder Sonderschule L ist aufgrund der Gutachten nicht möglich.

Weil ich meine Familie vor drohendem Schaden bewahren möchte, bemühe ich mich
schon seit einiger Zeit, für E█████ einen Heimplatz zu finden. Meine Bemühung
sind aber bis jetzt erfolglos geblieben. Mein Hilfegesuch an das Sozialamt ist
über die Verbandsgemeindeverwaltung D█████, die Kreisverwaltung A█████████
zum Sozialamt in Mainz gegangen. Der Leiter der Arbeiterwohlfahrt Bildungsstä-
ebenso wie dessen Vorgänger haben sich für meine Familie bemüht, desgleichen
das Sozialamt in Mainz. Leider bislang vergeblich. In Siegen wurde mir von Lis
mit 800 Namen gesprochen.

Blatt -2-

Auch das kirchliche Sozialamt hat sich durch eine Beauftragte davon
überzeugt, daß der andauernden Anspannung meiner Familie, hervor-
gerufen durch unseren kranken Sohn E███████, rasch ein Ende gesetzt
werden müsse. Die Bemühungen um eine Heimstelle, die auch diese
Stelle sich machte, blieben bis jetzt ebenfalls ohne Erfolg.

Rasche Hilfe ist nötig, für E███████ und für meine Familie insgesamt.
Deshalb bitte ich Sie, mein Ersuchen wohlwollend zu prüfen und zu
unterstützen.

Ich danke Ihnen schon jetzt für Ihre Mühe.

Hochachtungsvoll

███████████████

The Federal President's office has appealed — up to now without success — to a
variety of nursing institutions for a place for the sick boy.

Ponyhof „Zur Sonne"

Hans Jörke

Fremdenzimmer mit fließend warmem und
kaltem Wasser - Pension - Liegewiese -
Garagen - Saal für 50 Personen - Gute
Küche - Bestens gepflegte Getränke -
Ganzjährig geöffnet.

3541 Flechtdorf / Waldeck
Ruf Adorf 170 (870)

Datum 24.2.1970.

Sehr Geehrter Dr. Heinemann

Hinrich Kopf Minister von Niedersachsen und meinem Kollegen Herrn Kram
Willinngen / Waldeck Im Willinn== Waldecker Hof einen Skat gespielt,
nach vorgerückter Stunde,Termin ist mir entfallen , es war am Weltkirc
tag, Ehrlich! Wier haben Sie beschissen, Herz Bube 2 + gezogen
1 Runde 1 Picollo und 4 Pils = 5.-DM   hatten Sie verloren
zu Unrechtcht
Ich möchte es wieder gutmachen da ich sehe das Sie Als Bundespräsident
doch höhere Ausgaben haben als ich.
5.-DM lege ich bei damit die Sache mal in Ordnung kommt.

Ich Wünsche Ihnen auch im Namen meines Kollegen allzeit

Gute Fahrt

Mit Freundlichen Grüssen

co-ordination and financial support for all those engaged on peace studies in the Federal Republic. A year later to the day the inaugural meeting of the "German Society for Peace and Conflict Studies" took place in the Villa Hammerschmidt.

Before the society came into being, difficult disputes between researchers and those holding the purse-strings had to be overcome in relation to the financing of peace studies, the academic definition of the object of investigation and methodological and organisational problems of this new discipline. Heinemann took no part in these arguments, nor has he subsequently sought to influence the work of the peace researchers. He has made no secret of the fact that he is not particularly interested in sterile arguments about method, but hopes for cool-headed, practical research work in the field. It was his concern that his initiatives should help to raise peace studies out of the shadowy existence the discipline had led up until that time. As late as May 1969, just before Heinemann entered office, Johan Galtung of the Oslo institute for peace research had spoken of the "relatively low level of interest for peace studies in the Federal Republic." Since then, as active scholars have testified, there has been "a vitalisation which has caused peace studies in the Federal Republic to participate in international scholarly discussion."

Heinemann's foundation of the "German Forum for Development Policy" also had practical aims in view. The proposal originated from the Federal Minister for Economic Co-operation, Erhard Eppler, who hoped to use this forum to broaden the discussion of policies in the developing countries. Heinemann took up the proposal of his friend and longstanding political associate and, at the instigation of the Federal government, called together prominent figures in public life to form this group. The Forum came out into the open for the first time on 23 October 1970. In his speech of welcome, Heinemann said that he expected new ideas would be put forward by its members, and that it would effectively communicate to the public the need for and tasks of development policy. Without the understanding and

critical collaboration of their citizens, the industrialised nations cannot set
their sights upon policies which are directed, not at the short-term interests
of their own foreign and economic policies, but on the long-term interests
of the developing nations themselves. Because Heinemann is well aware of
how difficult this kind of information exercise is, he gave it public
support by calling together the Forum. And he continues the task of information in his speeches.

"The time is short in the face of the problems we confront, many of which
now seem insoluble", he said to the German Forum. What he was referring
to in relation to development policies equally holds good for a politically
guaranteed world peace and for the control of technical progress in the
industrialised nations. These three areas are interrelated. They are exposed
to the same threat that mankind will not survive if a solution is not achieved
within the course of the next few decades.

Early in 1972 the German translation appeared of a research document
which scientists of the famous Massachusetts Institute of Technology had
drawn up for the Club of Rome. It bears the title "The Limits to Growth".
In this study the American research workers predict the end of mankind for
the year 2100 if the present rate of economic expansion is maintained
unchecked. The growth in population, the food requirements, the consumption of raw materials and the pollution of the environment will, according
to this prognosis, bring about the collapse of technological civilisation,
because it is not possible, in a world with finite resources of raw materials,
water and energy, to expand industrial production indefinitely. The first
copy of the German edition was presented to the Federal President in
May 1972. The weekend after he had received it, Heinemann read it through
at a single sitting.

This study has evidently made an enormous impact upon Heinemann. Up
until then he had warned, encouraged, occasionally urged action. But now
he sounded the alarm. (The phrase is his. At a luncheon for members of
the order Pour le Mérite he exclaimed: "Here and now . . .the time has come

to sound the alarm so that no one will fail to be aware of the gravity of the situation.")

Heinemann had first drawn attention to the gravity of the situation in April 1972, in a speech in Oberhausen entitled "Quality of Life." He spoke of the fact that we had for far too long made the environment bear the cost of our prosperity, and now we were threatening to choke it; that many of the things we thought were advances had turned out to be illusory; that the life style and standard of living of the industrialised nations could become questionable if things continued as they were. Then Heinemann drew the consequences:

> The time has come to make clear and state it to all that no one — I repeat, no one — can any longer draw back from a thoroughgoing investigation of the principles on which we live and our systems of value. All politicians, whatever their status and whatever their country of origin, scientists, teachers, businessmen, agriculturalists, housewives, and all the workers who in their various ways contribute to our material well-being: the challenge goes out to each of us.

No longer can the material standard of living be taken as the sole yardstick for the "good life". No longer can the technical feasability of a project be taken as conclusive proof of its desirability. No longer may the natural riches of the earth be thoughtlessly exploited. And above all: no longer may private wealth be increased at the expense of public poverty. Heinemann's demand that the citizen should transform his way of thinking and his mode of life is directed at his most sensitive part — his purse. The enormous public tasks of conservation of the environment, educational policy, health systems and transport can only be financed if the taxpayer is prepared to make substantial sacrifices.

Heinemann makes a particularly urgent appeal to those people whose work is most directly related to whether the world will further deteriorate or take a turn for the better: the scientists. Because of the threat to the survival of mankind, the former division of labour between scientist and politician no longer holds good, namely, that the former thinks out problems and the latter takes the decisions. The social responsibility of the scientist no longer permits him to withdraw into "the pursuit of knowledge for its own sake." Science becomes a mere absurdity if it does not accept its responsibility for the future and leaves it to the politicians to use the results of their research as they think fit. Heinemann campaigns among scientists to persuade them to accept their new role, without which it would not be possible to persuade the politicians to accept a new scale of values.

The fact that, if present developments continue, the future will not be living in, that worth it is essential to undertake a thoroughgoing re-evaluation of our standards — convictions such as these form the major motive force behind Heinemann's "productive restlessness". And at the same time they are the reason for which the young respect him so greatly.

Heinemann has often recognised that his own impatience gives him a large measure of understanding for the impatience of the young. But this common stance is not of itself sufficient to explain his affinity for the younger generation. It is those very critical voices among the young, who normally claim to have nothing but mistrust and scorn for the older generation, who respect the man who does not dismiss their moral outcry against outmoded educational institutions, injustice and lack of peace as mere youthful rebelliousness. As Federal President, Heinemann has made special efforts to establish and maintain contact with the young. In the many conversations he has held with groups from all areas of society, it has struck his attention time and again that the younger members of the party were more concerned with the wider public problems, whereas the older people present tended to be preoccupied with their own group interests. Heinemann applauds this moral commitment among the young, even when he cannot approve of the methods or objectives they are pursuing.

Heinemann does not try to tell the young what he thinks they would like to hear. Speaking to apprentices in Coblenz, he said:

> All genuine concern about outmoded notions, prejudices and the
> forceful preservation of anxious taboos loses all credibility when it

results in a refusal to play an active part in the state and in society. Paint bombs and acts of violence, shouts of support for Mao and Che Guevara neither improve the lot of the individual nor do they make our world one iota more humane, more just, or more rational.

Heinemann speaks with particular feeling when he is addressing the young on the subject of the inviolable freedoms which the Basic Law guarantees. Those in their twenties today are far more strenuously opposed to the injustices of this world than the sceptical young of the fifties. What they have not themselves experienced is the absence of freedom. Heinemann regards the undervaluation of the citizen's freedoms by critically-minded young socialists as a particular danger. He fears that these young people would be all too ready to sacrifice the basic rights of freedom and the principles of peaceful resolution of conflict in their endeavours to achieve a greater measure of justice in the world.

Heinemann shares the impatience of the young, but not their readiness to believe in Utopias here on earth. Political majority brings with it, in Heinemann's view, the ability to live with the fact that it is not given to man to bring about qualitative changes in his nature. All that are possible are relative improvements, and stern ideologies are as unlikely to bring about such improvements as adherence to outmoded attitudes. Between these two, between the revolutionary and the reactionary scorn of the notion of gradual step-by-step improvement, Heinemann recommends the difficult path of reform. He exhorts people to positive patience, calm reason and a sober sense of proportion.

But because of the severe limitations imposed upon political action in a world exposed to so many threats and the limited time at our disposal to resolve them, even slight improvements can be brought about only at the expense of supreme efforts, and because such efforts are impossible unless the citizen is prepared to undergo a radical reassessment of his attitudes, Heinemann exploits the opportunities the authority of his office affords him to prepare the way for this essential change of heart among the entire population.

Conversation with Gustav Heinemann

Dr. Joachim Braun: Mr. President, the office which you fill exposes its holder to constant public interest, but at the same time it isolates him. It is not thought proper for a Federal President to call in on old friends in Bonn of an evening, but by the same token his position is too superior to that of his former colleagues for them to visit him of their own accord. Do you find the loneliness of office a burden?

Dr. Gustav W. Heinemann: Even though it is not so easy to maintain the same unforced relationships with friends as used to be the case, that doesn't necessarily imply that I am any the lonelier. It is up to me to fix a time and invite my old friends here. And they usually show no reluctance to come.

Braun: The loneliness of office is, of course, not just a private thing. The Federal President is largely cut off from political happenings in Bonn, that is, from the discussion of live issues as they are being dealt with. If the President is to maintain neutrality, he must stay aloof. But are you not tempted now and then to return to the fray?

Heinemann: I must confess that I am. If Federal elections were to come upon us now, I should be more than tempted to take an active part as I have always done in the past.

Braun: In theory, the Federal President also has the role of political adviser. How does this work out in practice, and are you actually asked for advice?

Heinemann: If the government has certain intentions, it is up to them to carry them through. The government does not come round asking advice as to how that is to be done. If on the other hand I should like to see something dealt with, it is up to me to speak to the government, either to the Federal

Chancellor or directly to the competent Minister. The latter is what usually happens.

Braun: As Federal President you hear far more than other politicians of individual suffering and privation in whole groups of people in our society. You yourself have said that the President is a kind of Federal wailing wall. How much are you able to do to alleviate suffering and to reduce privation?

Heinemann: I am constantly having brought to my attention complaints, cases of distress and suffering by letter and in personal interviews, particularly when I am travelling around. In the office I hold, it is not possible for me to deal with them directly. For example, I am not in a position to grant a free pardon to someone who has driven a car with an illegal alcohol level in his blood. Something like that can be passed on to the appropriate Land or federal offices. So it is only in a roundabout way that anything can result from a letter to me or an interview.

Braun: And do you have the opportunity to draw attention publicly to areas of need in society?

Heinemann: Yes, that can happen, for example, when I am invited to a particular conference, let us say of the war wounded. In that case I should be able to make some statement of principle in relation to the social conditions of this group, and I have done that sort of thing on many occasions.

Braun: You have, for example, very often put in a word on behalf of the handicapped, foreign workers, and on behalf of other groups such as drug addicts, and those punished of criminal offences. Many of your critics maintain that this continuous emphasis upon fringe groups in our society is not really compatible with an office which is supposed to be there for everybody, an office which might be expected to be a force for social integration. Does it worry you when people call you a President of the Minorities?

Heinemann: It is part of the nature of things. Those who are capable of helping themselves hardly need outside assistance. But the groups you have referred to are as a rule not even capable of organising themselves. As a result, we have to approach them in order to find out what is worrying them, so that we can pass the information on to society at large.

Braun: And you would see the task of the Federal President as being one of integrating society by bringing these fringe groups to the attention of the community at large?

Heinemann: Precisely. Society tends to forget about many of its members, but everyone should be kept informed about them. These groups can only do this for themselves within the strict limitations of their own resources. Where there is a need, they must be given help, and that is the point of my drawing attention to their problems.

Braun: Another subject, Mr. President, that appears time and again in your speeches and which has at times caused some criticism to be directed against you, is our relationship with the past. You said once that the time had come for a free democratic Germany to re-write its history, down to the school-books. Is it up to the head of state to commend a revised image of history to the nation?

Heinemann: I regret the fact that many events in our past are not widely enough known. What I am thinking of in particular are movements in earlier times in the direction of a freer society or towards an improved level of social justice in our country. There are many more precedents than we are generally aware of. Where are they to be found in the schoolbooks, where do they still live on in the minds of our contemporaries? There is a very large gap here, and one which I should like to see filled.

Braun: Not only have you drawn our attention to things which have been forgotten, you have also taken things which are very familiar and re-interpreted them in your own fashion. Should you not call a halt to your efforts towards revising the past at events — and there are precious few of them — of which the majority of Germans can feel a little proud, for example Bismarck's foundation of the German Reich in 1871?

Heinemann: Pride at the foundation of the Reich in 1871 by Bismarck implies something like this: At long last we have turned into a national state and have emerged out of particularism. What I should like to see added to what is known and spoken about 1871 is the fact that the Bismarckian empire was badly organised from within.

Braun: We Germans have even less to be proud of in our history when it comes to the twentieth century. There are many who would simply like to see those dark times forgotten. You have repeatedly warned against this. Even when abroad you have spoken about German guilt. For this reason some have dubbed you the Penitential President. Does that kind of criticism embitter you?

Heinemann: Not in the least, all I should like to say to that is that it means there are still many of our contemporaries who are unwilling to face up to our own history.

Braun: You never tire of urging the German people on to political responsibility, more democracy, and greater social justice. Are you not afraid that your continued encouragements in this direction will result in too great a burden of responsibility being imposed upon the population?

Heinemann: If we want to be a free democracy, people must be repeatedly reminded of the fact that it is up to them to take an active and effective role. That is something which cannot be said too often.

Braun: In the normal run of things, as long as the parliamentary system is functioning, the political effectiveness of the head of state is restricted to an informative role, particularly in public speeches. But the Basic Law has given the President the task of giving emergency assistance in times of crisis. Such a crisis has been with us since the end of April 1972. The Chancellor had no majority in parliament, nor could the leader of the opposition muster one. At that time you were swift to make it known that in your view the best democratic solution would be new elections. But you did not have the right to dissolve parliament. Does not a situation like this call for greater effective powers of intervention on the part of the President?

Heinemann: I have always taken the view that the present status quo in broad terms should not be changed. The bulk of the political responsibility must lie with the Chancellor. As a result, it must remain a matter for him to make the first move in the direction of a parliamentary solution by instituting a vote of confidence in the Federal parliament.

Braun: At that time I wrote some commentaries to the effect that this was the hour of the President. Is the role of the President in times of crisis not a fiction if he is unable to act on his own authority in a stalemate situation like that?

Heinemann: What I am able to do in such an eventuality is to hold discussions with those involved, and that includes the opposition leader, of course. Such talks have taken place.

Braun: In July 1972 you expressed the view in public for the first time that when things have calmed down again, the legislators should think again about whether the dissolution of parliament should not be made easier. What kind of solution do you have in mind?

Heinemann: For example, the Federal parliament might be able to dissolve itself by voting for dissolution by a given majority.

Braun: The image of parliament has taken something of a knock because this crisis has been precipitated by some delegates crossing the floor to the opposition benches. In public discussion, several suggestions have emerged which might point the way towards a solution of this problem of members of parliament changing horses in midstream, for example, that a member who changes party should surrender his mandate to his old party. Do you take the view that the position of the member of parliament in this respect should be subject to new rules?

Heinemann: No, I should prefer to leave things as they are. Of course, a member of parliament does become part of a political team. He belongs to a party and is selected by that party for the parliamentary elections. But he is not bound to that party so strictly that he forfeits his personal freedom of movement. Neither the constitution nor electoral law forbid members of parliament from retaining their mandate when they change parties, even though it may cause considerable offence. But I can see no way of putting a complete stop to it.

Braun: You have frequently stressed that the Basic Law should not be changed lightly, because it is a good constitution. But do you not think that modifications should be introduced at points where the Basic Law seeks to lay down political objectives conditioned by the time at which it was drawn up? For example, is the reunification clause of the Basic Law still a meaningful injunction in a political situation in which recognition of the DDR is more or less inevitable?

Heinemann: Despite recognition of the fact of two German states, despite recognition of the DDR, I hold fast to the hope that one day we as a German nation will once more be able to live together under a common state.

Braun: And so you take the view that the preamble to the constitution is not in opposition to this policy?

Heinemann: No. This has shown itself not to be the case.

Braun: One thing that distinguishes the Federal Republic from the old Weimar Republic is its determination to protect itself against enemies of the state. In January 1972 the Prime Ministers of the Länder which make up the Federal Republic came to an agreement, the effect of which was to exclude from entry to public service all those forces inimical to the constitution. This resolution has been the subject of public controversy, because the concept "inimical to the constitution" is an elastic one and there is the fear that it might be employed in order to keep unwelcome critics at a distance. Where do you yourself draw the line here?

Heinemann: You are right in saying that this resolution has given rise to some disquiet. But the first thing I should like to stress is that the the Federal Ministers and Home Affairs Ministers in the Länder have not said or done anything new. It has formed part of our civil service law for a long time that anyone who seeks to enter the public service must be positive in his attitude towards our free democratic system. Anyone who cannot sincerely make such an undertaking is not suited for civil service work. And that must be decided by objective criteria through the appropriate procedures.

Braun: May I put the question to you again: Where do you draw the line on hostility towards the constitution, in the case, say, of a future judge or teacher?

Heinemann: The key features of our social system, as we understand it, are clear enough. The basic rights must be maintained. There must be no one-party system. Opposition must remain possible, as must the unrestricted right to form political parties. There must be no erosion of the right of all to vote secretly and directly. A change between government and opposition must be possible. But even these are questions which are seen in a quite different light by certain groups, and are treated differently in the countries to which these groups are politically sympathetic.

Braun: And you would take the view that such critics of the system are, of course, free to express their opinion, but should not be accepted into public service?

Heinemann: That is correct. There should be no curtailment of the free expression of opinion.

Braun: Is a radical opponent of our economic and social system an enemy of the constitution?

221

Heinemann: Certainly not as such. Our economic and social systems are not as such laid down in the Basic Law so rigidly that it is impossible to criticise them. And it is not beyond the bounds of possibility that there are concepts of an economic order which do not correspond to the one we have now, but which none the less would be admissible within the framework of the constitution.

Braun: Do socialist views of, say, the nationalisation of the means of production or the nationalisation of land fall within the terms of the constitution?

Heinemann: In my opinion they are possible within the framework of our system. The lines of demarcation are to be drawn in other areas. They lie in the directions which I referred to a few moments ago. There is, of course, a great deal that could be added to the list: for example, the independence of judges and courts must be preserved.

Braun: Now there are people, and there are some fairly big names among them, who consider that even the Soviet system falls within the possible forms permitted by the constitution.

Heinemann: First of all I should like to know what precise form that system would take. The constitution does not exclude every new or supplementary form of democratic expression — let us say, a referendum. But, in this context, our Basic Law requires a representative democratic system, that is to say, free, secret and direct election of members of parliament, with no continuous direct line between the elector and the elected.

Braun: So elections every four years, asking the population if they are prepared to entrust the current government with another term of office?

Heinemann: Certainly. That is the meaning of the representative system, that certain citizens, men and women, are placed in office for a particular period of time, and when this period has elapsed they have to account to the electorate for what they have done or have neglected to do.

Braun: Mr. President, the discussions on Baader and Meinhof have caused the question of the viability of our democracy to be concentrated in one particular area. Once again the demand has gone out for a strong state, for a police force which does not have to wear kid gloves, for stricter regulations governing custody and similar matters. Do you consider that the state is too weak?

Heinemann: No, the state is not too weak. The success of the action taken against the Baader-Meinhof group has demonstrated that.

Braun: As Minister of Justice you devoted a great deal of effort towards persuading the public to accept more liberal practices in the criminal law and forms of punishment. Do you not fear that the pressure of public opinion will cause the advances you have made in this area to be lost?

Heinemann: I hope that any advances will not be lost in the future. But we must continue to make a determined effort to clarify what kind of punishment we want to see imposed, and one that is appropriate to the age we live in. The old penal system sought to make the criminal repent his misdeeds; the present system, on the other hand, seeks to educate him. In the first instance this is achieved by threatening punishment for illegal actions, that is to say, by operating a deterrent. But when an offence is committed despite the threat of punishment, the criminal must be faced with the responsibility for his actions, the object being to reinstate him in society. The punishment should therefore take on an educative role. So this could include training for a particular trade, or, in the case of sexual offenders, medical treatment. In those unfortunate cases where remedial action remains ineffective, the ultimate resort is protective custody.

Braun: The public agitation over Baader and Meinhof has led to pretty wide-ranging suspicion of the intellectuals in our country on the part of conservative elements. Writers like Heinrich Böll and theologians like Helmut Gollwitzer are accused of doing the intellectual groundwork from which the bomb planters drew their inspiration. Do you consider that the intellectuals share any part of the culpability for the development of this politically motivated brand of criminality?

Heinemann: No. Anything can be misapplied. Social criticism is a necessary thing at all times and should never be taken as a priori evidence of support for criminal actions. We have to go deeper if we are to discover the true causes of such phenomena.

Braun: So you are drawing a clear line of demarcation between intellectuals who publicly direct criticism, however sharp, against our social system and those who set about attacking the system by force?

Heinemann: Precisely. The free expression of opinion, including unfavourable opinion, is and must remain permissible as one of our basic rights. Incitement to violence or the application of violence — that is quite a different matter.

Braun: But on the other side of the coin, a figure of the prominence of Heinrich Böll has stated that the spiritual climate in this country is rendering intellectual work increasingly impossible. Do you think that there is a real threat to intellectual activity in this country?

Heinemann: I regret that Mr. Böll finds cause to express himself in such a fashion, yet I cannot subscribe to his generalisation.

Braun: In recent months the polarisation of public debate has been much deplored, and there has been a call for a "common front of democrats." Is it not true to say that in these exhortations there lurks the ghost of an old anti-democratic neurosis, namely, a fear of conflict?

Heinemann: Well, we have not had as long to get accustomed to the democratic game as, say, the British, so we have so far failed to learn not to think about changing the rules of the game every single time a tricky situation crops up. To put it another way, we are a little too inclined to revert to an authoritarian mode of thought.

Braun: So you accept that even a stand-up fight among the parties is in your view a necessary part of democracy. But would you not say that the methods employed sometimes go a little too far?

Heinemann: Yes, the methods employed are sometimes far from acceptable, but strenuous opposition to an impending decision can and should have the effect of ensuring that the decision is all the more thoroughly considered. It is not a good thing for a politician to become so caught up in suspicions about his opponents that he loses sight of the common task that lies before us all of preserving and advancing our democratic system.

Braun: The intensity of the political debate will in the future become even sharper, if politicans summon up the honesty to demand of the citizen the sacrifices that will be necessary if the tasks of the future are to be faced successfully. Public expenditure will have to rise much more sharply than private investment, because the needs of our society will have to be met to an ever-increasing extent by public institutions. Do you believe, Mr. President, that the nation can be persuaded into accepting such a radical change of direction, particularly when their own pockets will suffer?

Heinemann: If it is a matter of raising taxes for clearly defined purposes, there is at the present time a clear and widespread readiness to accept such impositions. Besides, the only good political platform is one that has the good sense to point to where the needs lie. This is something the politicians must not shirk. It is not always easy; but we have no other real way of dealing with one another.

Braun: Little by little we are being obliged to recognise the fact that we in the industrialised countries have for far too long been making the environment pay the cost of our prosperity. Many of us are beginning to suspect the very notion of progress. But is not progress itself our destiny?

Heinemann: Progress has now become suspect in the sense that we should continue to follow our present developmental path indefinitely. There are plenty of examples for this ready at hand. If it is correct that in the last quarter of a century more of the earth's natural energy resources have been exploited than in the entire history of mankind, then we must inevitably ask ourselves how long things can continue in this fashion. How much longer can we continue to plunder the earth? We should not be prepared to allow ourselves to live our present lives to the detriment of future generations.

Braun: The free constitutional state makes great play on the fact that it protects the individual against arbitrary intrusion by the state. No one wants to see that altered. But in the future the point will be reached at which the common interest of society will have to be promoted at the expense of individual interests. Does that not signify that in the future we shall need a stronger state than we have had up to present?

Heinemann: Anyone who seeks to persuade the citizen that he should demand a "stronger state" must first of all make clear in what areas this strengthening of the state should take place.

Braun: May I offer two examples: At the present time it is still more or less impossible to compulsorily take over private land and property, without long drawn-out litigation which takes years to complete, when that land is required to fill a community need. Secondly, it is equally the case that the Federal monopolies commission has the greatest difficulty in getting its decisions implemented for the common good. Should not the state possess greater executive powers in these two areas?

Heinemann: I completely agree with you there. As far as ownership of land is concerned, I have reminded a conference of the association of urban authorities in Munich that our Basic Law regards ownership as a social and moral obligation. We really must work out the direction in which this obligation should move. And in answer to your other point, I would say that competition is part and parcel of the market economy. Limitations upon competition imposed by agreement among interested parties act against our economy.

226

Braun: If it is the case that more and more tasks in the community will have to be undertaken by the state and that the state must be provided with the necessary means for carrying them out, does it not signify that the demand for more democracy, for more effective participation by the citizen in the political decision-making processes, is an illusory one?

Heinemann: I think we must draw a distinction here. As far as the large-scale political decisions are concerned, these will have to be taken in parliament. But there are innumerable other things going on on a smaller scale, for example, at the local government level. It should be a profitable exercise for those who are planning the construction of a school or a refuse processing plant at the appropriate time to bring into the discussion the citizens who are to benefit by the construction or who will be affected by it in one way or another. It should not be necessary to wait until the citizen himself comes along to voice his opinion. Where that happens, his views should be gratefully received, but it could and should also happen that the planners themselves take the initiative in discussions with the citizen.

Braun: In your opinion, then, the demand for more democracy can best be realised within the clearly-defined bounds of the local authority?

Heinemann: Precisely.

Braun: You once said that the magnitude of the tasks which the future confronts us with will oblige us to undertake a radical rethinking of the basic principles of our lives and of our whole system of values. Do you believe that the average citizen has sufficient capacity for relearning to be able to cope with such fundamental changes?

Heinemann: The citizen will not be prepared to face such developments or necessities off his own bat. They must be carefully presented to him. This is a process that can be begun in the schools. At the end of the day, it is something which must develop within the context of an on-going dialogue between elector and elected.

Braun: In relation to peace studies you have stated that we need not only new modes of thought, but also different forms of conduct, if a dignified human existence is to be made possible for future generations on our planet. Are you suggesting that it is possible for qualitative changes to take place within man?

Heinemann: No, I don't believe that at all. Everything that history teaches us points to the contrary view, and this is also demonstrated to be so in periods of human history in which more strenuous efforts have been made to educate or enlighten the population than was the case in the more distant past. Man remains fundamentally what he has always been.

Braun: What did you have in mind, then, when you used the term "forms of conduct?"

Heinemann: If we are to prevent conflict situations or wars, it is necessary for the one side to try to arrive at a genuine understanding of the point of view and interests of the opposing side. Only by so doing shall we be able to find possible means of arriving at a peaceful solution to our problems.

Braun: It would be tantamount to a direct transfer of Christian attitudes into politics to see a problem with the eyes of one's enemy.

Heinemann: Yes, it may well be Christian! But it is at one and the same time part of the general currency of good sense to recognise that I cannot make progress with an opponent — unless, of course, I use force — without taking pains to find out who he is, what his motives are, and what makes him tick.

Braun: So you do not believe that it is possible for qualitative changes to take place within man. Is this the reason for your sceptical reaction to the Marxist hope that the inhumanity of society can be swept aside by changing the system of ownership?

Heinemann: None of the possibilities for restructuring the nature of society can be capable of altering the nature of man. Man will always seek to carve out his own individual destiny and then try to move mountains, whatever the social conditions, even if the ownership system is different; and man will never be made free of conflict.

Braun: Is that not a secular expression of the Biblical notion that man is a sinner?

Heinemann: You can put it that way if you like. Man cannot extricate himself unaided from the position in which he finds himself.

Braun: Without substantially increased productivity, it will not be possible for us to accomplish the tasks of the future which we have been talking about. But it is this very concept of productivity which makes our society appear so inhuman in the eyes of so many of our young people. A group of young psychologists even goes so far as to take the view that the concept of productivity in our competitive society is a basic cause of discontent and violence in the community. Do you think it is possible to reconcile an ethos of productivity with a positive attitude to peace?

Heinemann: Productivity is the precondition for prosperity in any shape or form. If men compete to achieve some objective, it will always happen that one individual or another gains a temporary advantage. But that should not give rise to discontent nor to an inhuman lack of concern for those who have not been able to keep pace with the competition and the achievement of the majority, let us say, because they lack natural gifts. Constant efforts must be made to achieve and attain a state of overall balance.

Braun: Anyone casting an eye over the magnitude of the tasks before us, our limited resources and the shortness of the time at our disposal, must inevitably feel anxious about the future. There has never been the feeling in your case, Mr. President, that you might be prepared at any time to resign. Is resignation something you would ever contemplate?

Heinemann: Absolutely and categorically not.

Braun: So it is something which it is not within you to feel, or something that you simply do not feel?

Heinemann: The latter. I do not feel that way. I know that every day we must strengthen the floodgates wherever they are threatening to burst in upon us. That is an unceasing necessity; it is part of man's destiny.

Braun: Mr. President, twenty years ago you substantiated certain political decisions directly on theological grounds, relating them to the demand for obedience to God's command. Nowadays this kind of direct link is no longer to be found in your speeches. But you remain now as you were then, a convinced Christian. What has brought about this change?

Heinemann: I think what has actually changed is the way I conduct my arguments. Even in those days I did not base my arguments directly, that is to say, solely, on theological grounds, but on the basis of the two offices I hold — I was a politician as well as holding a position in the church — and so I developed my lines of thought by drawing on both backgrounds. On the one hand, I might be referring back to God's command to us to obey Him, on the other side, which does not fall within the Biblical sphere, I have sought to employ only rational grounds in argument.

Braun: And your present office causes you to turn more to the latter, to arguments based on reason?

Heinemann: Yes, that is very much in the nature of things. It is all bound up with the possibilities and obligations of my office. I am supposed to be here for the benefit of all, and so I must devise a language which is not just comprehensible to a small section of the community.

Braun: So this change has nothing to do with the fact that you might have become more sceptical of employing any one of God's ordinances in order to decide in favour of one course of action or another?

230

Heinemann: It is not a question of scepticism. I can see no sense of contradiction here. Wherever there is common ground, I try to make use of both, but with particular emphasis upon the one which can be of the greater value to the group of people I am addressing. It depends entirely on the occasion. In a Christmas speech it is naturally easier to bring Christian elements to the fore than in the course of a speech to a conference on a purely political occasion. But even then some traces of Christian reference are to be detected in what I have to say. It seems to me that it is up to anyone who so wishes to perceive the basic premises which guide my thoughts and words. It doesn't have to be shouted from the rooftops. It is readily perceptible to those who have ears to hear.

Braun: If I have properly interpreted the path you have taken as a politician, your interests have changed in the course of the last twenty years. At the beginning of the fifties your political interest was directed principally towards foreign policy and the German question, and your views on social policies tended to fade into the background. But now social issues dominate your speeches. How do you account for this change?

Heinemann: My involvement in the fifties in foreign policy and the German question derives from my participation in the debate that was taking place at the time over the correct approach to a policy for Germany. Today this debate is not part of my present office. It is a matter for the government and opposition. In my position, it is inevitable that I should refrain from involving myself in current issues relating to German or foreign policy, and should instead direct my attention to the other areas you have been asking me about.

Braun: Mr. President, in his new book (Tagebuch 1966—1971) Max Frisch has voiced the malicious idea that a politician has less need to fear old age than a worker, an intellectual or an artist, because it is in the nature of political power that one can exercise considerable influence upon others

231

without being creative. The fading of the imaginative powers, says Frisch, and a lack of fear for the consequences makes an ageing politician the ideal person to be head of state. You are now over seventy. But in your case there is no sign that your imaginative powers are on the wane, but instead you are restless, constantly posing questions, and demonstrating an unceasing ability to adapt yourself to an ever-changing pattern of new and unfamiliar tasks. How have you experienced the process of growing older?

Heinemann: Growing old means constantly enriching one's experience and hence increasing the possibility of adopting the right approach to the constant flow of new demands made upon one. What has helped me so much in my office as President is the unusual range of my own experience and activities. I have had an independent career as a lawyer, and I have been engaged in the management of a large industrial company. I have been involved in all forms of political office from the humblest to the highest. In the church, I have held every office open to someone who is not ordained. I have been an academic teacher — and much more besides. At no time in my life have I worked within one single limited area, but have always been engaged in a variety of activities. Whenever I am faced with a new problem, I do not find it unfamiliar, but almost part of my current experience. This is why I feel able to deal with the problems which are brought to me now, because I have experienced either the same thing or something similar.

Braun: But there are many contemporaries of yours who have done perhaps as many different things as you have, but who in their old age begin to feel that there is no sense in life any more; they resign, become tired, find it difficult to see another generation going its own way. But for you this kind of experience has not been associated with growing older?

Heinemann: No, I have not become tired. But giving responsibility into younger hands is a matter which is always open to discussion.

232

Braun: A popular cliché has it that it is the privilege of the young to be rebellious, and the privilege of the old to be inoffensive and conservative. Would you contradict this?

Heinemann: Yes indeed, why should it be a privilege? It may be natural for young people to be more forceful than their elders. But I have said on many occasions to young people: You are the future, but your future is also your own old age. That should not set the generations at odds with one another, but rather bind them together.

Braun: But the approval and respect that you enjoy among the younger generation may none the less be mainly attributable to the fact that you have dealt with the problems of this generation with unprecedented frankness.

Heinemann: Every society has to learn to come to terms with its own young generation. We cannot let ourselves drift apart from one another. If I can in my own way make any useful contribution in this respect then I am all the happier.

Braun: But still, Mr. President, the passing years have left their inevitable mark on you. Is it your intention to take upon yourself a second term of office as Federal President?

Heinemann: When the question of my election arose for the first time, I excluded any such intention from my plans for the future. I said then that no one who votes for me the first time should feel himself in any way obliged to vote for me on a second occasion, simply because my precedessors in this office have both served two terms. I wanted to make it clear that from the outset there was complete freedom of movement on both sides, for those electing me as well as for myself, and that re-election would be a matter for discussion when the time came for the issue to be raised again.

Braun: So you have not yet arrived at any firm decision about your possible candidacy for a second term?

233

Heinemann: No. Both sides will have to consider very carefully whether I should embark on a second period of office at the age of seventy-five.

Braun: You have now arrived at an age, Mr. President, at which the thought of death can no longer be brushed to one side. What is the meaning for you of the Christian belief that, although death cannot be done away with, it can be conquered by the faithful?

Heinemann: There is no disputing the fact that we must all die. Federal Presidents are no exception to this rule. If you like, that is a great act of wisdom on the part of our creator. Naturally, as I get older, I see more and more of my contemporaries passing away. This does make me feel increasingly isolated. But this is something that must be accepted. What happens to us after our death upon this earth we cannot tell, but we can but hope or place our confidence in our faith.

(This interview between Dr. Joachim Braun and Dr. Gustav W. Heinemann took place on 28 June 1972.)

The Third President

Theodor Heuss once said of the office of Federal President that it was a legal fiction which could only be brought to life by the bearer of the office. The three politicians who have held this office up until now in the history of the Federal Republic have filled it in very different ways indeed.

For many Germans, Theodor Heuss represents the ideal embodiment of the Federal President. He was an educated man. He was thoroughly conversant with German history, and as a young man he had hiked throughout the German countryside. He embodied a type of politician rare in Germany, a man who had strong links with literature and the arts; and in both of these areas he had scored noteworthy achievements on his own account. By background and conviction he was a liberal democrat, and a civilian through and through; all forms of sabre-rattling militarism were abhorrent to him. He knew the art of speaking with the voice of a mediator and was capable of acting the dignified representative of the state at home and abroad. But the borderline between private life and the conduct of his high office became blurred, and increasingly so as time went on. He did not regard his restricted power as a limitation, quite the contrary. He enjoyed being removed from the deadly earnest of the political struggle by virtue of his office and became carried away by the spell of his own powerlessness. In addition, he had a friendly sense of humour with an unmistakable Swabian streak which readily overcame the distance between the citizen and the head of state. Heuss was a popular figure without there being any trace of demagogy about him. There is no denying his achievements in the consolidation of a young and uncertain democracy which had come into being under the most difficult circumstances. He made virtually no political impact on his successors.

Heinrich Lübke, on the other hand, found it hard to accommodate himself to the modest opportunities for political influence which the Basic Law allows to the head of state. He had not sought this office, and did not feel himself suited to it. But once President, he sought vigorously to extend his powers. He lacked both the talent and the vanity for stylish representation of the highest office in the land in the manner of his predecessor. His ambitions lay in the direction of becoming a political President. By this he meant exercising a direct influence on the decisions of day-to-day politics. When the authority of the ageing Konrad Adenauer began to decline, he worked to bring about his release from office. When Ludwig Ehrhard's leadership in the office of Chancellor was clearly weakening, he publicly campaigned for the grand coalition whose architect he sought to be. He resisted the appointment of Gerhard Schröder as a Minister and publicly censured the Cabinet. All these are marks of a sincerely-held tenacity, but this is not in the spirit of the constitution. Lübke's efforts to upvalue the Presidency politically effectually so missed their mark. In conflicts with the government he came off worse. The fact that he was elected for a second term in 1964 was nothing to do with recognition for his activities to date, but was rather the result of a discreditable tactical manoeuvre on the part of the Social Democrat opposition who hoped to gain from his re-election a share in the government at long last. The bitter irony of his terms of office lay in the fact that his authority as head of state expired at the moment when his old political goal, the grand coalition, was finally realised. The people valued his simplicity, his sense of duty and his straightforward character. But they were never able to warm to the second President.

Gustav Heinemann succeeded in making the office of Federal President politically effective without taking politics into the private sphere as Heuss did, and without overstepping the bounds by becoming involved in day-to-day politics like Lübke. From the outset he had declined to play the purely decorative role of the substitute monarch. The changes in the style of his conduct in office were the consequences of the political views he held about his office. His disregard for protocol, his efforts to achieve direct contact with his fellow citizens, his tours of the economically depressed areas of the Federal Republic, his visits to the handicapped, foreign workers, and other minority groups in society — all these things were directed at changing our awareness of the state which Heinemann represented, and making it more democratic.

Heinemann conscientiously observes the party political neutrality which his office prescribes to him. But he does not consider that this requires him to abstain from politics. There are more than enough political issues which are centred on a higher plane than that of day-to-day political conflict. Without infringing the rights of government or opposition, the Federal President is fully capable of taking a stand on issues such as the German past, the development of a social democracy, the greater involvement of the citizen in the political decision-making process, or the re-evaluation of the tasks confronting the community. It is in these areas that the possibility for political effectiveness lies which Heinemann is seeking to attain as President.

But he is no brilliant speaker. At times the opening words of his speeches leave a great deal to be desired: "I should first like to express my respect and gratitude to the metalworkers' union for having made this international congress possible." Nor are the closing words of his speeches exactly designed to evoke a storm of applause: "I hope you will have fruitful discussions here." He is not concerned with stylistic refinements, dramatic rhetoric and the like. He does not indulge in dazzling his audience with bold metaphors, relishing to the full a carefully placed pause, or flirting with heroic gestures. And he has no card-index of western culture divided up into convenient lengths for quotation purposes with which to arouse respectful admiration in his audience. His choice of words and his manner of address remind one more of the former chairman of a synod than a popular figure seeking to arouse the enthusiasm of the nation.

Heinemann does not try to stimulate enthusiasm but to convince with arguments. What gives his speeches their quality is their moral seriousness, their intellectual rigour, and Heinemann's ability to put across even complex issues in a few straighforward sentences. He is not interested in being original: he did not invent the notion of the "quality of life", nor that of peace studies, his historical insights are to be found in the scholarly literature, and even the task of bringing greater reality to the idea of a social state is not his idea. Heinemann's achievement lies in the fact that he has explained to the public at large matters which had previously remained within the province of the expert, that he has familiarised the citizen with issues which would otherwise have remained outside their experience, and that he makes them face up to awkward questions.

By not keeping silent on the important tasks of the political community, Heinemann is running the risk of being exposed to attack. Whether the state should be more or less prominent, whether there should be more rights for the individual or greater sacrifices for the sake of common goals, whether the scientist should be pursuing knowledge for its own sake or facing up to his social responsibilities — none of these issues is neutral, each is hotly disputed among the population, and even though they may not include among the live party political issues of the day. A head of state who takes a stand on these issues exposes himself to the risk of criticism.

But those who provoke must expect to be challenged in return. A Federal President who seeks to exercise some influence on the life of the state cannot simply react to other views, more concerned to avoid treading on anyone's feet than exercising real public influence. Naturally the Federal President should not heedlessly offend broad sections of the population — and that is something Heinemann does not do. But neither does he restrict himself to what is already accepted by the majority of the people. He regards it more fitting to his office to say what needs to be said and to campaign for support for it, rather than to rehearse truisms. Heinemann regards his office as one which should influence standards of judgement through argument, and this is what he does. His integrity, his credibility and his intellectual approach have bestowed upon Heinemann a kind of authority which none of the paragraphs of the Basic Law can offer him.

238

Heinemann has achieved this against all the rules of popularity. Whether or not he is popular with the public is uncertain; he himself does not worry a great deal about it. But he is certain of their respect and support. A sample poll early in 1972 produced the result that 84 % of the West German adult population approved of his conduct in office. Only 19 % took the view that any other politician would be better suited to the office of President.

When he took office, Rolf Zundel wrote in Die Zeit that not only would the new President have to prove himself in his office, the political community of the Federal Republic would have to prove itself to the President. This statement, particularly its second part, could be taken as a kind of Brechtian arrogance: if the people do not suit the President then he must dissolve them and elect new ones.

This was not the idea behind Zundel's observation. He was referring to the exceptionally favourable judgements which had been expressed abroad on Heinemann's election. He was asking if political developments would justify what the Bonn correspondent of the Dutch radio wrote about Heinemann's election that it "heralded in a new period in the history of West Germany, a period of political maturity for democracy." There are many signs that this is indeed the case. A republic which, in free elections, votes into the two highest offices in the land the former outsider Heinemann and the one time emigré Willy Brandt, has clearly emerged from its infancy. Brandt's policy of coexistence with eastern Europe, which a few years before would have been shouted down as defeatism, met with a greater measure of approval among the public at large than in parliament. The anti-parliamentarian and anti-democratic forces which had grown to dangerous proportions towards the end of the sixties, disappeared from the political arena on both left and right. The integrating power of the democratic parties won through. The CDU absorbed the lost members of the NPD and thereby rendered it harmless, and the SPD was equally able to assimilate the critical forward thrust of the student opposition. The crisis of the Social Democrat and liberal coalition of summer 1972 was not regarded as a state crises, as would have been the case in previous years. The Federal Republic has taken a great step forward in the direction of normalisation.

But there still remains good cause for scepticism. The call for a strong state, which was to be heard loud and clear during the search for the Baader-Meinhof group; the continuing desire for stability which is more concerned with calm and order than with an open resolution of political conflict; the embittered relationships with political opponents which all too often burdens political conflict; problems about democratic morality which have arisen among many politicians and organs of the press; the unresolved questions of social minorities — all these things indicate that democracy in the Federal Republic may still be in its infancy. No one can yet say whether the new democracy in Germany is so firmly rooted that it would be able to withstand the severe shock of a serious economic crisis.

Seen from this point of view, only half of what Rolf Zundel said after Heinemann's election has been achieved: Gustav Heinemann has proved himself in his office as Federal President; but the Federal Republic itself has yet to pass the test.

Speaking in the Olympic stadium in Munich during the memorial ceremony for the victims of the Arab terrorist attack

State visit in Bonn: meeting the Indonesian President General Suharto at Wahn airport

◁ State visit in Bonn: reception for King Baudouin and Queen Fabiola

In conversation with soldiers of the Federal army

Selected Speeches by Gustav Heinemann

Not less, but more Democracy . . .

(Address given to the Federal German parliament on 1 July 1969 the occasion of Heinemann's taking office.)

With the oath I have sworn here today I now assume the responsibilities of the office to which the Federal assembly elected me on 5 March.

First of all I should like to extend my gratitude to you, sir, as President of this assembly, for your welcome and for the good wishes you have expressed on behalf of this assembly for my assumption of office, and I should also like to thank you, Dr. Lübke, for the most friendly and helpful manner in which you have transferred the reins of office into my hands. I should like to repeat the words I used in Berlin: I thank all of those who voted me into office for the confidence that they have shown in me. I respect the fact that others have cast their votes elsewhere. I hope — as I said on 5 March — that it will also be possible to collaborate fruitfully with them in dealing with the common problems that confront us all.

As Federal President I have no governmental statements of intent to make. I have left the government and the Federal German parliament; I have surrendered all my positions in the Social Democrat party. In accordance with the will of the Basic Law, I now stand on the sidelines watching those who have to carry out and bear responsibility for the political decisions that have to be taken. But I feel it is not inappropriate for the Federal President to say a few personal words at this moment.

I enter office at a time in which the world finds itself confronted with the most extreme contrasts. Man is about to land upon the moon, but he is far from solving the problems of war, hunger and injustice upon his own planet. Man seeks a greater voice in his own affairs, and yet there are so many questions which he is still incapable of answering. Uncertainty and fatalism mingle with a hope for advances in the future. Will such hope ever be fulfilled? That is a question that faces us all, especially those of us here today who, by virtue of the mandate they hold, are responsible to their fellow citizens. I see our first obligation as one of serving peace. It is not war which should be regarded as the hour of crisis in which man has to stand the test, as my generation in the days of the Kaiser learned on their school benches, it is peace that is the time of crisis in which all of us have to stand the test. There is no alternative to peace any more.

Twenty-four years after the Second World War we are still having to face the same problem of coming to terms with our neighbours to the east. All-party talks on a secure peace in Europe are well overdue and must inevitably take place. I know that the German people, the Federal parliament and the Federal government all unite with me in a common desire for peace. I call upon the leaders of the power blocs and the individual powers to put their faith for security, not in the arms race, but in coming together for the purpose of mutual disarmament and arms limitation. Disarmament demands trust. Trust cannot be forced into being. Only someone prepared to trust others can be expected to be trusted himself. It is one of our noblest tasks as politicians to create a climate of trust. All our powers, both civil and military, should be subordinated to this task.

The Federal armed forces are not an end in themselves. We know that they are in no position to impose any political solutions. It is their task to prevent aggression upon us from outside. This is why we are maintaining our defensive effort. So we should respect all those who devote themselves to this task.

I wish to do all in my power to assist the efforts of those working towards an international peace system which includes our nation as a whole. On the long road towards this objective, it is appropriate that the ties between the people who make up our nation should be strengthened and improved. It would be of extreme value if we could give a proper measure of attention to peace studies, that is, to scholarly investigation not only of the military connexions between armament, disarmament and the securing of peace, but also of all the many other factors involved, for example, the social, economic and psychological aspects of the problem.

In this context, we are no longer faced with just an east-west conflict, but to an increasing extent with a conflict between north and south. Hunger and suffering in the world cry out for our help. The industrialised nations, whatever their politics, must not shy away from this challenge. I owe a particular debt to Dr. Lübke, my predecessor in this office, for having repeatedly drawn our attention to this obligation of ours.

Our nation can point to many things in its history which can make us feel proud and happy. Our contribution to the enrichment of humanity has not been meagre. But the name of our nation was also taken in vain and associated with the unleashing of the catastrophe of World War Two. Only when we really face the question

246

of how the terrible Nazi chapter in our history came about will other nations no longer be able to reproach us for this period in our past. It is a time which must never be allowed to return, for the sake of the millions of Jews, and the further millions of war dead throughout the world, and not least for the sake of those of our own nation who fell victim to the Nazi terror, the war and ultimately suffered expulsion from hearth and home. When the war finally came to an end in 1945, when, as Theodor Heuss said at the time, the paradox of our simultaneous liberation and destruction took place, the past was about to be transformed into the impetus for the dawn of a new age. But after all the material reconstruction and despite the constant procession of new generations, we must still continue to explore our past for the sake of our future.

We find ourselves in the early years of the first period of genuine liberty that Germany has ever enjoyed. Free democracy must in the long term become a cornerstone of our society, for only then shall we be able to come face to face with the paradox of our age which, as I see it, lies in the fact that the area of influence of the individual is becoming ever smaller, whilst at the same time individual self-determination is gaining ground.

What I mean is that mankind is conquering the world and the universe beyond at an unprecedented rate. But the individual is becoming less and less powerful. The economy continues to make great strides. Bureaucracies — which are big enough already — continue to mushroom. My question is: what is going to happen to the freedom of the individual? His role in the business of production and consumption becomes ever more insignificant, impersonal and controlled by others. But is it not true at the same time that after centuries of exclusion a new floodtide of self-determination has burst among mankind? The way had been paved for this breakthrough in various areas since the waning of the Middle Ages. But it is only now that it is reaching such breadth and intensity. Everywhere authority and tradition are being compelled to justify their existence. Neither the Christian churches with their doctrines and their hierarchies, nor the state with its constitutional agencies such as parliaments, nor yet customs and morality as such or in relation to penal or family law or to the structure of society — especially in the areas of marriage and family, property and work — none of these things are exempted from a searching critical examination.

In the main it must be said that our age is filled with a desire to be free from the old ties and to become actively involved in the affairs of the community. It is a matter of dialogue, of events and of decisions being made clear to all. My question is: are we ready to face the consequences? My view is that we are in a position to see our way through this great transformation from dictatorship to self-determination and individual responsibility with no attendant danger that our communal life might go off the rails. An additional factor, of course, is that the individual does not simply regard himself to be at the mercy of outside controls in his work and in his activities as a consumer; as a citizen he demands a real voice in the democratic process. In the mass societies of the industrialized nations, however, the only real possibility is representative democracy.

This is why our Federal Republic was deliberately instituted as a representative democracy. I consider its structure, reposing as it does on human dignity and human rights, to be the basis and framework for the best social order in our history. But the fabric is not yet complete. All the necessary features are there: a free democracy, social justice and a constitutional state — but these things demand ceaseless effort by the free citizen towards maintaining constant improvement.

I am aware of the fact that not everybody is happy to hear such words. Some still yearn for an autocratic state. We have long been burdened with it, and it ultimately dragged us into the whirlpool of the Third Reich. Others regard our present society as a particularly subtle form of deviation and suppression which must be countered in the sternest possible terms. They behave as if it were possible to realise the kingdom of Heaven here upon earth or to regain paradise lost. In this world, the nearest we shall get to the ideal is the relative Utopia of a better world, which is the sole sensible model for all our actions and aspirations.

The secret even of great revolutionary actions lies in seeking out the one small step, the strategic step, the step which causes further steps to be taken in the direction of a better world. That is why there is little point in pouring scorn on the imperfections of the present or in preaching the absolute as the order of the day. Let us rather change our circumstances step by step through constructive criticism and co-operation. I fully understand the anger about all the inertia to be found in human society at large, and even in the churches. All my life I have been an impatient man. I still am. Perhaps this is why I tend not to appear at engagements at the right time, and frequently turn up too early. In my own impatience I can recognise and understand even the impatience of the radical young. But I must counsel them to direct their endeavours towards joining the long march to reform which has long since been started and which the marchers are firmly resolved to continue.

Some groups of young people have chosen to conduct their revolutionary campaign by seeking to prejudice the viability of the Federal army by refusing to undertake military service. Everyone is familiar with the fact that I have consistently supported a fair practical implementation of the Basic Law on the refusal to undertake military service on either religious or ethical grounds of conscience. This I have continued to do right up to my time as Federal Minister of Justice, both here in the Federal parliament as well as within the context of the church. So I find it all the more deplorable when this right is abused. It is these very opposition groups who enjoy the protection of our basic freedoms who should be more than usually wary of making light of these freedoms.

In our society very many different groups are pursuing any number of divergent goals and ideologies, and each of these groups wishes to attract the support of all citizens. This multiplicity can be burdensome. But at the same time the underlying philosophy of our constitution would not countenance their suppression. They enrich our human existence. Our free system of a philosophically neutral state represents a supreme offer to us. It regulates the decision-making process in relation to matters of concern to the community at large through the medium of majority decisions. Working together within a democratic framework demands a willingness to compromise. But our system does not permit issues of goodness, beauty, truth and belief to be negotiable or subject to compromise. The poet Emerson says that every man has the choice between truth and sleep; we must choose wisely, because we cannot have both.

On the occasion of my election large numbers of letters have come to me from people from all occupations and at all levels of society in which high expectations — far too high expectations — are placed on my assumption of office. I take these expectations seriously. In so far as they relate to personal matters, they represent calls for help in the manifold difficulties of everyday life, from those in need and sickness, those with housing problems, those in trouble with the law, those who suffer loneliness or injustice. Such needs are evidently far greater than our prosperous society is generally prepared to concede. But many of the letters also express a fear for the future, about job security, a fear of old age.

Much has been achieved in the last twenty-four years; but one day's achievements count for little even on the day after. But these achievements are not enough nor will they be in the future, if they do not encourage us to outstrip them. Social change marches onwards. Thus it is incumbent upon all of us to make ever-increasing efforts to bring reality to the injunction of our constitution that we should develop social democracy. We shall have to recognise that the freedom of the individual must be protected, not only against the power of the state, but equally against economic and social pressures. The influence of organised bodies and their lobbyists is often enough in conflict with our social system, in which

249

justice claims to do away with privilege, although privilege does none the less continue to exist as a social reality. In our society, based upon achievement, advancement and education, we must realise the vision of freedom for all by giving each and every individual his own concrete personal opportunity.

Not less, but more democracy — that is the demand, that is the great objective which we, and above all the young, must dedicate ourselves towards achieving. There are some difficult homelands. Germany is one of them. But it is our homeland. This is where we live and work. Thus we wish to make our contribution towards mankind as a whole by and through this land of ours.

In this spirit I greet all the citizens of Germany from this rostrum.

The Third Reich was no Accident

(Extracts from a speech given on the occasion of the twenty-fifth anniversary of the revolt of 20 July 1944, given in Berlin-Plötzensee, 20 July 1969.)

... 20 July 1944 was a significant day for all Germans and must remain so, if the word nation is to retain its meaning for us despite the division of Germany. In this one date the worst and the best traditions of our history confront one another with full force. We are constantly drawn to seek to unravel the drama of their involvement. How was it possible — we must ask ourselves this question once more today — that people from our nation could become so consumed with arrogance, racialism and a lust for conquest in the so-called Third Reich? How was it possible that the freedom of the citizen, the dignity of man and the right of self-determination could be so barbarically spurned? We cannot fight shy of this question if we truly seek to come to terms with ourselves. To find an answer to this question we must reach far back into the broad history of Europe as well as the history of Germany itself.

It is a task facing many other nations. We are not the only ones who have experienced nationalism or are experiencing it now. The persecution of the Jews can be traced right back to Christian anti-Semitism, which the second Vatican Council denounced once and for all. As far as we Germans are concerned, there is no denying the fact that our people have right up until the present time been brought up to conduct themselves with obedient submissiveness in the face of all authority, and this can even go so far as submission to a criminal authority. Nor

250

can we seek to conceal the fact that even before the appearance of Hitler we were particularly susceptible to a violent form of nationalism, as the rejoicing at the outbreak of the First World War demonstrates.

... The purpose of these scattered observations is to suggest that the Third Reich was, in my considered view, not an accident, that is to say, that it was not entirely attributable to the unemployment around the year 1930 nor to the reparation burdens imposed by the 1919 Versailles Treaty. The events leading up to and immediately following upon 20 July 1944 represent a culmination of central trends in our history. They paved the way for the wretchedness that caused the men and women of 20 July 1944 to act. They indicated the unutterable vileness with which these people and many of their associates who were not directly involved were done to death.

But 20 July 1944 also stands for our participation in the best western traditions and in the great European manifestations of the struggle for the rights of man and for human dignity. True, we cannot trace a line back to a thirteenth-century Magna Carta like the English, nor to proclamations of human and civil rights, such as those produced by the American declaration of independence or the French revolution. The peasants' wars at the time of Luther and St. Paul's church in 1848-1849 represented movements in that direction. But they were defeated. We must confess that we did not succeed in bringing a free democracy to Germany by dint of our own unaided efforts. On two occasions foreign victors have brought democracy to us after lost wars. After a short existence, the Weimar Republic foundered. Shall we be able now to preserve a free democracy, to develop it further in the direction of social justice and make it an integral part of ourselves? That is one of the questions posed to us by 20 July 1944. The resistance fighters during the Nazi period were admittedly motivated by a whole range of different political and social aspirations. But they were united in their resolve to bring an end to subservience and war. The failure of their action in practical terms can in no way diminish the noble example they set. They were all fully aware of the gravity of what they were undertaking, and yet they still dared to act. All of them had to overcome doubts and uncertainties as to whether it was right and proper to raise a hand against the very man whom so many of the people adulated.

... But in this context, many of those in whose honour we are gathered here today must have had to come to terms with a much more weighty issue of conscience. Many of them had sworn before God an inviolable oath of personal obedience to the very man whom they were now seeking to attack and kill. The oath of loyalty sworn by soldiers to Hitler ran as follows:

251

> I swear before God this solemn oath, that I shall offer unconditional obedience to the Führer of the German Reich and nation, Adolf Hitler, and shall at any time be prepared as a courageous soldier to stake my life upon this oath.

Thank God, we no longer have such an oath of personal loyalty. The present-day oath of loyalty sworn by soldiers relates strictly to their duties. It takes this form:

> I swear to serve the Federal Republic of Germany loyally and bravely to defend the justice and freedom of the German people, so help me God.

In the same kind of way the members of the Federal government also swear an oath, like the one I gave on 1 July:

> I swear that I shall dedicate my efforts to the well-being of the German people, to work towards their benefit, to turn away harm from them, to preserve and defend the Basic Law and the laws of the Federal Republic, shall conscientiously perform my duties and deal justly with all my fellow men, so help me God.

When I had sworn this oath, a friend of mine said to me, "Don't forget that this oath will confront you again on judgement day word for word." word for word. word for word. He is quite right. The only question is whether any kind of oath is admissible in our philosophically neutral state.

It is all too easy to say today that the oath imposed by Hitler was a violation of public authority. And there can be no doubt that the unconditional vow of obedience demanded by Hitler was self-contradictory. The obligation to God sworn by the individual essentially releases him from the obligation to Hitler the man. Ultimately the oath of loyalty foundered on the absence of that reciprocity of obligations so essential to such an undertaking. But at the time it was all interpreted quite differently, and the oath had to be honoured word for word as it had been delivered. The soldiers who were involved in 20 July 1944 had first to reason this out within themselves and towards society so convincingly as to achieve the clear conscience necessary for the attack on Hitler. "We have examined ourselves before God and before our own consciences; it had to happen." Those were Graf Stauffenberg's own final words.

... I turn now to make a few observations on the question as to what aspects of those resistance fighters we should hold in our memory. The first is a most earnest warning against a renewal of nationalism. The men and women of 20 July 1944 truly loved our homeland. They acted out of this love. The violent nationalism

252

which had been cultivated in our nation since the Franco-German war of 1870 in our people has burned itself out in the course of two world wars. It has wrought enough harm to ourselves and the world at large. Such a disaster must never happen again. We must be extremely vigilant in suppressing each and every new movement in that direction. Here in Berlin especially it must never be forgotten that our present distress caused by the division of our country is the direct result of national arrogance. A good German cannot be a nationalist. Nowadays, a German with a sense of nationalism can only be a European.

War is in any event no longer a possibility, because there is no longer any viable alternative to peace. Thus conciliation is our national obligation, as it was also in the eyes of the resistance fighters. They all acted and died for a better world, for justice and human rights. The Hamburg workers' leader Fiete Schulze, in whose honour the GDR have named one of their ships, wrote before his execution in June 1935 in a farewell letter to his sister:

> You quarrel with the circumstances that take your brother away from you. Why will you not understand that I am dying so that many others will not have to die an untimely and violent death? Those days are not yet with us, but my life and my death will make some contribution in that direction.

Such a heritage obliges us to face up to the never-ending obligations of a democratic constitutional state. The resistance fighters, who were simply done to death with only a semblance of justice, make us ask ourselves the question as to whether we can remain immune against anti-democratic movements of the spirit, whether we are maintaining a climate of calm reason in politics, whether we are allowing justice and human rights to prevail in every individual case.

I close on a personal note. I cannot shake myself free of the question as to why I did not offer more resistance during the time of the Third Reich. It was this question that made me personally, as a former member of the council of the Evangelical church of Germany, associate myself with the Stuttgart declaration of October 1945, which includes the following:

> What we have often borne witness to in our parishes we now speak out in the name of the whole church: it is true that we have for long years fought in the name of Jesus Christ against the spirit which has found its terrible expression in the violent régime of the National Socialists; but we accuse ourselves of not having confessed our faith more courageously, prayed more loyally, believed more happily and loved more passionately.

When I swore the oath on 1 July I said that our free democratic system of a philosophically neutral state was a supreme offer to us. One of the legacies of the German resistance is the recognition and realisation of this offer.

Making a new Start

(Radio and television speech given on the thirtieth anniversary of the outbreak of war, 1 September 1969.)

Thirty years ago today, on 1 September 1939, the curtain was raised on that terrible drama which we call the Second World War. After a week-long conflict with Poland over Danzig and the Corridor, Hitler announced on that day in Berlin before the Reichstag to the delegates who were cheering and beside themselves with enthusiasm the beginning of "the struggle for the justice and security of the Reich." From a quarter to six hostilities were under way.

But despite — or perhaps even because of — the pact on mutual spheres of interest signed between Hitler and Stalin a few days before, it was all too clear that our nation was being dragged into a wild adventure. It is hardly necessary now to analyse in detail the origins of the Second World War. They are clear for all to see.

Since the twenties Hitler had given speeches, written, agitated and incited — stating that it was his declared intention to resolve the Jewish question and to extend German rule over his Slav neighbours and beyond to Russia. Danzig and the Corridor were only the preliminary bouts on the programme of Greater Germany extending German mastery over the so-called Slav thugs. Nor do I have to talk about the outcome of the war. But we must not allow ourselves to forget that over 55 million people throughout the world lost their lives in the Second World War. Even more lost their homeland as refugees or expellees. In the territories beyond the Oder and the Neisse and in the rest of Eastern Europe alone 17 million Germans met with this fate. Even today there still seems to be no end to the after-effects of the National Socialist adventure. How long shall we remain a nation divided along the line which separates the big powers in the east and west? How long will Berlin remain a torn city?

When will Europe emerge in a peaceful system with an independent role to play in the world? Even now, thirty years after the outbreak of the Second World War, these and other questions remain unanswered. But one thing is clear enough. None

254

of these questions will be answered if we do not make our peace with all our neighbours and establish a new relationship of trust.

What we, to our great satisfaction, have achieved with our former "arch-enemy" France remains as an uncompleted task with regard to our eastern neighbours and especially Poland. Poland was the first victim of the onslaught of 1939. Her contribution alone to the death total in the war amounts to some six million, of whom 700,000 died as soldiers, the remaining five million and more were the victims of arbitrary extermination. Whatever the Polish government may have done in 1939 to give Hitler arguments to support his actions, and however hard the lot of our fellow countrymen was who in 1945 had to suffer the loss of their homes to the east of the Oder and Neisse, nothing must divert our attention from the fact that things cannot remain as they are between Poland and ourselves. Here too the old war memories must be buried so deeply that no one will be able to disinter them ever again. The right conditions for this must be established.

Since 1945, that is, since the end of the Second World War, many new wars have taken place throughout the world. Some of them are currently flooding the world with news reports and pictures of the sufferings they are causing. When the bloodshed of these wars comes to an end in armistice, they will be found to have resolved few, if any, of the problems which caused their outbreak. Is the time not long overdue when the world at large, and ourselves in particular, directed our resources to the academic study of peace, that is, of the preconditions necessary for peace, inclusive of the social and economic structure as well as the psychological factors, as the basis for all fundamental research? Up until the present time, the greatest achievements of the human spirit have been in the investigation and conquest of nature. These achievements are the basis for the ever-growing population of the world. The actual danger for humanity no longer lies in nature, but within man himself. But man knows less of himself and his abilities to threaten life than he does about his natural environment. The causes of conflict among the nations and the human aggressive drives have been less researched than the laws of atomic structure.

Although war can be the result of the attitudes of individuals, it is evidently most frequently rooted in the social structures and hierarchies of given communities. Its causes are, despite any war profiteers who may be around, not private, but political in nature. They derive from social customs, prejudices, social structures and systems of authority. This is why research into these factors is so necessary. We need peace research. And we need new structures and new habits, new rules and new patterns of conduct. One of these new structures is the United Nations,

255

which, in view of the collapse of the League of Nations, needs to be strengthened. It would be worth acquiring the new habit of judging a conflict situation with the eyes of one's opponent as well. One of the new rules must be a willingness to compromise, to surrender the notion of getting one's own way whatever the cost in favour of a resolve to replace a state of enmity handed down from one generation to the next with a willingness on the part of both sides to make a fresh start. One of the new patterns of conduct ought to include trying to come to an understanding of the fears and sufferings, the pride and sensibilities of the other side.

War is not one of nature's laws, but the result of human action. This is why we must investigate these actions. Peace is not a law of nature, either — we have experienced that all too clearly. Is it an illusion? What do we seek and what are we doing, what is the goal of human existence, and how does man so order his life that he can prevent war with its deaths and killings from coming round once again? There is no absolute answer to this question.

But there is an answer which everyone can give, and that is to strengthen those forces which are pursuing a credible policy of peace and to turn away from those who are already assuming the mantle of nationalism and preaching the spirit of intransigence. Camus once said:

> Perhaps we cannot do anything to prevent the fact that this creation is a world in which children are martyred. But we can at least reduce the number of martyred children.

That holds good for war too. Let us, therefore, on this the thirtieth anniversary of the day on which the Second World War broke out, reflect on these two things: first, we must make a new beginning with our eastern neighbours and particularly with Poland; and, secondly, we must resolutely set our face against the scourge of new wars.

No one among us is the State

(Speech on the occasion of the presentation of the Brandt-Scheel cabinet, 22 October 1969.)

When a new government takes office, it can either be of great significance or amount to very little at all. A new government can simply be continuing the work of its predecessor in office. But it can proclaim a change of power and political will. And all the signs in this case point to the latter.

Looked at from outside, we are now witnessing the replacement of a grand coalition with a small opposition by a small coalition with a big opposition. Under the grand coalition there were ten members of government parties to every one opposition party member. From now on, there will be at least nine opposition party members confronting every ten government party members. That is the external appearance of the situation. But of far greater importance is the fact that, for the first time in the Federal Republic and after an interruption of nearly forty years since the Weimar Republic, the other great party of our country, the Social Democrat Party of Germany, holds the reins of government, and this means that the alternation between government and opposition so essential to the preservation of our democracy has been initiated.

I will go no further than to raise this one fact. I am sure that you are well aware of the magnitude of the task which you have undertaken. This will confront you from your first working day in office, in particular when you are considering the form of your government declaration of policy.

It goes without saying that every citizen wishes you success in the tasks before you. For you, Mr. Prime Minister, and the members of your government stand for us all during the period of your office. For this reason everyone should follow the path and the actions you take. Following should mean encouragement and also criticism. There will be no lack of opposition from those who simply want you out of office. But opposition too must take place within the context of our Basic Law, that is, within the system of a free, socially aware and democratic constitutional state. You, who are now taking over government, are the very ones who in the past have set the example for opposition within the framework of the Basic Law of our Federal Republic.

No one among us is the state. And you too have been entrusted only with limited power for a certain span of time. Make good use of this time! . . .

A common European Future

(State visit to the Netherlands: extracts from a speech at a state dinner given by the Queen in honour of the Federal President and Frau Heinemann, Amsterdam, 25 November 1969.)

. . . My visit to your country, which I have already seen on various occasions as a private individual, is not the fulfilment of some obligation of protocol. Its purpose is to make a public declaration of the fact that we in Germany remain aware of the sufferings we have brought upon the Dutch people in the past. It is the acceptance of a hand of friendship which seeks to overcome once and for all the residue of restraint that still remains between us despite all the new initiatives already undertaken in many different areas by our two peoples. My gratitude for this opportunity is all the greater since the only practical path into the future is one of common effort. We gratefully recognise the fact that, despite the grave experiences of the war and the occupation, the Netherlands have gained confidence in the Federal Republic and have resolved to work together with us in building a common European future.

If we have succeeded since 1945 in creating once more a democratic and constitutional community in one part at least of our country, this has come about, apart from our own efforts, in large measure as a result of the support of other democratic nations like the Netherlands. This moral, spiritual and — in the early years — financial support has given us much of the strength we needed to construct a viable state and bind it indissolubly to the free world.

Hardly any other country, your Majesty, can lay a stronger claim than yours to being a sanctuary for the concept of freedom and the democratic tradition. You can point with justifiable pride to the fact that your country has kept faith with these noble values throughout the changing course of a long history. And this makes it a model for us all. We were not resourceful enough to avert the Hitler régime nor to defeat it from within. This is why many people in Germany as well as elsewhere regarded its collapse as a moment of liberation. Since then a new generation has emerged. Over half of the people alive now in Germany were born too late to experience or remember what happened in the Nazi period.

May it prove possible for both our peoples to continue to live according to the principles of peace in an era of peace which we confidently hope will never again be broken. There would be no finer justification for our common efforts now than if future generations were able to say that peace and democracy had become as secure a tradition in the whole of Europe as it is now in your country. In this sense, my visit can serve as a symbol for the esteem and high regard in which the Germans hold the Netherlands. And it can equally serve to express pleasure at the fact that we have similar views, interests and also problems in the great political questions which affect Europe both directly and indirectly. We are most deeply indebted to the government of the Netherlands for the continuing and particular understanding they have shown for the tragic division of our country and for their wholehearted support for the right of self-determination of our nation . . .

Historical Awareness and Tradition in Germany

(Extracts from a speech at a dinner in Bremen City Hall, 13 February 1970.)

... I know that some conservative elements have long since come to suspect me of being an iconoclast, because I have criticised or just called into question many things which have remained unchallenged in the past. But I cannot take it very seriously when, for example, my aversion against red carpets or against the complete domination of the New Year's receptions at the Federal President's residence by politicians and senior officials is taken to be evidence of my opposition to tradition as such. I am well aware that our spiritual, social, cultural and political present is founded upon tradition. Even what we call radical changes, revolutions or reforms not infrequently base themselves upon a re-evaluation or extension of what had been recognised or demanded in previous times.

In other words, traditions are by no means the privilege of conservative forces. Even less can they be said to be the inherited province of reactionaries, although these are the people who hold forth about them most volubly. And it is not impossible to interpret specific events in quite different ways and to enlist them in the service of diametrically opposed concepts of tradition, an exercise which it can be fascinating to observe. In my view, the central question is not whether we are for or against tradition. The alternative is rather one of which traditions are to be taken up and the way in which we regard the historical process.

... The view of tradition which appears most reasonable to me is the one which the Frenchman Jean Jaurès, murdered for his opposition to the war in 1914, expressed once in these terms: "Not to preserve the ashes, but to keep the flame burning."

But what flame? And in what spirit? That should be our constant theme whenever we discuss tradition. It is my belief that we possess an undiscovered treasure of predecessors who merit being brought out into the open and fixed far more firmly in the minds of our nation than has been the case up to now.

For years in the course of visits to the towns and districts of our country, I have made it my practice to investigate on the basis of chronicles and church records the kinds of peace movements or even local uprisings that have taken place in the various parts of our native land. It is an astonishingly meagre crop that one can gather from the copious volumes of city records and the like. My interest was not only aimed at the predecessors and local ramifications of the revolution of 1848—1849, for example, the Hambach Rally of 1832 or the fighting at the barricades in Elberfeld or around Rastatt in the 1848 Baden uprising, in which men from the generation of my great-great-grandfather on my mother's side were involved — this might be claimed to explain my interest.

Fortunately there have been a not inconsiderable number of individual men and women in Germany concerned about freedom and social issues, as well as whole groups and classes of people who were not content to let the entire political voice rest with their rulers. I am thinking, for example, of the Steding peasants, who were finally defeated in 1234 by the Archbishop of Bremen. Or the so-called "salt-petremen," who fought for their freedom as peasants in the first half of the eighteenth century in the Hotzenwald at Säckingen and Waldshut in the southern part of the Black Forest, principally against the abbot prince of St. Blasien, until their leaders were banished to Hungary by the Austrian Emperor. One of the duties which the Emperor sought to compel them to perform was carting away stable manure in order to manufacture from it saltpetre for gun-cotton for his wars. It seems to me characteristic of our lack of historical awareness that even the inhabitants of the southern Black Forest area know virtually nothing about the saltpetre campaigners, although their battles were fought almost outside their own front doors, and in many instances their own ancestors were actually involved. Events like that ought to mean far more to them than those wars waged by Emperors and Kings for the extension of their power.

I think that even today it ill becomes a democratic state to regard the rebellious peasants of the past as nothing more than gangs of rabble who were swiftly brought to heel. That is how the victorious side recorded what happened. It is high time that a free and democratic Germany rewrote our history right down to the schoolbooks.

... Sometimes we find it amusing, sometimes painful, when we see how all the freedom movements in our country have been recruited willy-nilly into the ranks of the forces in power. Historical materialism, applied in such a simplified form to German history, distorts more than it reveals the truth. But nothing can prevent us from tracking down and doing full justice to those in the history of our people who lived and fought to bring political suffrage to the German nation so that they could control and administer their own affairs ...

260

Nothing is wasted

(Extracts from a speech given at a ceremony during Brotherhood Week, Cologne, 8 March 1970.)

... Are we being Utopian, are we refusing to face the facts of the world by celebrating Brotherhood Week once again? I should say that such criticism might be justified if this celebration reposed on the notion that well-meaning encouragement and insistent moral appeals were enough to persuade all mankind to feel for their fellow mortals. That is not what this Brotherhood Week is all about. It is not preaching an idyllic state of harmony and has certainly nothing in common with that good-intentioned phrase which it costs so little to say: "Be nice to one another."

If we trace the word brotherhood back to its original meaning, it will be found to signify an injunction to us all to treat one another as brothers because we have in God the creator a father common to each and every one of us. Friends can be selected on the basis of personal preference, but it is open to no one to choose his own brother. We are born into brotherhood as we are into the rest of our family circumstances; and there is no escaping the fact. But do not be tempted to argue that faith in God the creator has ceased to be a force among us today. On the contrary, understanding of our fellow men, which results from this attitude of faith, has shown itself to bear such strong conviction that the demand for brotherhood has all but become an integral part of the general currency of humanitarian and political movements.

... But has brotherhood really come to be taken for granted in the free societies of the present day? Since the French revolution freedom and equality have been able to make much greater strides foward than the sentiment of brotherhood. This is all to do with the fact that the two former rights can be secured by constitution and law and, if the need arises, they can be enforced. But a brotherly frame of mind can neither be imposed nor enforced. After the experiences which we have been through, we are forced to doubt whether it is possible in practice to establish systems of society and standards of justice which would make brotherhood into a generally accepted yardstick for human conduct.

... But in talking about the future, let us not forget about the present. We must not shrink back from speaking out frankly and openly wherever a lack of brotherhood threatens to poison the life of the community. In a free constitutional state, crimes and atrocities, such as take place under a régime of a National Socialist stamp with the support and at the command of its rulers, are impossible. But the guarantee of basic rights given by the constitution and liberal laws cannot prevent social groups and minorities in particular from becoming pariahs in private and public opinion even in a free society.

How, for example, do we speak of foreign workers? Are we prepared to regard them as equal social and human partners who are contributing to our prosperity through their work? How do we regard children born out of wedlock, and what is our estimation of the mothers who gave them birth? Who is prepared to set an example and actually do something about rehabilitating released criminals in society? How deep-rooted are prejudices against men whose skin is a different colour, who have a different faith, or different political convictions?

These are the things we should call into mind when we are asked what the meaning of Brotherhood Week is. It has nothing to do with declarations of principle. It confronts us with questions about our personal behaviour. We should be asked to make an account of what we are doing to break down prejudice and unmask jealousies. Do we let ourselves be comfortably borne along on the tide of public and private opinion, or do we have the courage to speak out wherever spiritual lethargy and arrogance are to be found in our community?

Nothing is neutral. Nothing is wasted. Everything we do or neglect to do can have immeasurable consequences. Evasion can never succeed in the long term. Everything returns sooner or later. The question: "Am I my brother's keeper?" is one of man's oldest utterances, handed down to us by the Old Testament in the account of Cain's fratricide of Abel. What is our answer to this question?

Our Constitution demands Freedom of the Press

(Extracts from a speech given on the twentieth anniversary of the German journalists' association, Frankfurt, 6 April 1970.)

... One of the most vital preconditions for the proper functioning of our democratic system is a free press. There can be no questioning of the guaranteed freedom of opinion for each and every individual journalist, a right which is specifically guaranteed by the Basic Law. It is an inviolable constituent of our society.

Equally inviolable is the right of each individual citizen to have free and uninterrupted access to information. In this respect he is aided by the multiplicity and efficiency of the different competing mass media in the Federal Republic. From the right of free expression of opinion and the right of each individual citizen to have full access to information it follows that all those involved in the business of passing on information should report events as fully as possible. That means that the freedom to express opinion guaranteed by the constitution contains within it an obligation to provide the consumer of news and information with the most comprehensive possible framework within which opinion can be formed. This can only happen on the basis of a very wide choice of sources of information.

If it is the case that centralisation in the press brings with it the danger of a limited range of opinion and style in newspapers, the solution of the resultant problems should not be left to the journalists alone nor should we rest content with appealing to their individuality. Freedom of the press is not simply a basic right under our constitution, it is also something which our constitution demands should be actively maintained. If such movements towards centralisation restrict the independence of journalists, then parliament, the government and the constitutional court are obligated to take an active part in the resolution of any resultant conflicts. I am clear in my own mind that the legislators and the administration of justice can for the most part can do little more than lay down general guidelines and points of reference. It is impossible to lay down everything under a rigid set of guarantees. A great deal depends on willingness and ability to co-operate on the part of those directly involved, that is, the publishers and journalists on the one hand, and the politicians on the other. At this point, you will be more than justified in stressing the fact that, in this respect, the role of journalist is of particular importance. In recent weeks and months a great deal has been talked about what has been called the internal freedom of the press. There are evidently no ready-made solutions to this problem. It is my view that we must all of us undergo a period of experimentation and feeling our way. But there are two points which seem to me to be important none the less: first, it is not possible to carry on doing things the old way out of sheer inertia. That means that ways must be found, whenever the need arises, of maintaining the independence of journalists come what may. And secondly, the decisive matter will be one of maintaining and increasing choice in the press. It is not enough to seek to secure this range of choice by means of economic and administrative measures alone ...

Reconciliation — the European Task

(Extracts from a speech on the occasion of the twenty-fifth anniversary of the end of the Second World War given in Bonn before the accredited heads of foreign missions, 6 May 1970.)

... When we look back over the last twenty-five years, we must not forget what it meant to take a demoralised population in devastated cities and millions of homeless and destitute refugees and to set about fashioning a free and democratic society which, despite the sacrifices it had to endure, despite the fact that the national unity had been torn apart, has remained immune against sentiments of hatred and revenge. It should not be forgotten that the majority of our citizens, in contrast to the situation in 1918, had not fallen foul of the temptation to embrace a new shortsighted brand of National Socialism, but turned their minds to a vision of European solidarity and collaboration with all nations. And this today is the foundation on which is built the political thinking of a nation which has learned to contemplate its own destiny with sober moderation.

The governments elected by this people in the Federal Republic, on the basis of a free determination of democratically will, have accordingly task of working within the content of a complex world towards a peaceful future by means of rational politics. Against the background of a democratic parliament, they have done their best to make good past injustice and to reconcile themselves with former enemies. We have entered into close relationships with other like-minded nations. The Federal Republic of Germany, like the German Democratic Republic, has become part of a system of military alliances in which weapons of atomic annihilation balance one another out. The great task which we were charged with at the end of the Second World War is thus only half completed. No one deplores this more than the German people as a whole. This recognition must form the starting point when we look into the future. We know today that we shall get nowhere by weeping over what we have lost in the past, but that it is our principal duy to work towards bringing the process of reconciliation with the East to a satisfactory conclusion. This is just as important for those who themselves lived through the horrors of the last war as it is for those members of our younger generation to whom it is all an historical fact rather than a personal memory.

This task is more than just a national concern. It is a European obligation. It can be made a reality only with the assistance of all men of good will throughout the world. We feel a particularly strong sense of responsibility in working towards the as yet unattained comprehensive and enduring peace system in which, we further hope, our nation as a whole will be able to come together once more and play its part. We shall also further the scientific work directed towards the securing of peace, which is nowadays called peace studies and the investigation of human conflict and seek to ensure that this research is carried on in an international collaborative effort . . .

Exploit every Opportunity

(Extracts of a speech to apprentices who had completed their apprenticeship, Coblenz, 1 September 1970.)

. . . The world of tomorrow will be one of ever-accelerating change and radical transformations. Values and institutions which have for generations been respected are being called into question. It is the young particularly who today must ask themselves what they can hold on to in the midst of the spiritual, political and social tensions and conflicts of our age. One of the basic reasons for the unrest among the young, the protests of students, of secondary school pupils, and now among some apprentices, is surely this lack of certainty . . .

. . . I have constantly stressed, and I repeat now, that I have a great measure of understanding for the unrest among the younger generation and that I regard it as a healthy sign. But all genuine concern about outmoded notions, untenable prejudices and the forceful preservation of anxious taboos loses all credibility when it results in a refusal to play an active part in the state and in society. Paint bombs and acts of violence, shouts of support for Mao and Che Guevara neither improve the lot of the individual nor do they make our world one iota more humane, more just, or more rational.

Understanding that is clearly not just a matter of age. How else would it be possible to explain the fact that the overwhelming majority of our young people, recognising the pointlessness of doing no more than protesting, unquestioningly take upon themselves the tasks which must be accomplished if a system as complex as our technical economy is to continue operating within the framework of a world economic system for the good of all?

Little is spoken about this section of the younger generation. Those who are much more adept at attracting publicity to themselves draw the big headlines. This makes it all the more imperative that we should not, in our statements and judgements on the younger generation, pass over the majority who, although by no means uncritical, are not impervious to reasonable demands.

These young people should themselves be wary of slipping into the frame of mind of the silent majority. But this will inevitably happen if they deprive themselves of the opportunity to make their voices heard and their opinions felt by withdrawing from the public scene, instead of putting their views forward openly and backing them up with arguement.

The ancient Greeks used the word "idiot" to describe those people who insulated themselves from public life and who had no thought for anything outside their own immediate circle. Nowadays the meaning of the word has shifted in a different direction. But it still remains an appropriate descriptive term for an individual who withdraws completely into his own circumscribed private world or even resorts to drugs.

But it is only the need to participate, the urge to become involved with other people and groups in the community in order to gain an effective and active voice that is the mark of the true citizen of the calibre indispensable to a democracy.

Democracy means involvement in the process of government. Only someone who seeks to voice his opinions and tries to get them put into practice has a right to participate in the decision making processes. Make good use of the opportunity which our constitution offers you. It is up to you alone to make the decision. Anyone who refuses out of sheer idleness is assisting those forces which are ever ready to exploit the political timidity of the mass of people in order to advance their own self-interest. Those who refrain from participation in politics cannot complain if forces gain the upper hand which they utterly reject.

1871: Outward Unity without inner Freedom

(Television broadcast on the centenary of the foundation of the German Reich, 17 January 1971.)

I

Anniversaries come round unbidden. They make their presence particularly felt when the total of years after an event amounts to a round number. And it will be a hundred years ago tomorrow that the King of Prussia was proclaimed German Kaiser in Versailles. So 18 January 1871 is regarded as the day on which the

German Reich and thus the German national state came into being. For generations this anniversary has been regarded as a big day in the history of our nation.

But nowadays we are in no mood to celebrate such a centenary. The German Reich, which then expressed the final attainment of unity among our people, although it did not include the German Austrians, has now been transformed into two German states, neither of which bears any resemblance in its system of government to the German Reich of 1871. Prussia, the dominant and motivating power behind those events in 1871, is no more. Berlin, the capital of the German Reich, has been carved up. Important areas of the Reich in 1871 no longer belong to us. Sobering thoughts like that do not permit us to celebrate 18 January tomorrow in the same spirit as we used to many years ago.

Does our past still have some lessons for us? The younger generation is not anxious to hear much about history. In any event, their interest only begins with the year 1933, and their main concern is with the future of our society.

But the future grows out of the past. And if we refresh our memory a little, we may yet learn something from the past.

II

There are many ways in which our history can be said to have followed a quite different course from that of our neighbours. We have been called a "belated nation." And it is true that we attained our national unity in 1871 much later and in a more imperfect form than other nations. The call for unity was raised in the wars of liberation against Napoleon, among the restless students at the Wartburg rally in 1817, in the great popular gatherings in the castle of Hambach in 1832, and particularly in the turbulent years 1848—1849. But on each and every occasion the call was stifled by those dozens of little princedoms into which Germany was still divided.

Ought we to celebrate 1871? Emanuel Geibel has done so on behalf of many in a line which has found its way right down into the schoolbooks: "As Pallas Athene once sprang from the brow of Jupiter, so the Reich sprang armed ready from the head of Bismarck."

Bismarck was presented as the creater of unity with blood and iron, and depicted as such in the wealth of monuments dedicated to him that are to be found throughout Germany.

We must recognise that this is a simplification, and should be treated with due caution like every generalisation as being both true and false at one and the same time. It is true that Bismarck forced unity upon the particularist federation with

267

the exclusion of the Germans in Austria. But Bismarck is not one of the black, red and gold tradition of those who sought to bind unity with democratic freedom. So it would be a distortion of history to seek to trace a line from the wars of liberation and the Wartburg via Hambach, St. Paul's church in Frankfurt and Rastatt as the concluding point of the 1848—1849 revolution, and thence to Sedan and Versailles.

In our national anthem penned by the Democrat Hoffmann von Fallersleben in 1841 we sing about unity and justice and freedom. But that was not how it was before the Weimar Republic. In the Kaiser's Reich until 1918 we also sang "Hail to thee bearing the victor's garland."

When the German Reich was proclaimed one hundred years ago in Versailles, none of the men of 1848 were present. Yes, men like August Bebel and Wilhelm Liebknecht and other Social Democrats, who had expressed themselves against the nationalist arrogance of the victory against France, were in prison. In Versailles, the Kaiser was surrounded by princes, generals, court officials, but there were no representatives of the people there.

The foundation of the Reich had sundered the links between the aspiration towards democracy and that towards nationhood. It had bound the German national consciousness lopsidedly to those monarchical and conservative forces which in previous decades had obstinately obstructed the progress of the democratic will towards unity.

It was a deep humiliation for our French neighbours that our national state was proclaimed in their country and that at the same time Alsace Lorraine was taken away from them. France was never able to forget this humiliation.

III

What was achieved in 1871 was a superficial unity with no internal freedom for the citizen. The power of the state did not originate from the people, it lay with the princes and the senates of the Hanseatic cities. It is true that the people elected the Reich parliament. But the Reich parliament did not constitute the government and exercised only a marginal influence upon foreign and military policies.

That is why it is not by chance that we find very many peace-loving, liberal and democratic forces in opposition to Bismarck's Reich. The three serious struggles in the Bismarck period in Prussia and later in the Reich were directed against three groups of the German population who had a quite different conception of national unity. I refer to the Prussian constitutional dispute of the years 1862—1863 against the liberals, Bismarck's struggle between 1872 to 1880 against the Catholic portion of the population and the conflict with the Social Democrats who were pilloried as "enemies of the Reich" and "rootless cosmopolitans" by the laws against socialists of the years 1878 to 1890.

Many people were early to recognise and warn against the dangers inherent in this internal rift. Our nation seemed united and resolute only when the First World War broke out and Kaiser Wilhelm II proclaimed: "I know no parties any more, I know only Germans!" But soon it became clear that the equality of dying a soldier's death was not to be followed by equality of civil rights.

The three groups which opposed Bismarck emerge once more at a later date in our history. It was they who a year and a half later helped to translate the Kaiser's Reich which had suffered military defeat into the Republic of Weimar. This, rather than Versailles, is the historical link with the Frankfurt national assembly of 1848.

The Weimar Republic had the opportunity of at last adding democratic unity to the unity which had been handed over in the Versailles treaty. But it failed.

The severe burdens imposed upon the Weimar Republic, when it came into being, allowed reactionary and nationalist forces to extricate themselves from their responsibility for the First World War and the military collapse of the Kaiser's Reich. Instead of looking critically and ensibly at our history, these forces exploited the legend of the "stab in the back," that is, that Germany was supposedly traitorously robbed of victory in the First World War by the enemy within — a poisonous slander which had enduring evil effects. Large areas of the population did not unreservedly support the Weimar constitution. As early as 1920 those parties which did not belong to the Weimar coalition of SPD, Centre, and German Democratic parties gained the majority in the Reich parliament and maintained their position until the Republic lay in ruins and fell into the hands of Hitler.

Even from this point of view our historical image of Weimar demands critical revision. Those who speak of the First World War as a straightforward misfortune in which Germany has no share of the blame and seek to excuse the National Socialist coup d'état on the grounds that the Versailles Treaty was unjust, have not satisfactorily explained the collapse in 1918. A hundred years since the founding of the German Reich: this means not once, but twice Versailles, in 1871 and 1919, and it also means Auschwitz, Stalingrad and unconditional surrender in 1945.

How was it all possible? That supposed line of descent from Arminius and Luther via Frederick the Great and Bismarck to Hitler has long since been dismissed as a fancy.

But people forget all too readily the social conditions especially of Bismarck's Reich and the Weimar Republic, which were both torn apart by internal division and foundered not least because of that division.

But from where we stand now, we can look back with hope.

IV

We have lost our national unity, yet the thought of regaining it still lives on amongst us. But the life patterns of our people have changed in the course of a hundred years.

However much Germany may have been divided before 1871, its people none the less all lived within the context of the same kind of social systems. And for this reason all that had to be overcome was particularism if Germany was to be turned into a unified economic system and the way paved towards the first industrial revolution.

But today the Elbe-Werra line is not just the border between two state authorities, but between two radically opposed social systems. So our task is vastly different from that of 1871. Our objective is a system embracing the whole of Europe, in which states and nations, despite differences in internal structure, not only live alongside one another, but also exclude war and the use of force against one another and work jointly towards solving common problems in the widest variety of different areas: for example, transport, ecology and pollution, research, and aid for development. In these areas there are vast opportunities before us.

The inner unity of the Federal Republic of Germany has, by contrast, made good progress. The republican state system, its symbols and its democratic pattern in the spirit of the Basic Law, has a substantial measure of support such as has never before been known in our history. Important though this may be, this does not release us from our duty to seek constantly to measure up to the standards which our Basic Law lays down for our society. Our society should not only have a democratic constitution but also a strong social conscience. In this respect there is a long way to go. History teaches us that the consequences of neglecting to establish a just social order are grave in the extreme.

There are widely divergent conceptions of how our society should be fashioned in the future. It is a conflict between the parties, the generations, the different

270

groups of the working population and their organisations. But there is one thing that must be retained with all vigour as we look back at 18 January 1871. And that is the fundamental right of freedom for all citizens. In the constitution we have unreservedly committed ourselves to basic rights such as freedom of belief, speech, assembly, and movement.

All these things have been the subject of fighting and suffering in the course of our history. It must be our common task to preserve and enhance the practical realisation of such things within a context of social justice.

Obedience to God in the political Sphere

(Extracts from a speech in recollection of the Diet of Worms of 1521, 17 April 1971.)

... Whatever one might have to say about Luther's ideological standpoint, justice can certainly only be done to him if one takes full account of his religious motives and aims. He was concerned to restore a debased church back to first principles. That is why he stressed the Bible as the only true yardstick. That is why he translated it into German for his contemporaries. That is why he placed the emphasis on Christ the mediator and restored Him to His position as the sole focal point of the gospels. But Luther was not concerned about overcoming feudalism in favour of a new social order in which all men are equal under the law. Any ideological evaluation of Luther on these lines is too restricted and hence falls short of the mark.

But, on the other side of the coin, the theologians and the Lutheran churches should pay a greater measure of attention to the significance of social factors in ecclesiastical history than is normally the case. In the history of the church God works through men, and indeed men caught up in the situations and attitudes of their age. In this regard there is no need for a stress on religious motivations and goals and a stress on social situations or forces to be mutually contradictory. In fact, they might well cast light on one another.

... A social factor such as the power of the state, which plays an important role in Luther's reformation in contrast to previous times, can be particularly illuminating.

... It is not only the political development of Germany that has suffered from an interpretation of the teaching of the two kingdoms of the state and church which is false because it is too inflexible. In the social sphere it has also prevented a proper view of where the duty of a Christian church should lie: namely, in taking the part of the oppressed and exploited. The fact that, in the nineteenth century, many workers turned to Marxism, and the conviction among intellectuals which is still widespread today that atheism and progress are inseparable, can be traced back to the impotence and inadequacy of Lutheranism in the face of the problems of this world.

... It is of course not difficult to cast oneself in the role of prosecutor against the inadequacies of former generations. And by the same token, this does not exclude the possibility that we might not fare any better when we come to be judged by future generations.

One thing at least has happened, and that is that we now have lost the self-satisfaction which prevented Luther's followers in the past from being properly aware of the realities of life and the duties that lay before them. We can see more clearly the dangers which derive from an over-ready acceptance of the close bond between the state, the power of the state and the church. We have recognised that there can be no Christian politics nor a Christian state; but on the other hand, we also know that it is the duty of the Christian also to practise obedience to God in the political sphere.

We have also learned to recognise that the schism in the church is an expression of the disobedience of the Christian, a demonstration of the fact that in the past and even today questions of power and false authority have tended to dominate the church rather than the question of listening to the word of God ...

Albrecht Dürer and the Germans

(Extracts from a speech celebrating the five hundredth anniversary of the birth of the painter, Nuremberg, 21 May 1971.)

... Anniversaries and anniversary celebrations tempt us to exploit the name and fame of the individual being celebrated for the benefit of those living today. I wonder if we can lay any claim upon what Dürer created, and by we I mean Nuremberg, Franconia, the Federal Republic of Germany, or if, in our festive mood, we overlook the division of our country, Germany as a whole.

I think not. It is true that creative work and the environment are always related one to the other. One might well ask whether Albrecht Dürer would have become what he is without Nuremberg. The answer would have to be in the negative even if we take note of the fact that Albrecht Dürer's forebears can hardly be reckoned among the most longstanding families of Nuremberg. Dürer's parents only settled in the city in 1455, that is, a mere sixteen years before the painter's birth.

Leaving that on one side: would the Nuremberg of our day have the right to look upon Dürer as a product of the city, rather like the equally world-famous Nuremberg Lebkuchen spice cakes?

Permitting the five hundredth anniversary of the birth of Albrecht Dürer to redound to the greater glory of this city could lead to many other things that happened in Nuremberg being principally credited to the city itself. In general I do not think much of the idea of drawing up a balance sheet for a city, a country or a nation. So I shall not take Dürer away from the Nurembergers, the Franconians, nor yet from the Germans. What I am concerned about is that the great son of this city should be restored to what he can lay proper claim to: his own individuality, his personal destiny, his unalterable personal achievement, and his utterly original genius.

These are the very things he has long been deprived of by a Dürer cult which, on closer inspection, turns out to be directed less at him than at those busily heaping praise upon him in order to show themselves off in a favourable light.

... We wish to have no part in such abuse of Albrecht Dürer. Let us leave him exactly as he is, as a great artist, whose paintings, woodcuts and engravings offer a penetrating picture of the world of the sixteenth century, and at the same time give us an insight into the hopes, faith, difficulties, cares and self-doubts of a sensitive spirit in which creative power and destructive fears held one another in mutual balance and dependency.

Albrecht Dürer owed a debt to his contemporary Martin Luther, whose sermons and writings lifted a great weight from his mind. Let us be grateful that we have had in our country a Dürer who has shown us right down to the present day the beauty of the world, but also the threats to that beauty. To reveal this should be one of the objectives of this exhibition of his works, which I now declare open.

How is our civil Courage?

(Extract from the radio and television Christmas broadcast, 1971.)

... We have learned a few things. We have learned that the state is not some kind of higher being which can lay claim to submissive obedience. The state is there to help us all to live an ordered life in society as free citizens.

We have often been reproached for lacking in self-assurance as citizens and for being as a consequence easy prey to tyrannical régimes. But how is our civil courage?

We possess a splendid brief for freedom in the form of our Basic Law which, for the first time in our history, has promised each and every one of us inviolable rights to freedom above and beyond any power invested in the state. Do we respect this brief, and are we exploiting its possibilities to the full?

From year to year the number of those of our fellow citizens who lived through the enslavement of Nazism grows ever smaller. And by the same token, the number grows ever larger of those for whom every aspect of our present system is taken for granted. Many of our citizens, particularly those among our younger generation are all too keen to show scant respect for the rights of others, particularly their freedom of conscience, in their proposals for the betterment of our social system which, it is beyond doubt, certainly can be improved upon. Where that kind of thing happens even in isolated pockets, the whole system can soon come under threat.

When I was staying in Sigriswil above Lake Thun in Switzerland, I came across a community hall. In it are preserved old documents which testify to the fact that 600 years ago the ancestors of the citizens of Sigriswil bought their freedom from their Habsburg masters. Outside the house is a sign stating: "I preserve the old letters of freedom of Sigriswil, but it is up to you to preserve freedom itself!" This saying gives us too food for thought. Are we fully aware of the extent of our own rights as free men?

We all have the freedom to live according to own our consciences.

We all have the freedom to express our own opinions, and this includes the freedom of the press, of assembly, of organisation.

We all have the freedom to chose our own place of training, work, and residence.

I too am aware of the fact that justice and reality are not always in harmony one with the other. And it is in those places where this is so that it is incumbent upon us to work towards improvement, step by step.

Lübke did not bear his Office lightly

(Extracts from a speech in the German Federal parliament in memory of the second President of the Republic, 13 April 1972.)

... Only someone who knew Heinrich Lübke in those days long ago, before decades of hard work and a severe self-discipline had drained his spiritual and physical reserves, is competent to pass judgement on his abilities, his energy, and his inner and outward steadfastness. Heinrich Lübke is a penetrating example of the demands high political office impose upon those who undertake it, not out of ambition, but out of a sense of duty.

... It is certain that this office bore heavily upon him. Lübke, who gladly took on responsibility as a Minister, clearly suffered because he now had to stand by while others took the decisions. Unlike his predecessor Professor Heuss, it was not given to him willingly to restrict his activities to that circumscribed area permitted to the Federal President, although the Basic Law does not define its exact boundaries in detail. As a result, his relationship with Adenauer and Adenauer's successor was not without tension. It is true that it never came to a crisis, but it must have pained and grieved him as the weaker party under the constitution.

... We all have good reason to take seriously his statement that he assumed office as Federal President with the full intention of serving the common good. He took his own obligation seriously of standing above the parties and their natural state of conflict. For this reason, he bore up under the danger allied with this obligation that his own party would now and again regard him as an inconvenient admonisher ...

Filling the Treaties with Life

(Extract from a radio and television broadcast on the occasion of the signing of the ratification of the treaties with the East, Bonn, 23 May 1972.)

... This treaty system has been the object of debate throughout our nation. We have all sensed that this was one of the most serious national and international problems of the post-war period for us to overcome.

The debate was hard-fought. Certain aspects of it should give us all cause for thought. But a past battle must not be fought on and allowed to prejudice the future. For this reason we must allow the decisions which have been taken to stand as valid.

After a period which has brought our nations an immeasurable burden of suffering and mutual injustice, the treaties should play their part in allowing our children and grandchildren on both sides to live from now on in a peaceful Europe.

I turn now particularly to address those of our citizens who had to leave their homes after the collapse of Hitler's dictatorship. Life has passed by the hope that many of them have cherished of ever being able to return once more to their homes. We owe a debt of gratitude to all those who have contributed towards reconciliation, despite the fact that they have suffered from the loss of their homes. It is essential that we respect the present frontiers of Europe . . .

What we must now do on both sides is to fill the treaties with life. If the nations do not make the treaties into a part of themselves, they will be nothing more than lifeless letters on the page. The confrontations of past years must now be translated into collaboration for the future.

Help us overcome Hatred

(Speech in the Munich Olympic stadium during the memorial ceremony for the Israeli victims of the Arab terrorist attack in the Olympic village, 6 September 1972.)

Eleven days ago in this stadium I declared the Munich Olympic games of 1972 open. They began as truly happy games in the spirit of the Olympic idea. There was a magnificent response to them throughout the world, until yesterday morning when murder cast its shadow over them. And last night fear and terror spread when the attempt to rescue the Israeli hostages went wrong.

Faces that up until now have been gay and carefree are marked with shock and horror. We stand helpless before a truly despicable crime.

In deep sorrow we pay our respects to the victims of this attack. Our sympathy goes out to their families and to the entire Israeli nation.

This is a blow that has struck us all. Could the attack and its outcome have been avoided? At this moment, no one can give a final answer to this question.

Who are responsible for this crime? In the first place, it is a criminal organisation convinced that hatred and murder are legitimate means of political struggle.

But the countries which permit such men to live in their midst also bear a heavy responsibility.

The past few hours have demonstrated to all people throughout the world that hatred is inevitably destructive. The victims of this attack are a reminder to us that we must dedicate all our efforts towards overcoming hatred.

These new victims especially urge upon us the need to counter this fanaticism which has horrified the world by a determination to bring about a greater measure of understanding. The Olympic idea has not been refuted. We are bound to it more strongly than ever before. In the events we have lived through, the line of demarcation does not lie between north and south nor east and west, but rather between the solidarity of all those who seek peace and those others who place in mortal peril everything which makes life worthwhile.

Life must have reconciliation. Reconciliation must not be allowed to fall victim to terror.

In the name of the Federal Republic of Germany I appeal to all the peoples of the world: help us to overcome hatred, help us pave the way to reconciliation.

Acknowledgments

Photos

Antz p. 70
Associated Press p. 147
Bundesbildstelle pp. 72, 90/91, 133, 136, 146, 186/187, 214, 244
Darchinger pp. 89, 92, 93, 95, 134/135, 243
DPA p. 96
Luft pp. 18, 19, 20
Pabel p. 94
Private property President Heinemann pp. 17, 71
Schulthess p. 188
Stern pp. 69, 148, 185, 242
Jacket: Luft (front), Bundesbildstelle (back)

Documents

Auswärtiges Amt pp. 114/115
Bundesarchiv pp. 113, 166/167
Bundespräsidialamt pp. 116, 205, 206/207, 208
Lang, Ernst Maria p. 29
Private property Chancellor Willy Brandt p. 52
Private property Dr. E. Eppler pp. 50/51
Private property President Heinemann pp. 30, 31, 32, 49, 165, 168